The Tar Baby

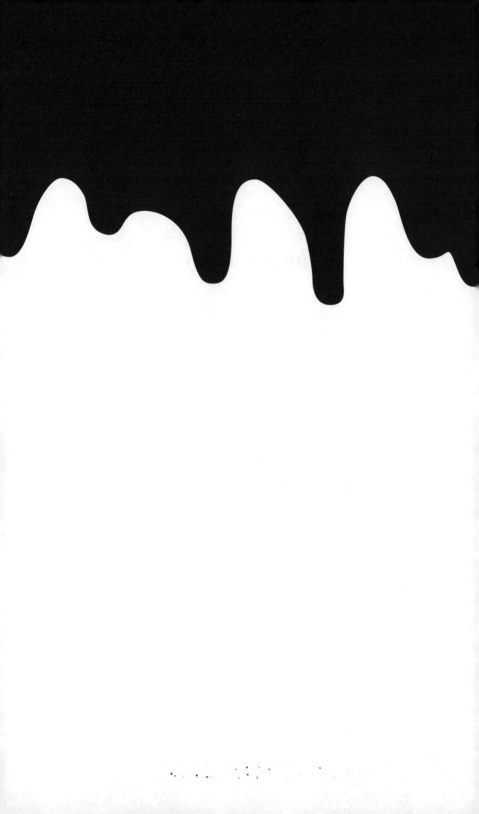

The Tar Baby

A GLOBAL HISTORY

Bryan Wagner

PRINCETON UNIVERSITY PRESS
Princeton and Oxford

Copyright © 2017 by Princeton University Press

Published by Princeton University Press, 41 William Street,
Princeton, New Jersey 08540

In the United Kingdom: Princeton University Press, 6 Oxford Street,
Woodstock, Oxfordshire OX20 1TR

press.princeton.edu

Jacket art: 1) *Planisphère, ou carte générale du monde* (1676)
by Pierre Duval, Bibliothèque nationale de France,
2) Type courtesy of Patricia M. / Flickr,
3) Black paint © Angela Waye / Shutterstock

ISBN 978-0-691-17263-7

Library of Congress Control Number: 2016945502

British Library Cataloging-in-Publication Data is available

This book has been composed in Bodoni Std, Ultra and
Adobe Garamond Pro

Printed on acid-free paper. ∞

Printed in the United States of America

1 3 5 7 9 10 8 6 4 2

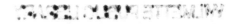

For **NORA** & **CAMILLE**

CONTENTS

PROLOGUE

The tar baby is an electric figure in contemporary culture. As a racial epithet, a folk archetype, an existential symbol, and an artifact of mass culture, the term "tar baby" stokes controversy, in the first place because of its racism. At least since the 1840s, "tar baby" has been used as a grotesque term of abuse, and it continues to feel like an assault no matter the circumstances in which it is employed. At the same time, "tar baby" has operated as a figure of speech suggesting a problem that gets worse the harder you try to solve it. The term takes both of these senses in the tar baby story, a short fable that was common in vernacular tradition before it was reproduced on the gilt-edged pages of illustrated children's books and on the silver screen.

By far the best-known version of the tar baby story is the one published by Joel Chandler Harris in his inaugural folklore collection, *Uncle Remus: His Songs and His Sayings* (1881). This was not the tar baby's first appearance in print, as other versions anticipated Uncle Remus by more than a decade, but it was "The Wonderful Tar-Baby Story," told in the manufactured voice of an imaginary ex-slave, that made the difference to the story's future transmission, documentation, and reception. Again and again, Uncle Remus's version of the tar baby was syndicated, translated, adapted, illustrated, excerpted, and interpolated in newspapers, magazines, folklore anthologies, and children's treasuries, as it was also repurposed in comic strips and advertising campaigns

FIG. 0.1. Edward Gorey, "[Rabbit Stuck to Tar Baby]." Colored pen and ink. From Ennis Rees, *Brer Rabbit and His Tricks, with Drawings by Edward Gorey*, (New York: Young Scott Books). By permission of the Edward Gorey Estate.

for products like Brer Rabbit Blackstrap Molasses. In 1939, Walt Disney Studios purchased the franchise rights to the Uncle Remus stories. Seven years later, the tar baby was featured in *Song of the South*, one of the first feature-length films to combine animation and live action. Following the film's release, Disney's management of the Uncle Remus franchise proved to be a successful experiment in convergence and cross-promotion. Content from the film appeared in picture books and read-along recordings, television programs and stereoscopic slides, board games and theme park attractions—all made possible by the deepening coordination between Disney and media corporations like Golden Books, Capitol Records, and the American Broadcasting Company. It is a measure of the extraordinary influence wielded by the culture industries at mid-century that the story is still strongly associated with *Song of the South* decades after Dis-

FIG. 0.2. J. M. Conde, "'I wish,' said the little boy, 'I wish I could fly.'" Pen and ink. From Joel Chandler Harris, *Uncle Remus and the Little Boy* (Boston: Small Maynard and Company, 1910), 12.

ney removed the film from commercial circulation. First through Harris and then through Disney, the tar baby has been reduced to a master outline that has predominated over all other expressions of the story.[1]

It is important to understand that there is more to the tar baby story than Uncle Remus. The disproportionate attention given to Remus's version of the tar baby has obscured the story's actual range. The tar baby exists in literally hundreds of versions derived over several centuries on at least five continents. Since the 1880s, collectors have claimed that they heard the tar baby "over and over" in the field, leading some of them to speculate that the story was "omnipresent" in world culture. According to some estimates, the tar baby was transcribed more frequently than any other story during the decades in the late nineteenth century when collectors were flooding into the field to transcribe stories, songs, and sayings they saw as the last vestiges of primitive culture. In these decades, the tar baby became a topic of intense concern in the emerging disciplines of professional social science, most remarkably in folklore and anthropology, where the story served as a paradigm case in the study of global culture, a trend that continued into the early twentieth century as the tar baby remained a sticking point in research undertaken by leading scholars including Elsie Clews Parsons, Franz Boas, and Melville Herskovits.[2]

The tar baby has been central to our understanding of cultural traditions that slaves brought from Africa to America. According to Herskovits, the tar baby was the "keypoint" in the debate over the nature and composition of black culture. The story's significance was magnified over time as it was cited as evidence against the views of sociologists such as E. Franklin Frazier, who argued that slaves retained little more than "scraps of memories" from the African past. The story was also invoked in arguments against Stanley Elkins, a historian who claimed that slavery destroyed the personalities of its victims, rendering them passive in the face of their oppression. As a counterexample to these claims, the tar baby showed that slaves were neither deracinated nor submissive. It was a story that survived the brutality of the Middle Passage, a story that was passed down from generation to generation and continent to continent, demonstrating the independence that slaves retained even under the worst conditions. Slaves learned to survive by imitating the trickster and using deception to overcome the strength of their masters. The tar baby showed that culture not only survived but thrived under slavery, and it showed that culture's purpose under slavery was practical, and even political, as stories like the tar baby taught slaves how to push back against their masters. It would be an overstatement to say that the tar baby was the origin for these new ideas about culture and politics, but there is no question that the story remained a leading case throughout the twentieth century, an example against which these new ideas were tested, refined, and reformed.[3]

One of the problems with this conventional approach to the tar baby is a matter of evidence. Scholars have attempted to determine the origin and chart the trajectory of the tar baby as a basis for interpreting the story's meaning. This approach treats the story's worldwide diffusion as something that can be measured, and thereby used as evidence, when in fact it is something that we can never know for sure. Oral traditions do not leave dated traces, which means it is impossible to reconstruct a story's movement based on the mere fact of its existence in more than one place. All we can say for sure is that the story was told in these places. How it arrived, and where it originated, are matters for speculation. Given the available evidence, which is unreliable and inconclusive, it comes as no surprise that the tar baby's diffusion has been subject to open-ended and acrimonious debate. If we want to interpret the tar baby in political terms, we need to reckon with the fact that the shape of its diffusion is not only unknown but likely unknowable. It provides no foundation for a theory of politics.[4]

First and foremost, this empirical problem returns us to the task of interpreting the tar baby, a task that had been suspended by some of its most astute commentators, who tried to make their objective knowledge of the story's circulation into the basis for a theory of politics. Critics have worked out the metaphysical problems of political agency posed in the tar baby by invoking the story's mercurial transmission as evidence for the cultural autonomy of its storytellers, but in my view, the theory of politics generated by this critical approach remains inadequate to the story's complex meditation on the problems of action, identification, and consciousness. We have put the right questions to the tar baby, in other words, but our answers have been insufficient.

This book aspires to be more comprehensive than previous accounts of the tar baby, looking beyond oral tradition to discover examples of the story's narrative elements outside the domain claimed by folklorists. We know that the tar baby was circulating at the same time, and in many of the same places, as the new thinking about property and sovereignty that developed in colonial law and political economy. One of the purposes of this book is to demonstrate that the story addresses many of the same problems—labor and value, enclosure and settlement, crime and captivity—represented in the tracts and charters conventionally associated with the so-called great transformation in world history.[5] Interpreted in this broader comparative context, the tar baby looks less like an ethnographic example and more like a universal history that seeks to grasp all at once the interlocking processes by which custom was criminalized, lands were colonized, slaves were captured, and labor was bought and sold, even as it also meditates on the feeling of disenchantment and the impact of science on the conflict over natural resources. We should understand the tar baby, in other words, not only as an artifact of globalization but also as an account of globalization whose scale of reference matches the scale of its diffusion.

This book departs from previous thinking about the tar baby, but it relies on critical precedents established as the story was taken up by various disciplines in the humanities and social sciences. For the purposes of this study, I have been willing to engage with any example previously seen as a version of the tar baby story. I am especially interested in versions collected and published during the major phase of collection between 1865 and 1945, as these are the examples that supplied the material for the standard interpretation of the story. A bibliography of examples from this major phase of collection appears at the back of the book. In addition, I have retained the tripartite model used by folklorists, which divides the story into three stages: a beginning, in which a trap is set to catch a thief; a middle, in which the trap is sprung; and an end, in which the thief escapes or receives comeuppance. I have also retained the anatomy of narrative elements (such as the "stickfast motif," the "mock plea," and the "no-reply formula") commonly used by folklorists, even as I have abandoned their attempt to trace the story's diffusion in space and time.[6]

My interpretation of the tar baby mostly ignores the dialect that is one of the story's most notorious features. Intended as entertainment, this dialect almost always denigrates the people who told the story. Collectors justified their use of nonstandard spelling and syntax on the grounds that they were reproducing the story "verbatim." Dialect was meant to preserve the tar baby's authenticity, its connection to an oral tradition that was supposed to be untouched by books, newspapers, and other modern technologies. However, as many scholars have pointed out, the simulation of spoken language in these ethnographic works has less to do with phonetic accuracy than with adherence to artificial literary conventions that imposed rules for substitution ("d-" for "th-," as in "dat" for "that") and transformation (the subtraction of postvocalic "-r," as in "mawnin'" for "morning") even as they also encouraged liberal use of eye dialect, a term of art that refers to a misspelling phonetically identical to its root (as in "wuz" or "soshubble"). These dialect conventions are artifacts of ethnographic representation, and as such they are worthy of study, but they are extraneous to my main concerns.[7]

The book is divided into five chapters. The first is devoted to reception history. It addresses both the longstanding controversy over the direction of the tar baby's diffusion and the implications that followed from this controversy in intellectual movements ranging from the new social history to symbolic anthropology. The next three chapters correspond to the three stages in the story: the setting of the trap, the springing of the trap, and the trickster's escape. In each chapter, the analysis seeks to understand the tar baby in relation to its cognates in natural law and political economy. In an epilogue, I turn to the story's self-conscious representation of the speaking animal, a figure that condenses the story's general reflection on personhood and property.

The book concludes with twelve examples of the tar baby story chosen to illustrate the story's conventional features, its variation, and the scale of its geographical distribution. I have included a map indicating where the stories were collected as well as the dates on which they were published. The map illustrates how rapidly scholars discovered how far the story had traveled. It should not be necessary to refer to these sample stories while reading the chapters, but obviously they are available for consultation. They are intended to provide a highly selective and concentrated exhibition of the story's range and ambition.

The Tar Baby

Chapter One

IDEAS OF CULTURE

A rabbit and a wolf are neighbors. In the summer, the rabbit wastes his time singing songs, smoking cigarettes, and drinking wine, while the wolf stays busy working in his fields. The rabbit then steals from the wolf all winter. The next year, the wolf decides he will catch the rabbit by placing a tar baby, a lifelike figurine made from tar softened with turpentine, on the way to his fields. When the rabbit meets the tar baby in the road, and the tar baby does not reply to his greetings, the rabbit becomes angry and punches, kicks, and head-butts the tar baby until he is stuck at five points and left to the mercy of the wolf. The rabbit is not, however, trapped for long: he tricks the wolf into tossing him into the briar patch, where he makes his escape.

This composite obviously, perhaps inevitably, fails to capture the true range of variation in the oral tradition of the tar baby. In the hundreds of versions on record, the thief is sometimes a rabbit, other times a spider or a monkey. The owner is sometimes a wolf, other times a possum or a lion. The thief sometimes takes grain from a field, other times fruit from an orchard or water from a well. This flexibility is normal in any vernacular tradition, and any interpretation of the tar baby needs to account for the regular substitution of characters, props, and incidents that occurs as the story is related again and again. Accordingly, one of the central tasks undertaken by scholars interested in the tar baby has been to explain how the story traveled so widely, and why it changed, when it did, along the way.[1]

FIG. 1.1. A. B. Frost, " 'Gracious Me! An' den He Howl.' " Pen and ink. From Joel Chandler Harris, *Told by Uncle Remus: New Stories of the Old Plantation* (New York: Grosset and Dunlap, 1903), 44.

This longstanding interest in the tar baby, in where the story has been and how it has moved from one place to another, has proven extraordinarily fruitful. This chapter outlines the tar baby's intellectual reception in anthropology, literature, history, and folklore—disciplines that were being professionalized in the same decades when collectors were publicizing their surprising discoveries about the scale of the story's worldwide circulation. Although the most elementary questions asked about the tar baby—how it traveled from location to location, why it traveled as far as it did—have never been, and likely never will be, answered empirically, this has never put a stop to speculation. Indeed, it has always been the things we cannot say for sure that have inspired the most influential discourse about the tar baby. The mystery of the story's diffusion, in particular, helped to shape the terms in which it became possible to think more capaciously about culture.[2]

During the late nineteenth century, the tar baby was one of the examples most often cited by collectors interested in the cul-

FIG. 1.2. A. B. Frost, "'Brer Rabbit, he Put his Han' ter his Head.'" Pen and ink. From Joel Chandler Harris, *Told by Uncle Remus: New Stories of the Old Plantation* (New York: Grosset and Dunlap, 1903), 45.

tural traditions that slaves had transmitted from Africa to America. Joel Chandler Harris, in particular, was convinced that the tar baby, like the other tales told by Uncle Remus, came from Africa, and in his introductions to the Uncle Remus books, he sought to substantiate this connection by comparing the stories he collected in Georgia to stories collected by Wilhelm Bleek in South Africa and Charles Hartt in Brazil. Based on the similarities among these stories, Harris suggested that they represented the culture that united the African diaspora. According to Harris, stories like the tar baby expressed a racial point of view. They were political allegories in which the relative position of the weaker animals corresponded to the global perspective of the race.[3]

Others followed Harris in this interpretation, looking for analogues to Brer Rabbit wherever there were people of African descent. Some scholars, such as Thomas Crane and Héli Chatelain, recognized prototypes for the tar baby in trickster tales found in Liberia, Congo, Mauritius, South Africa, and the Gold Coast, and they tracked the changes that occurred in the story as it traveled to such places as Cuba, Jamaica, Mexico, and Louisiana. Like Harris, these collectors were committed to an approach that they inherited from Johann Gottfried Herder and the Brothers Grimm, an approach that assumed folk traditions conserved national or racial identity as they were transmitted from generation to generation. In 1892, David Wells put the point succinctly. It was possible, Wells noted, to reconstruct the "history of a race" by tracing the "alterations" in its "typical legends." In 1896, Alice Bacon agreed with Wells, suggesting that stories like the tar baby were the "chain" that linked "the American with the African Negro." "Every story in Uncle Remus," Bacon elaborated, "can be shown to exist in a more primitive shape in Africa, and among people who cannot be suspected of having imported it." As early as 1877, William Owens was prepared to affirm what seemed obvious: that stories like the tar baby were "as purely African" as the "faces" of the people who told them. Summarizing this prevailing wisdom in 1914, Charlotte Sophia Burne noted the importance of the "African slave-trade" to the "dissemination of folk-tales," citing as her main example the "Tar-Baby story," which was known to have been "inherited" by the "coloured population of the United States" from the "tribes of Angola and the Congo." Writing in 1933, Alice Werner makes the same point. Not only "the Tar-baby" but literally "every story in 'Uncle Remus,'" she proposes, "can be shown to exist in a more primitive shape in Africa, and among people who cannot be suspected of having imported it from America or elsewhere."[4]

At the same time as these various critics and collectors were casting their argument for the diasporic provenance of the tar baby, others suggested that the entire tradition concerned with speaking animals, including the collection of ancient fables attributed to Aesop, could only have come from Africa. As early as the thirteenth century, a Byzantine scholar named Planudes speculated that Aesop was a black man from Ethiopia, but this idea did not gain broader acceptance until the nineteenth century when writers like William Godwin and William Martin

Leake developed an argument based not only on the evidently false etymological connection (Aesop to Aethiop) that Planudes had made, but also on specific examples, such as "Washing the Ethiopian White," and on the flora and fauna that recur in the fables. While these claims about Aesop's blackness remained conjectures, they were common enough to shape the interpretation of the trickster stories that had become, thanks to Harris, strongly associated with African Americans. Some critics, like Arna Bontemps, have even argued that the only "question" is not whether but how Aesop's fables were turned into the animal stories told by slaves, with others, like J. H. Driberg, suggesting that "if Aesop was not an African, he ought to have been" given the powerful correspondence between his fables and the modern trickster tradition.[5]

The tar baby's importance to the African diaspora was also emphasized in later studies, including James Weldon Johnson's *Native African Races and Culture* (1927) and Melville Herskovits's *The Myth of the Negro Past* (1941), which made the case for the influence of African retentions in New World slave societies more comprehensively and systematically than had previous collectors, like Harris, whose research was limited in its coverage and frequently based on specious generalizations. Even as scholars broadened their base of evidence, the tar baby story remained an important touchstone in the argument for African cultural survivals. According to Herskovits, the story was a primary example of the "cultural luggage" that Africans brought with them to America. These claims were supported by field research, as the tar baby had in fact been recorded in locations throughout the African continent from peoples including the Makua, Mbundu, Duala, Dinka, Manganja, Hausa, Fantee, Baronga, Namwanga, Nyungwe, Yao, Temne, and Ewe. As Herskovits notes, the tar baby was considered "so characteristic of West Africa" that collectors had used the version narrated by Uncle Remus as a "point of comparative reference" when seeking out their own folklore on the continent. Collectors sometimes substantiated their claims for the tar baby's diasporic provenance by citing informants who learned the story in Africa before coming to America, as is the case with Lattevi Ajaji, who told the story to John Lomax in Texas. Other times they explained that their informants had learned the story from a friend or relative who had heard it in Africa. Collectors also argued for an African origin by tracking cognates—elements whose strong similarity suggests direct transmission or a common source—marking parallels between "The Wonderful Tar Baby Story" and stories like "The Leopard in the Maize Farm" (collected by John Weeks in the Lower Congo) or "The Spider and the Farmer" (collected by Alfred Burdon Ellis in the coastal territory later known as Ghana). Even when there was no evidence for direct transmission, it seemed plausible to assume a link between stories with such similarities, especially when the stories in question were shared by a racial population presumably related by blood.[6]

This line of argument has always been controversial. Right from the beginning, some scholars disputed Harris's claim that the tar baby story came from Africa. Even before Harris published his first book, he received a letter from John Wesley Powell, the head of the Smithsonian Bureau of Ethnology, proposing another possible origin for the Uncle Remus stories that Harris had been printing in the *Atlanta Constitution*. Encountering "The Wonderful Tar-Baby Story" when it was syndicated in his own evening newspaper, Powell recalled that he had heard versions of the story during his fieldwork with the Southern Paiute in Utah, though at the time he had no idea that the tar baby was also being told by slaves. Powell asserted in his letter to Harris that the tar baby story, like many other Uncle Remus tales, was not in fact invented by African Americans but borrowed from American Indians.

Others noticed the similarities between "The Wonderful Tar-Baby Story" and the trickster tales that geologist Charles Hartt had collected among the Amazonian population in Brazil. Although Harris maintained that the Amazonians had been taught the story by Africans recently imported as slaves, other scholars, such as James Mooney, held that Hartt's evidence actually supported the opposite conclusion and that the tar baby story was in consequence not an ancestral inheritance from Africa but instead a cultural compound that could only have been made in the Americas.[7]

Things only became more confusing as collectors continued to find versions of the tar baby in far-flung regions of the world that were assumed to be culturally distinct from one another. The realization that African Americans and Amazonian Indians had culture in common was one of many discoveries from this time that challenged prevailing wisdom about the circulation of culture, during which it was revealed again and again that people from different lands, speaking different languages, were telling the same stories. Such revelations raised basic questions about the relationship between race and culture. In 1906, William Wells Newell detailed the potential implications. Rather than a "closed race handing down from generation to generation its own stock of ideas and beliefs," Newell imagined bits and pieces of information that were continually "differentiated into new forms" as they drifted from place to place with "disregard" for "barriers" of "descent or language."[8]

Without standard units of measurement or other methodological controls, folklore collectors were free to sketch any number of speculative itineraries for the tar baby story. Following Powell's argument in his debate with Harris, many claimed the story was invented in America by the Cherokee, Natchez, or some other tribe before it was borrowed by slaves. Also common was the hypothesis that the tar baby was formulated in Europe, where it was supposed to have descended from the Roman de Renard, a medieval story sequence that was alleged to have traveled from France to Haiti to Louisiana. According to F. M. Warren, the similarity between the two stories appeared to indicate a "very close connection," or almost a "translation," the "Roman de Renard being written 700 years ago and Uncle Remus some fifteen years ago." Elsie Clews Parsons suggested another theory, holding that the tar baby had once belonged to the "Master Thief" story cycle transcribed by Herodotus, and that its independence came relatively late in its passage from Europe to Africa to America. Others believed they had located the story's origin in Spain, Portugal, or Lithuania. Franz Boas took the time to try out several theories about the tar baby's "peculiar distribution," the most striking of which was the idea that the story was carried to places like Mexico and the Philippines by European sailors who had learned the story from slaves who had come to Spain and Portugal direct from Africa. "It is not improbable," Boas concludes, that European settlers were ultimately "instrumental" in "disseminating tales of Negro origin."[9]

No matter where these arguments turned, they retained the same stakes. If the tar baby originated in Africa and was carried to other continents by Africans, its transmission could be conceived as diasporic and therefore discernible, across time and space, as a kind of heredity. On the other hand, if the tar baby came from somewhere other than Africa, or if it was transformed during its global diffusion by some intermediary influence, then the strong claim about the story's connection to racial identity did not hold. If you could track the story's derivation to Europe, Asia, or America, it followed that there was no necessary connection between culture and race. Whether culture follows or crosses over lines of descent, whether culture is racial, or race is cultural, whether culture constructs or transcends racial identity—these questions have persisted in something like their original form in a range of disciplines including folklore, anthropology, history, musicology, religion, literature, and geography, not to mention interdisciplinary fields such as African American Studies and Ethnic Studies that have made the problem of culture into one of their foundational concerns.[10]

After Harris, the most influential theory about the story's origin and subsequent diffusion was offered by Joseph Jacobs in his book *Indian Fairy Tales* (1892). Responding directly to Harris's hypothesis about the story's racial descent, Jacobs rejected the idea that the tar baby story came from Africa, proposing instead that it came from India, where it had derived from another story called "The Demon with the Matted Hair," the fifty-fifth installment from the Jātakas, a cycle of legends recounting the previous lives of the Buddha. In this story, Buddha is a prince who battles a demon, striking it repeatedly and becoming stuck at five points to its syrupy hair. Jacobs cites circumstantial evidence to build his case that "The Demon with the Matted Hair" is the precursor to "The Wonderful Tar Baby Story," but his claim rests mostly on the oddness of the five-point attack, which is so "preposterously ludicrous" in both tales as to suggest that they could not have been "independently invented." For Jacobs, the fact that there are tar baby variants in South Africa in regions where there are also Buddhist symbols woven into the local culture "clinches the matter." The story, he decides, must have been invented in India more than 1,500 years before it was taken to Africa by Buddhist missionaries and then brought to America through the slave trade. Over time, other scholars agreed with Jacobs that the story came from India even as they imagined new pathways for its diffusion—suggesting that its arrival in Africa, for instance, might have come as late as the sixteenth century, with the arrival of Portuguese sailors. Others argued the story went from India to Europe before it was taken to America and taught to slaves by their masters. Others still found versions in Japan, Indonesia, and the Philippines that appeared to have been transmitted directly from the Indian subcontinent.[11]

During the first half of the twentieth century, scholars led by Aurelio Espinosa further subdivided the tar baby by adapting techniques from the so-called "historical-geographical" method in folklore studies, an approach championed by Archer Taylor and Stith Thompson in the United States, which was supposed to provide the tools for breaking down any story (or "tale type") into its "fundamental motifs" ("motifs" in this case referring to the smallest elements in a story "having a power to persist in

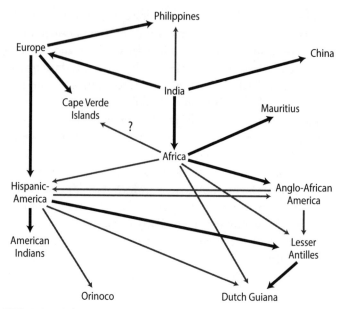

FIG. 1.3. Aurelio Espinosa, "[Chart Showing the Direction of the Tar Baby's Diffusion]." From Aurelio Espinosa, "More Notes on the Origin and History of the Tar-Baby Story," *Folklore* 49 (1938), 180.

tradition"). In a monumental series of essays published between 1930 and 1944, Espinosa gathered together every version of the tar baby he was able to locate, two hundred and sixty-seven by his count, and parsed them using statistics, tables, figures, and graphs to reveal the sequence of the story's development as well as the course of its global diffusion. Charts measured versions of the story in which the thief is a rabbit against others in which the thief is a spider, a monkey, a jackal, or a human. Calculations were performed to demonstrate how the thief's role in the story pivots around the changing mechanism of the trap, which in some cases involves artifice (a figure made from tar, wax, or bird lime), in others a naturally occurring entity or substance (a rotten stump or an ogre's unwashed hair), and in others still a supernatural agency (a cursed amulet or vodou doll).[12]

Although Espinosa and his associates presented their methods as if they were scientific, their thoughts about the development of the tar baby were shaped by the controversy over its origin, which dated all the way back to Uncle Remus. There is no question that Espinosa was a partisan dedicated to proving the tar baby's links to South Asia and Europe. Given his assiduous research methods, Espinosa's willingness to disregard evidence to the contrary is all the more striking. He makes no mention, for instance, of stylistic devices, like the ideophone ("lippity-clippity") or the use of honorific titles ("Brer Rabbit") that others have invoked to suggest the story's connection to Africa. Espinosa admits that his conclusions will be subject to revision as new versions of the story surface, but he remains convinced his claims are incontrovertible in light of the available evidence. This certainty comes at a cost, because it ignores the extent to which his conclusions are prefigured by his own assumptions. At the same time, Espinosa ignores the notorious unreliability of ethnographic sources. The corruption of these sources has been a cause for concern as scholars have enumerated flaws resulting from manipulation, condescension, evasion, reticence, mishearing, and failed memory, not to mention the eye-catching inconsistencies introduced by editors. Even the classification system used by Espinosa to correct for this unreliability has been shown to carry its own bias in the provincial standards it applies to stories from the rest of the world.[13]

Ethnographic documentation is inconclusive even under the best circumstances, and many leading accounts of the tar baby have made insufficient allowance for this contingency as they have connected the dots between the remote sites where the story happens to have been transcribed. The best that can be said for many of these arguments is that they are "not improbable," to borrow the term that Franz Boas uses to describe his own hypothesis. In the 1888 inaugural issue of the *Journal of American Folklore*, reflecting on the controversy over the Uncle Remus stories, Thomas F. Crane was already worrying that folklore collection was being contaminated by the "prejudice" of scholars who brought a "preconceived theory of the origin and diffusion of popular tales" into the field. The tar baby was transcribed repeatedly by collectors eager to confirm, deny, or elaborate some hypothesis about its derivation, and by extension, some theory about the relationship between culture and race.[14]

Even as Espinosa, Herskovits, and other thinkers were quick to insist that their conclusions were based on incomplete evidence and were therefore subject to revision, they continually deferred to a projected moment in the future when they felt they would have enough data to reach a definite conclusion about the story's circulation. Herskovits and Espinosa had little doubt that their knowledge of the tar baby would eventually be "systematic" and "complete," and their approach to classification took for granted that each new discovery brought them closer to this horizon. Others, including Ruth Benedict, were less sanguine, insisting that the "direction of diffusion" could be established only by using "special kinds of data" that were absent in this case. Some things about the tar baby, perhaps, were unknowable, though this possibility has never kept scholars from speculating about the story. Indeed, one might even argue that the story's unknowability has been a spur to theoretical innovation, starting with the rudimentary ideas that nineteenth-century scholars posited in relation to the tar baby, such as the age-area hypothesis, which says a story's age can be deduced from the distance it has traveled, or the rule that says the probability of a connection between two stories increases with the complexity of the elements they share. Speculation did not stop with these early theories, as new conjectures about the story continued to attract interested commentary from leading scholars.[15]

Increasingly in the twentieth century, these ideas about cultural circulation were adapted by historians and anthropologists eager to think more expansively about politics. It was hoped that sources like the tar baby could provide a way to understand the politics practiced by the colonized, the unwaged, and other groups whose contributions had been undervalued by previous generations of scholars whose attention had been trained on political elites. At stake in this new approach was the identification of a new political perspective that was formed outside state institutions and outside the cash nexus, a perspective that could bring focused attention to a history of violence that was obscured in disciplines like law and political economy that had little interest in people whose primary records were oral traditions. This was an expansive politics that spread across jurisdictions—a cultural politics for want of a better term—that was less likely to bind itself to a territory than to spiral outward, operating alongside established institutions wherever landless people happened to find themselves.[16]

As scholars worked to substantiate this new approach, they looked to vernacular traditions that featured speaking animals as their trickster protagonists. According to James Scott, these trickster traditions were "hidden transcripts"—ephemeral sources, usually coded or concealed, that recorded the arts of everyday resistance. Taken in combination and read back into the contexts in which they circulated, these traditions were said to have been shaped at a time when European commoners were being expelled from the land, American Indians were being conquered and pillaged, and Africans were being kidnapped and transported across the ocean as slaves. Certainly in many instances, the stories predated the onset of modernity, but their utility in recent centuries, as they were adapted to the struggle over expropriation, remained a predominant concern in this interpretation, and the stories were understood accordingly as Manichean political allegories in which the repeated battles between speaking foxes, rabbits, spiders, and wolves were supposed to represent entrenched conflicts in human history.[17]

This orthodox interpretation assumes that identification in these stories was routed through the weaker animals, who had to rely on their wits when outmatched by their stronger opponents. It was acknowledged that these stories had universal appeal, as we all like to root for the underdog, but it was also suggested that commoners, natives, and slaves had specific reasons for identifying with the weaker animals given their own struggles against their oppressors. Returning to a stock situation in which the strong attack the weak only to be tricked in return, these stories revealed the elementary aspects of a previously unacknowledged approach to politics, an approach that was geared neither to the graduated advance of reform nor to the flashing forward of revolution but instead to the repeating waves and cycles of everyday existence. This was an approach based on tactics rather than principles and deception rather than disputation, an approach that found its own justice by seizing every advantage and surviving to fight another day.[18]

During the 1960s and 1970s, this interest in cultural politics became strongly associated with the new social history, a movement that looked to unconventional source materials like broadside ballads, anonymous letters, confessions, rumors, and folklore to document the consciousness of non-elite groups whose experience was not reflected in the actuarial tables and statute books that had previously been the preferred sources for scholarship. This approach borrowed from the established interpretation of the trickster tradition, looking to the rabbit in particular for insight, and it drew explicitly, if not always systematically, from recent developments in historical materialism, symbolic anthropology, and the sociology of everyday life. The central theme in this research was that the capacity of common people for self-directed action had to be taken into account in order to gauge the course of history. This was a capacity that could not be grasped by looking to the usual places in the usual ways. It required new kinds of evidence, and it also required a willingness to expand the domain of politics to encompass the entire range of human activity.[19]

The crux of this new thinking about politics centered on everyday life: scholars from a range of disciplines worked to reconstruct the reasoning behind small acts of resistance like breaking tools, burning crops, adulterating food, hiding out, slowing down, poaching, pan toting, and pilfering—acts, in other words, that occurred not on the grand stage of history, where revolutions were plotted and worlds were transformed, but in the obscure confines of ordinary situations where individual tactics were either inferred or improvised and formal organization was not required. Because they involved taking opportunities when they presented themselves and reacting on the spot to miscalculations or lapses in surveillance, these acts of everyday resistance were in every sense contingent and circumstantial. There were skeptics, including the historian Eric Hobsbawm, who said these acts were "pre-political," meaning that they were performed by people who had not yet found a way to conceptualize their aspirations, and there were others, including Eugene Genovese, one of the preeminent scholars of North American slavery, who argued that these acts were detrimental to the development of political consciousness, as they focused on routine conflict between individuals rather than a principled critique of systematic exploitation. Increasingly, however, these skeptics were holdouts within intellectual movements that had begun to concentrate much of their critical attention on the quicksilver politics of everyday life.[20]

Some thinkers, such as Michel de Certeau, went so far as to say that acts of day-to-day resistance were always *sui generis*. "Lacking a view of the whole," these tactics were "limited by the possibilities of the moment." They could not be modeled, generalized, or planned in advance. Based on a situational ethics, they were not supposed to be taken as norms to be followed in every instance. They were justified only under certain conditions. It was also invariably the case, according to Certeau, that these practices did not, and could not, take place on their own terms. By definition, they were performed by individuals who lacked the capacity to impose themselves on the world. It did not make sense to conceive politics in universal principles when the circumstances susceptible to influence were so restricted and uncertain. This was a politics about day-to-day survival, a politics that saw abstraction as an absurdity, rebuffing talk of rights and prerogatives to focus on here and now, always returning attention to situational necessity.[21]

Exemplified in oral traditions like the tar baby story, this was a politics that was often cast symbolically—or *culturally*—so that it could be concealed in plain sight. Zora Neale Hurston famously describes her own culture as fitting like a "tight chemise" that she could not see while she was wearing it. Stories about "Brer Rabbit's capers," Hurston continues, were like second nature to her, but their full meaning was easiest to grasp when they were viewed in context from a distance. Hurston's metaphor affirms that every culture needs to be understood in relation to its own particular assumptions, adding the ironic twist that these assumptions are often invisible to cultural insiders because they are so prevalent as to be taken for granted. These are ideas that Hurston learned from her mentor Franz Boas, ideas later elaborated during the 1960s and 1970s by symbolic anthropologists like Clifford Geertz, who argued that traditions and rituals needed to be understood in light of the symbolic meaning they held for participants. Culture, Geertz believed, was a story people "tell themselves about themselves." It expressed a worldview endemic to a locality, with stories and rituals deriving their embedded meaning from their coexistence in a "web of significance."[22]

The tar baby story has been interpreted in precisely these terms as situational and metaphorical rather than rational and abstract, with its symbolic significance keyed to actors and objects present in its immediate environment. Moving freely from location to location, the tar baby is thought to remain tuned into its changing local circumstances, embodying the culturally specific values associated with particular locations and particular peoples. Based on these premises, traditional stories like the tar baby have been seen as political, and even inherently political, to the degree that they resist assimilation to the universal designs that others would impose on them. Stories like the tar baby in-here in their stubborn particulars. They are irreducible. As such, they provide a basis for claiming autonomy against usurpers. This resistance is not only exemplified but expressed thematically in the tar baby, as the story both performs and figures its commitment to culture through its conventional recourse to the briar patch, the ancestral home that gives the rabbit refuge from the enemy.[23]

The theory of cultural politics associated with this interpretation of the tar baby has remained influential, especially in interdisciplinary fields focused on race and ethnicity, where it has served as a *lingua franca* for scholars seeking a common approach to their objects of study. At the same time, others have expressed reservations about this theory, especially its account of political agency, which is thought to take too much for granted. To its skeptics, this account fails to explain the motivation for resistance. Moreover, the account appears circular to the extent that it defines the politics practiced by peasants, natives, and slaves in idealized abstractions, like freedom and self-determination, that were themselves defined over centuries in opposition to the material exploitation suffered by peasants, natives, and slaves.[24]

These objections about vague or circular reasoning ultimately come down to the complaint that thinking about cultural politics has emphasized the embedded and contingent practices of everyday life to an extent that has obscured a fundamental question about the perspective from which these practices are put to use. Sometimes this thinking appears to assume a free-standing individual that exists fully formed apart from society, an individual whose perspective can be taken for granted. Other times this thinking seems to reduce the vagaries of individual intention to a mechanical process where categories of interest derive automatically from circumstantial inequalities. In both of these respects, the new thinking about cultural politics can seem substantially weaker in conceptualization than the political theories it seeks to supplant, as it dispenses with the ways that others have accounted for the emergence of political consciousness without offering anything in their place. In contrast to the old myths about individuals throwing off the dead weight of tradition or classes coming to consciousness as contradictions are revealed from the point of production, it would seem that the new social history and its associated intellectual movements are content to take individual agency for granted, thereby leaving us without the backstory we need to understand how politics becomes possible in relation to objective circumstances.[25]

I remain interested in these questions about culture and politics, and I believe we have been right to look to the tar baby for answers. My sense, in fact, is that the tar baby anticipates more than we have assumed about the claims that have been made in its name. Restored to its full breadth, the story may even help us solve some of the problems that have beset the political theory it helped to establish. In this book, I depart from the orthodox interpretation of the tar baby, which has been repeated over generations to the point where it has become common sense. If the story's contingency has often been understood as a virtue, and even as an antidote to the universal designs projected by colonial dictate, my sense is that this standard interpretation has kept us from perceiving the scale at which the story pitches the disagreement between its characters. The story thinks locally and tactically, that much is true, but it also thinks broadly and indeed philosophically about the world in ways we are likely to miss if we are not willing to credit its capacity for integrated thought. Ultimately, it is at this higher level of abstraction, in the recurring conflict among its representative characters, that the tar baby story has perpetuated, over centuries and around the world, an intellectual tradition that rivals the most vaunted parables about the origin of property and the nature of politics.

This new approach to the story requires us to seek out common characteristics not only in myth and oral tradition but also in written records. Folklorists have always been willing to entertain the possibility that the tar baby is directly linked to vernacular traditions from other centuries and other continents, but they have not considered the possibility of its association to other intellectual domains. Treated as an example of culture, whether retained or remixed, and valued for its distance from the instrumental approach to nature represented in modern society, the tar baby has been interpreted in a way that obscures the circumstances under which it was characteristically collected. These were circumstances in which populations were mobile and mixed; labor was organized on a mass scale to produce commodities for export; and colonialism was long established. The tar baby is engaged from start to finish with these prototypically modern conditions. Too often reduced to something as vague as heritage or something as elementary as circumstantial self-preservation, the tar baby's political thinking is communicated in conventional tropes and scenarios that were adapted at the same time in other philosophical traditions in the attempt to come to terms with the disorienting experience of globalization.[26]

Approaching the tar baby in this manner, I have tried to keep in mind what is likely unknowable about the story. Probably we will never be able to say for sure where the story originated, nor will we be able to cut out the additives that compromise its authenticity, but admitting our uncertainty on these points is useful, if only because it returns us again to the task of interpreting the story. Rather than producing a theory of culture based on conjectures about how the tar baby came to be in the places it was told, I hope to show what we can infer about the story's meaning based on its common existence in places where people were struggling with elementary and unresolved questions raised by the onset of capitalism. If the tar baby's diffusion is often invisible and uncertain, its presence is felt again and again in places where the right to subsistence, the distribution of property, the legitimacy of contract, and the prerogatives of sovereignty are central questions. Elaborating on these matters, this book argues that the tar baby is best understood not as folklore but instead as a collective experiment in speculative reason keyed to problems of sociability in the natural world.

Chapter Two
STATES OF NATURE

In *To Make Our World Anew: A History of African Americans* (2000), their brilliant and wide-ranging survey of African American history, Robin D. G. Kelley and Earl Lewis outline the main points in the standard interpretation of the tar baby story. Situating the story in its canonical setting, Kelley and Lewis describe how slaves gathered by their quarters when work was done to share songs and stories, including the tar baby, a narrative that "begins," in their synopsis, "when the strong and powerful Wolf creates a sticky doll, or Tar Baby, to trap Rabbit, who is inquisitive and sly." After summarizing the rest of the story, concluding with the escape to the briar patch, Kelley and Lewis explain that the tar baby was an allegory of everyday life from which slaves learned many "important lessons." They learned, for instance, that "quick-wittedness was an essential survival trait" and that "deception" could give "the weak some control over the strong." The story "laid bare the concepts that might did not always make for right, and that rash behavior, like that indulged in by Rabbit, seldom yielded rewards." These were "lessons about life," Kelley and Lewis conclude, "not a life that was distant and abstract, but one the slave had to live every day."[1]

This interpretation has a long history. Before it was broadened into a general theory of slave politics, it surfaced in offhand commentary by some of the story's earliest collectors. Recurring themes in this interpretation include the affirmative emphasis on the independent culture of the slave quarters, construed as a counterbalance to the deadening routine of suffering and exploitation; the idea that stories like the tar baby were designed to instruct slaves in the methods necessary for survival, encouraging caution and modeling tactics of deception and misdirection; and the suggestion that there is nothing "distant and abstract" about the tar baby, as the story is grounded in everyday existence.[2]

The most important aspect of this interpretation, however, is the assumption that the rabbit is always the hero. Slaves, it is presumed, identify with the rabbit even in cases where the rabbit does not prevail. "It needs no scientific investigation," Harris writes, to discover why the slave "selects as his hero the weakest . . . of all animals, and brings him out victorious." The basis for the slave's identification with the rabbit, in other words, is self-evident, and it is the self-evidence of this identification that licenses the allegorical interpretation of the story. Abigail Christensen makes the point directly, even bluntly, in the introduction to her collection *Afro-American Folk Lore* (1892). "The Rabbit," she writes, "represents the colored man." Although the rabbit "is not as large nor as strong, as swift, as wise, nor as handsome as the elephant, the alligator, the bear, the deer, the serpent, [or] the fox," Christensen adds, "he is 'de mos' cunnin' man dat go on fo' leg' [the most cunning man that goes on four legs]—and by this cunning he gains success." And so it is with "the negro," she concludes. Lacking clout and education, the negro has one hope, which is to "succeed by stratagem."[3]

This interpretation extends to twentieth-century folklore anthologies, like *The Book of Negro Folklore* (1958), where the editors Arna Bontemps and Langston Hughes describe the vicarious satisfaction that slaves found by identifying with the underdog in trickster stories where "weakness [overcomes] strength through cunning." The "folk tales" shared by "Negro slaves," Hughes and Bontemps conclude, are "projections of personal experiences and hopes and defeats in terms of symbols." In the introduction to his own anthology, John Mason Brewer agrees that "the rabbit

. . . symbolized the slave." Whenever "the rabbit succeeded in proving himself smarter than another animal," Brewer adds, "the slave rejoiced secretly, imagining himself smarter than his master." Houston Baker pushes this point even further, arguing that the slave experiences an exceptional identification. "Black animal tales," Baker writes, "resemble the animal tales of other lores in their employment of the trickster, but the social condition of the folk producing them gives an added dimension, a certain psychical component which the slave narrator surely supplied and which his slave audience readily recognized." According to Baker, this intuitive identification was powerful enough to resolve the most difficult questions that have been raised about stories like the tar baby, including the question of their origin: "Any black man reading about Br'er Rabbit . . . realizes that this black American trickster has more to do with Denmark Vesey and Nat Turner than with Chauntecleer and Pertelote." This theme was also carried into the new social history of slavery. John Blassingame, for example, suggests that trickster stories like the tar baby were based on the slave's "personal experience." By "identifying" with the "weaker animals," Blassingame avers, slaves were able to indulge in "projection" and "wish fulfillment" while at the same time "holding on to the reality of [their] existence." Some critics, like Lawrence Levine, saw a subtle counterpoint in these stories, by which the trickster's occasional failures were used to teach lessons in restraint, but even in Levine's measured assessment, identification remains paramount.[4]

We will consider the issue of identification along with the other major themes encapsulated in Kelley and Lewis's interpretation, but first we need to address the crucial fact about their interpretation, which is where it begins. Kelley and Lewis follow an established tendency in the history of the tar baby's reception when they start their synopsis with the wolf making a "sticky doll" to trap the rabbit. This is where most political discussions of the tar baby begin, but it is not where the story usually begins. As best I can tell, this discrepancy results from the canonization of the original version told by Uncle Remus, a version that is atypical in its failure to provide a motivating context for the struggle between the animals. The majority of extant versions of the tar baby story begin with an account of what is at stake in the conflict, but Uncle Remus skips the preliminaries and starts the story with the predator's plan to catch the rabbit with the tar baby.[5]

Interpretation has too often followed the pattern set by Uncle Remus in the assumption that the reasons for the conflict need not be established because they are self-evident. Foxes and rabbits, it is presumed, are natural enemies. They are fighting because the fox is a fox and the rabbit is a rabbit. Fighting with rabbits is what foxes do, and fighting with foxes is what rabbits do. This is chalked up to instinct, and it therefore stands to reason that the rabbit and the fox will keep fighting even when there is nothing in dispute. According to this interpretation, the tar baby is a political allegory in which species difference corresponds to social difference. The attributes of the animals therefore only become meaningful as instruments in race and class warfare, a meaning that is elaborated only to the extent that physical advantages in size and strength are correlated with social advantages in prestige, legitimacy, and capacity for violence. Once the social is collapsed into the biological, and race is thereby collapsed into species, we are left with no way to draw other independent variables into consideration, making it difficult, if not impossible, to understand the predication of the opposing perspectives imputed to the rabbit and the fox. What we need to know, in other words, is how the rabbit became a rabbit and how the fox became a fox, and this is exactly what we cannot know, or even ask, if we accept the presuppositions that support the interpretation that has been around since the time of Uncle Remus.[6]

Most storytellers on record, however, try to explain why the animals are fighting, starting the story with the context that is frequently ignored in interpretation, a context whose very existence goes to show that the situation is neither natural nor inevitable and therefore requires some comment. In 1919, Elsie Clews Parsons identified what she took to be the dominant explanation given in the story. "In a comparison of the variants of the Tar Baby," she writes, "it is notable that the trap is almost always set to catch a thief." Whatever its circumstantial details, the tar baby characteristically has the same beginning (which establishes that the trap is set to catch a thief), middle (in which the trap is sprung), and ending (in which the thief escapes). Within this formula, Parsons adds, there is variety. Sometimes the theft is given in a concise prelude to the real action; other times the tar baby sequence is attached as a solution to another fully formed story with its own history of circulation, as is the case in the versions Parsons found on the Cape Verde Islands. In some cases, the owner is a king, as in the story collected by Charles Baissac on Mauritius in 1888, a variation that answers the riddle of ownership succinctly by appealing to the monarch's dominion over his territory. In all versions, the resource belongs to somebody. Whether the resource is possessed by an individual or held in common by a community, we are given some kind of backstory explaining how it came to be owned in the first place.[7]

A good example of the conventional backstory to the tar baby appears in "The Rabbit and the Tar Wolf," a story that was published in the 1840s in the *Cherokee Advocate*, a tribal newspaper in Oklahoma, and reprinted in James Mooney's *Myths of the Cherokee* (1902). Mooney uses the tar baby to support his claims about cultural diffusion, but as it appears in his book, the story's opening seems concerned less with culture than with access to nature:

> Once upon a time there was such a severe drought that all streams of water and all lakes were dried up. In this emergency the beasts assembled together to devise means to procure water. It was proposed by one to dig a well. All agreed to do so except the hare. She refused because it

would soil her tiny paws. The rest, however, dug their well and were fortunate enough to find water. The hare beginning to suffer and thirst, and having no right to the well, was thrown upon her wits to procure water. She determined, as the easiest way, to steal from the public well. The rest of the animals, surprised to find that the hare was so well supplied with water, asked her where she got it. She replied that she arose betimes in the morning and gathered the dewdrops. However the wolf and the fox suspected her of theft.

This passage is inserted into Mooney's argument that the tar baby was invented first by American Indians and subsequently borrowed by African Americans. Mooney writes that the tar baby has many variants not only "among the Cherokee" but also in "New Mexico, Washington, and southern Alaska—wherever, in fact, the piñon or the pine supplies enough gum to be molded into a ball for Indian uses." For Mooney, the primacy of this American Indian lineage is proven by the fact that stories similar to the tar baby are told by "widely separated tribes among whom there can be no suspicion of Negro influences." Even as Mooney contests the claims for African origin made by earlier collectors like Joel Chandler Harris, he shares with them the assumption that the tar baby's meaning derives from the pattern of its diffusion. Like Harris, Mooney also believes in something like a labor theory of culture: he asserts that culture is property that belongs to the race that created it. It may be borrowed by others, but it cannot be owned by them. According not only to Harris but also to Mooney, the story's meaning is conditioned by its existence as cultural property.[8]

Preoccupied with the problem of the tar baby's diffusion, Mooney has little to say about the meaning of its opening sequence. He does not bother to ask what this theft would have meant either to the Cherokee or to the other racial constituencies who began their versions of the story, it must be noted, in exactly the same way that Mooney's sources did. The great irony about Mooney's approach to the story resides in its willingness to take for granted an idea—property—whose composition is called into question in the story's opening scene. No less than other versions of the tar baby, "The Rabbit and the Tar Wolf" is a story about natural rights to property. The story does not presume anything about these rights. Instead, it begins by staging a scenario from which these rights can be deduced. In this case, the rights in question are based on individual labor and managed in common by a community.[9]

Following convention, "The Rabbit and the Tar Wolf" begins by establishing an original situation in which the rights to a particular resource, in this case a well, are shared among a group of animals who have organized themselves. Communal access to the resource and responsibilities for its maintenance are allotted among group members according to rules that have been established in concert. This collective arrangement seems justified for two reasons: first, it is the result of deliberation among interested parties, and second, it imposes not only rights but duties. It is the trickster, the "lazy one," who is the outlier in these situations, doing no work and stealing from the public trust, and thereby posing a challenge, by some lights an unanswerable challenge, to this attempt at organization, destabilizing the situation by shirking, infringing on others, taking more than his due, and even polluting or destroying the resource after he is done so that others can no longer use it. The community's capacity for self-regulation, which seems like a saving grace at the start, is called into question by the trickster, who often but not always makes an escape in the end.[10]

In this Cherokee example, the conflict involves the trickster's refusal to labor, but in some versions we see the trickster avoiding a greater sacrifice, as in "Why the Hare Runs Away." In this story, collected from the so-called Slave Coast in West Africa and printed by Alfred Burdon Ellis in 1890, the animals agree to cut the tips of their ears to extract the fat from them, so they can sell the fat to buy a hoe with which to dig the well. When it is the hare's turn, predictably, he refuses to clip his ears, but he draws from the well anyway, banking on the likelihood that the other animals will not take the trouble to stop him. The hare makes a racket with his calabash to scare off the other animals, then draws water and lowers himself into the well to bathe, stirring up the pool and leaving it muddy.[11]

In the Cherokee story reported by Mooney and the West African story reported by Ellis, the occasion is a drought, and in many other stories, the narrative is initiated in relation to some other natural disaster such as a famine or an earthquake. Sometimes in these stories there is an established system of governance, such as a monarchy, with a strong animal installed as king, but most of the time the animals organize themselves ad hoc to cope with the emergency. Whatever the mode of governance, we see the animals gather together to discuss a solution, a sequence often described in terms of political association, where we are told that they "deliberated a long time" over the distribution of costs, or where we see them "assembled in council" to decide on a public works project, such as the construction of a dam or a cistern to collect rainwater. Cooperation is also a common theme in other stories from the trickster tradition, where we see animals working together to gather grease for cooking, flatten a road, clear land for a corn field, or erect a kraal (a livestock enclosure with mud walls). We also see animals hunting and fishing in groups with an agreement to share what they kill or catch, and we see them storing their provisions in communal caches, trusting nobody will take more than belongs to them or more than they deserve. In every instance, the community's efforts at self-organization are disrupted by the noncompliance of one of its nominal members.[12]

The theft scenario in these stories is an example of the social dilemma that arises when an individual's short-term self-interest is placed at odds with the long-term interest of a group. As Mooney's story makes explicit, the problem in these situations is that defecting tends to be the "easiest" way to get what you need or what you want. Scarecrows and tar babies aside, it is extremely difficult to prevent tricksters (or "free riders") from obtaining benefits from a resource they did nothing to create or maintain. Any strategy guaranteed to prevent access, like hiring a round-the-clock guard, or standing watch yourself, or erecting a fortification under lock and key, is almost certainly too costly to be feasible. In most instances, the price of prevention is greater than the loss from theft. This so-called "zero contribution" problem is explored at length in Mancur Olson's *The Logic of Collective Action* (1965), a book dedicated to proving the claim that groups that try to work together for a shared benefit will inevitably fail, as there will always be free riders who take advantage of the labor of others without contributing to the common cause. The basic problem, again, is that it is difficult and costly, if not impossible, to exclude individuals from a resource once the resource has been made available. Self-interested individuals have little to no incentive to contribute voluntarily to the construction of a resource that they would be able to access anyway. Because cheating in these instances is the rational and self-interested course of action, Olson believes that all such efforts are doomed to failure, as everyone comes to suspect that everyone else is acting opportunistically whenever they are given the chance. As promises are broken and work is left undone, it becomes harder and harder to maintain an environment where norms can be developed and passed down over generations. In the tar baby, it is the trickster who plays the role of the free rider and who therefore stands in a larger sense for the impossibility of collective self-organization.[13]

Olson's argument has been extended to consider the environmental costs that result from the failure of cooperative resource management. Best known is Garrett Hardin's essay "The Tragedy of the Commons" (1968), which takes up a scenario where livestock is grazed in a common pasture, an example that Hardin adapts from a pamphlet published in 1833 by William Forster Lloyd on medieval land tenure. Hardin argues that herders in this situation are faced with a dilemma. It is in their short-term interest to maximize profits by grazing as many cows or sheep as possible, but if this strategy is pursued by more than a few herders, it will lead to disaster for everyone in the long term, as the pasture will be depleted, or even ruined, due to overgrazing. This outcome is "inescapable," Hardin says. Herders may try to establish norms to prevent overuse, but those norms will never be strong enough to prevent rational and self-interested individuals from defecting from the bargain, because such individuals will always seek to secure maximum advantage by expanding their own grazing on the assumption that others will follow the rules. Tragedy occurs when a majority of herders make the rational choice, and the pasture is destroyed. Because these herders are unable to police themselves, their tragedy can be avoided only by changing the structure of their situation—for instance by privatizing access to the pasture or else by investing sufficient power in an external authority such as a state.[14]

One theme that remains consistent in the tar baby is the general volatility that characterizes the society of the animals. As Bernard Wolfe writes in what is likely the best-known essay on the rabbit and his tricks, the world depicted in the story is a "jungle" where existence is little more than a "battle-unto-the-death." In this inhospitable world, Wolfe suggests, there are no conventions for conflict resolution. Society tends toward chaos. Or to combine Wolfe's interpretation with a term borrowed from Hardin, we might say that the story appears to have an "inherent logic" that leads inevitably to tragedy. Cooperative ventures are ill-fated, as someone will always choose to defect at the expense of his or her partners, and individual efforts will fare no better, as there is no way to protect property from the scroungers who are ready to seize every advantage.[15]

To put the same point differently, we might say that the story dramatizes the problem of sociability in the state of nature. As an opening, the theft scenario serves the same purpose that the state of nature has served in political philosophy, which is to show that the social dilemmas faced by self-organized communities cannot be resolved over the long term. The insolubility of these dilemmas is essential in each case. In the tar baby, as in political philosophy, the problem of free riding and the prohibitive cost of sequestering goods are invoked to demonstrate the ultimate impossibility of self-organization—to show, in other words, that moral norms and good-faith agreements are not sufficient to constrain liars, cheats, and thieves unless they are backed by the authority of state institutions. In the tar baby, the trickster is sometimes punished for his crimes, but the fact that he gets away most of the time is sufficient to prove the instability of the political setting. As the conflict in the story escalates, we witness the insecurity that is supposed to be endemic to primitive societies that have not yet developed the infrastructure needed for the rule of law.[16]

The tar baby is often concerned with common pool resources like pastures and springs, but in many examples, the story focuses on a conflict over private property. In these versions, there is no proposal to share the resource and no social arrangement governing access. Frequently in these cases the conflict is concerned not with common pool resources subject to joint appropriation, like water or wood, but instead with food supplies that are limited and perishable. Access to the resource depends exclusively on the labor that an individual devoted to its construction and maintenance. Characters in stories concerned with private property are introduced as conventional opposites: for instance, as "industrious" and "lazy" in a version of the tar baby from Nova Scotia, or as a "hardworking fellow" and a con artist who "lives off his wits" in an early-twentieth-century variant from Philadelphia.[17]

One example of a private property dispute comes in the story collected in 1913 by John Lomax from Lattevi Ajaji at State Normal and Industrial School for Negroes in Prairie View, Texas. In Ajaji's story, the plot begins when a man digs a well for his personal use. The rabbit then steals the man's water and bathes in it.

In this story, the conflict is between a man and a rabbit, but the property owner could just as easily be a leopard and the thief could just as easily be a monkey, as in a version told to Héli Chatelain by his black servant Jeremiah Curtain during a stay in Luanda, a seaport on the Atlantic coast of southern Africa. The resource stolen in Ajaji's story is water, but it could just as easily be turnips from a field (as recorded by Herminio Portell Vila in Cuba) or chile from a garden (as transcribed by Franz Boas in Oaxaca). In each of these cases, the principle at stake is the same.[18]

Another representative example of the conflict over private property appears in the version transcribed by Christensen on the South Carolina Sea Islands and published in 1874 in a regional newspaper, the *Springfield Republican*, while Christensen was a student at Mount Holyoke College, before it was finally reprinted in what would become her most famous ethnographic collection, *Afro-American Folk Lore* (1892):

> Now de Wolf, 'e bery wise man; but not so wise as de Rabbit. De Rabbit 'e mos' cunnin' man dat go on four leg. 'E lib in de brier-bush. Now, de Wolf 'e done plant corn one 'ear, but Rabbit 'e aint plant nuttin tall. E' lib on Wolf corn all winter. Nex' 'ear Wolf aint plant corn, 'e tink corn crop too poo'; so 'e plant groun'-nut. Rabbit, 'e do jes' de same as befo'. Well, Wolf 'e biggin for tink someting wrong. 'E gone out in de mawnin' look at 'e groun'-nut patch, look bery hard at Rabbit track, say: "I 'spicion somebordy ben a tief my groun'-nut." Nex' mawnin' 'e go 'gen, meet mo' groun'-nut gone, say same ting. Den 'e say, "I gwine mek one skeer crow for set up in dis yere groun'-nut patch, for skeer de tief." So 'e mek one ol' skeer-crow an' set um in de middle ob de groun'-nut patch. Dat night when Rabbit come wid 'e bag for git groun'-nut, 'e see de skeer-crow stan' bery white in de moonshine, an' 'e say, "Wha' dat?" Nobordy aint say anyting. "Wha' dat?" 'e say 'gen. Den nobordy aint say nuttin', an' he aint see nuttin

moobe, so 'e gone up leetle closer, an' leetle closer, tel 'e git close up ter um, den 'e put out 'e paw an' touch de skeer-crow. Den 'e say, "You aint nuttin but one ol' bundle o' rag! Wolf tink I gwine f'raid you? mus' be fool!" So 'e kick ober the skeer-crow an' fill 'e bag wid groun'-nut, an' gone back home to de brier-bush. Nex' mawnin' Wolf gone out for look at 'e groun'-nut patch, an' when 'e meet mo groun'-nut gone an' de skeer-crow knock down, 'e bery mad. 'E say, 'Neber you min', I fix ole Rabbit dat done tief all my groun'-nut. Jes' le' me show you!" So 'e mek one baby out o' tar, an' set up in 'e groun'-nut patch, an' say, "Jes' le' ol' Rabbit try for knock ober dis yere Tar Baby an' 'e 'll see! I jes' wan' um for try!"

Christensen's version follows the same pattern as Ajaji's story, treating the wolf's right to his groundnut patch as self-evident based on the labor he devoted to it. Christensen's story is also conventional in the difficulty that the wolf experiences attempting to protect his property. All the rabbit has to do is wait for the wolf to leave the patch unguarded. The scarecrow, like most of the enforcement mechanisms in these stories, is an ineffective deterrent. Although the wolf eventually catches the rabbit with the tar baby, in the end the rabbit manages to escape, again according to convention, into the "brier-bush."[19]

Thirty years after Christensen had her story printed in the *Springfield Republican*, a similar version was told more than eight-thousand miles away on Panay, an island in the Visayan region of the Philippines. Transcribed by W. H. Millington and Bertrand Maxfield in Iloilo and Mandurriao, two villages on Panay, this story was combined with other local versions of the tar baby and published as a composite in the *Journal of American Folklore*. It begins:

Masoy was a poor man. . . . [whose] little garden furnished him scarcely enough to live on. Every week day he went to town to sell his fruits and vegetables and to buy rice. Upon his return he noticed each day that someone had entered the garden in his absence and stolen some of the fruit. He tried to protect the garden by making the fence very strong and locking the gate; but, in spite of all he could do, he continued to miss his fruit. At length Masoy conceived the happy idea of taking some pitch and moulding it into the shape of a man. He put a bamboo hat on it and stood it up in one corner of the garden. Then he went away.

Millington and Maxfield report that this story was told by Visayan parents to their children and that it was also commonly conveyed by the public storytellers who worked the markets when people were out purchasing ingredients for the evening meal. There are obvious differences between Christensen's version, remembered from her youth in South Carolina, and the composite created by Millington and Maxfield in the Philippines, both in their respective settings and in the linguistic contrast struck by the eccentric spelling and syntax that Christensen uses to evoke Sea Island Creole English (or "Gullah" dialect). Christensen's version of the story is also at least one degree more elaborate than the Visayan version, as it repeats both the rabbit's theft, first corn and then peanuts, and the wolf's response, first scarecrow and then tar baby, to elevate the tension. What matters most in both versions, however, is not what distinguishes them but what they have in common. The fact that Masoy can grow papayas year round in the tropical climate of the Philippines, while the wolf must plant his corn and peanuts in spring, calculating an annual yield, is a contingency the stories capture to some minimal degree, for instance in how Christensen's version uses the cycle of the seasons to portray consequences. This difference, however, is circumstantial, leaving the conflict that structures the story intact.[20]

The principle at stake in Christensen's version is the same as in the other versions where Masoy assumes a natural right to the produce from his fields, or the wolf assumes a natural right to the water in his well, based on the labor that he expended. As best we can tell, they are the rightful owners of the produce and water that their lazy rivals steal from them. In each of these examples, the theft scenario is put to the same use: it offers what Jeremy Waldron describes as a "theory of historical entitlement" that explains why certain individuals or groups may have the right to exclude others from access to a given resource based on past actions. In the tar baby, this entitlement derives from the moral distinction established at the outset between the story's characters. In the version from the Philippines produced by Millington and Maxfield and in the version from South Carolina reported by Christensen, the owner's right to the produce from the land is based on the labor he devoted to its cultivation. In the first case, we are given details about Masoy's honest attempts to eke out a living from his garden, forming an identification that we cannot have with the heretofore unknown intruder, and in the second case, an explicit contrast is made between the wolf (who works for his subsistence) and the rabbit (who does not). In both cases, the claim to individual ownership is reasonable. The wolf works as the rabbit plays, and the rabbit's claim on the produce therefore appears insupportable, at least in this opening scene, which does not even attempt to justify the rabbit's actions.[21]

Across its many instances, the tar baby remains flexible enough to dramatize the problem of appropriation in a range of situations. Whether focused on property that is conventional or natural, communal or personal, the story also draws other variables into consideration. It makes a difference, for example, whether the resource is treated as functionally infinite, like fish in the sea or water from a spring, or limited, like the oranges in a grove or the wheat from a cultivated field—a difference that enables the story to imagine the exclusive claim to property under conditions of abundance (the water taken from a spring that, as far as the story is concerned, will never run dry) as well as conditions of scarcity (the fruit or grain that will not grow back until next season). By implication, the story also stretches to address matters such as the problem of waste and the prospect of improvement.[22]

Even labor, which sometimes seems like a constant across the tradition, is subtracted from the story in cases where ownership is taken for granted or being the first to stake a claim is counted as enough to give someone the rights that would otherwise follow only from a hard day's work. In versions like the one published by Mary Hose in 1867, no labor is depicted. Hose's story concerns a "pease-patch" that belongs to an "ole man," and as far as we know, the patch belongs to the man not because he worked to produce it, but simply because he says it belongs to him. The man's labor is neither presented in the backstory nor implied by the term "patch," which, unlike "garden" or "crop," implies a resource that could be either natural or cultivated, a resource that might well have been accessible before the rabbit was excluded by fiat.[23]

There are also composite versions of the story that merge narrative elements that are elsewhere employed separately. Consider the version published by William Owens in the essay in *Lippincott's* magazine that famously inspired Joel Chandler Harris to transcribe his own Brer Rabbit stories. Owens includes the backstory that Harris chooses to abandon:

> Buh Rabbit and Buh Wolf are neighbors. In a conversation one day Buh Wolf proposes that they two shall dig a well for their joint benefit, instead of depending upon chance rainfalls or going to distant pools or branches, as they often have to do, to quench their thirst. To this Buh Rabbit, who has no fondness for labor, though willing enough to enjoy its fruits, offers objections, and finally gives a flat refusal. "Well," says Buh Wolf, who perfectly understands his neighbor. "If you no help to dig well, you mustn't use de water." "What for I gwine use de water?" responds Buh Rabbit with affected disdain. "What use I got for well? In

de mornin' I drink de dew, an' in middle o' day I drink from de cow-tracks." The well is dug by Buh Wolf alone, who after a while perceives that someone besides himself draws from it. He watches, and soon identifies the intruder as Buh Rabbit.

This opening sequence gives two reasons for the wolf's right to the well. The wolf is justified, in the first place, because he offers to share the well with the rabbit, provided that the rabbit helps with its construction, an idea that fails through no fault of his own. He is also justified because he goes ahead and digs the well himself after his original proposal is rejected. Either of these justifications should be sufficient on its own, as the rabbit may have forfeited his claim on the water either by breaching a proposed agreement to manage the well in common or by avoiding the labor that is required to create the well. There is a similar redundancy in other versions of the tar baby, including a story recorded by Calvin Claudel in Louisiana in 1943, where the rivals are the lapin (French for rabbit) and the bouqui (adapted from the Ouolof for hyena). First, the bouqui offers to manage the well jointly with the lapin, but the lapin refuses this partnership, foregoing, we may assume, any claim on the water. Second, the bouqui goes ahead and digs by himself, becoming, we may assume, the owner of the well that was made possible by his initiative.[24]

As we have seen, in most cases one or the other justification is given, but not both. If the stories about common property tend to concentrate on the problem of political organization in a backstory that features a community deliberating and imposing duties on its members, the stories about private property focus instead on the natural rights that follow from labor. In both cases, the property right is challenged by a trickster who ignores all considerations other than his own self-interest. His actions are the cause of the conflict that consumes the rest of the story, most notably the setting of the trap.[25]

Chapter Two

Other themes and motifs recur across multiple versions the story, including the hollow excuses that the rabbit offers for his crimes, excuses that nobody is willing to take seriously. Often, the rabbit says he does not need to work as he is able to get everything he needs from nature. In the stories that concern access to groundwater, the rabbit explains he has no need to dig a well, because he gets all his water from the dewdrops. This excuse is given with some frequency, including in Calvin Claudel's version from Louisiana. "You go ahead and dig your well," the lapin says to the bouqui, "I'll drink the dew. That's all I need for my thirst, a little dew in the morning." In a Natchez version printed by John Swanton in 1913, the rabbit is caught toting water from a well he was "too lazy" to dig. "Where did you get your water?" the animals ask. "I gathered it from the dew on the weeds," the rabbit replies. This excuse also serves as an alibi after the fact in Mooney's version from Oklahoma, where the rabbit deflects accusations from the other animals, saying he has no reason to steal water as "the dew is enough" for him, and in a story from coastal Georgia, where the rabbit announces that he has "no casion fuh hunt water" as he "lib off de jew on de grass." In Taos Pueblo, the rabbit assures the coyote that he has "plenty of water" as he drinks "dew from the cabbage leaves." In Corsica, the rabbit tells the goat that he has what he needs as he drinks "dew from the cups of the flowers" at daybreak and the cream from the cow's milk in the "heat of the day."[26]

Even as the story pours scorn on the rabbit's assurances, there are cases where it gives some credence to the idea that reliance on nature's bounty is the only alternative to a world organized around the exclusive right to property. In the version published by Owens, for example, the natural store of freshwater is invoked not only by the rabbit but by the wolf, who unlike the rabbit finds it insufficient for his needs. While the rabbit is content to enjoy the world as it has been presented to him, drinking the dew from the grass in the morning and water from the puddles in the cow-tracks in the afternoon, the wolf is unsatisfied. He

FIG. 2.1. E. W. Kemble, "De Appile-Tree." Pen and ink. From Joel Chandler Harris, *The Tar-Baby and Other Rhymes of Uncle Remus* (New York: D. Appleton and Company, 1904), 19.

wants to make things better. Rather than "depending upon chance rainfalls" or trekking to "distant pools or branches" to "quench [his] thirst," the wolf wants the modern convenience of a well.[27]

In this exchange, the rabbit speaks for open access. The dew, he says, is a resource that should be available to everyone without limit. Because there is enough dew in the world to provide for everyone's subsistence, there is no need to regulate access to it. Through this exchange, open access becomes the measure against which the wolf's innovations are counted as improvements. Productivity is gauged in the tar baby in relation to these two extremes. Even when we see the rabbit's philosophy less cynically, as an artless approach to existence rather than a cover story for crime, it still looks like a miscalculation, as his world, when left unimproved, offers only a meager subsistence at best, a fact confirmed by the other animals in Swanton's version. "A person couldn't get that much water from the dew," they agree. This may be nothing more than a bad prediction by the rabbit about the amount of water he needs to survive, a miscalculation that leads him from desperation to crime, but at the same time, the claim also rings false. It sounds disingenuous, like a ruse premeditated to conceal a theft, or an alibi invented after the fact, with the consequence that the dream of living on nature's bounty is dis-avowed not once but twice by the story, as its inaccuracy is exposed along with the rabbit's deceit.[28]

There is nothing distinctive about the composition of these social problems as they are represented in the tar baby story. In the trickster tradition to which the tar baby belongs, there are many other stories that start the same way, finding their motivation in the practical dilemmas faced by self-organized communities. In the fables transcribed by Elsie Clews Parsons in the South Carolina Sea Islands, for instance, the rabbit is often caught defecting from communal arrangements, whether by taking more than his fair share of meat from a hunt, as he does to the partridge, or by stealing milk from a jointly owned cow, as he does to the alligator. In "Playing Dead Twice in the Road," a story that Parsons found in North Carolina, the Bahamas, and the Cape Verde Islands, we have an equivalent setup where the rabbit and the fox go fishing, and the rabbit, too lazy to put his own hook in the water, tricks the fox into leaving his catch unguarded on the roadside. Similar examples appear throughout *Nights with Uncle Remus* (1883), the sequel to the first Uncle Remus book, where in one story, the weasel outwits the guards standing watch over the communal butter supply, and in other stories, the rabbit is shown talking his way into other people's gardens, shirking duties, cheating friends, and double-crossing accomplices. In "Brother Rabbit Secures a Mansion," the rabbit fires a cannon, pours a slop bucket down a staircase, and plays other tricks to steal a house from the bear, fox, wolf, raccoon, possum, and mink who had cooperated in its construction. In a variety of similar stories, we see animals working together to build a shelter, grade a road, or construct a cistern only to have its benefits taken away by a trickster who contributes nothing.[29]

The social problems staged in the tar baby appear throughout the global trickster tradition, and they are also indispensable to other intellectual domains. From Aesop's fable of the industrious ant and the lazy grasshopper to the modern parables of market discipline spun by moral philosophers like Harriet Martineau, the theft scenario has cognates not only in folklore and mythology but also in natural philosophy and the law of nations. Moreover, as the science of political economy emerged in the eighteenth century on the heels of the theology of labor associated with the Protestant Reformation, the sin of laziness, the antecedent to theft, was summoned with ever-increasing confidence by thinkers like Adam Smith to explain the unequal distribution of resources in the present by referring to choices made by two archetypal individuals in a mythical past, one who secured his long-term prosperity by mixing his labor with the land, and another who stayed idle, and probably drunk, sinking ever deeper into poverty, becoming less contented by the day, sooner or later turning to crime. It was the chance meeting between these two archetypal individuals on the stage of history, one with savings to invest and the other with only his labor to sell, that is supposed to have sparked the invention of the wage contract.[30]

As a more sustained example, consider John Locke's thinking about the origin of property in *The Second Treatise of Civil Government* (1690), which shares the tar baby's interest in the disposition of resources that are hunted or gathered in nature. Locke infers the right to property from a series of examples closely related to the tar baby. Locke begins by insisting that "God gave the world to men in common," only to offer an immediate qualification. It was not, Locke says, God's intent that the world should remain "common and uncultivated." God gave the world to men for the benefits they could derive from it. Its fruits were meant to be developed, not idly savored, and it follows that the world was given in the fullness of time not to everyone but to the "industrious and rational," whose labor legitimates their title to the land. Left empty-handed are the "quarrelsome and contentious," whose competing claims are disqualified by their personal history of moral deficiency.[31]

Locke gives a series of examples to support his labor theory of appropriation, noting that acorns taken off the ground or plums taken from a tree become the property of the person who extracted them from nature. A person who shoots a deer has rights to the meat and hide it provides, and a person who clears the brush from a patch of ground can claim the land as his own. Most famously, Locke offers the example of a hungry person who goes looking for food. He finds some acorns on the ground, picks them up, brings them home, cooks them, and eats them. "When did they begin to be his?" Locke asks. "When he digested? Or when he eat? Or when he boiled? Or when he brought them home? Or when he pickt them up?" It is "plain," Locke concludes, that "if the first gathering made them not his, nothing else could." According to Locke, the person has a right to eat the acorns because he owns them, and he owns them because he devotes labor to gathering them. By mixing his labor with nature, he takes things that were previously available to everyone in common (acorns on the ground) and makes them into his property (gathered acorns). When the wolf digs his well or the fox tends his fields, their activity matches the theology of labor that Locke invokes in claiming that the world belongs to those who improve it. This scene also calls to mind Locke's comments concerning the relative productivity of improved and unimproved lands, exemplified in his calculation that ten well-tended acres in Devonshire would yield more than a thousand acres "left to nature" in the "wild woods and uncultivated waste of America." If the wolf appears in this analogy as the paragon whose labor brings earthly rewards of prosperity, the rabbit stands with the "needy and wretched" who are too careless to improve the world to meet their needs. According to Locke, the rabbit forfeits his existing rights to the world the moment he decides that the dew is enough for him.[32]

These ideas about the origin of property in the state of nature are often associated with Locke, but it is important to recall that they are not unique to him. In political philosophy, Locke is anticipated by thinkers like Hugo Grotius and Samuel Pufendorf—with Grotius, for example, writing in *The Law of War and Peace* (1625) that property emerges as individuals apply their labor to nature after becoming dissatisfied with the "spontaneous productions of the earth," and Pufendorf arguing similarly in *The Law of Nature and Nations* (1672) that property begins when individual labor removes an object from a natural situation in which all things "lay open to all men." This influential line of thought is extended in William Blackstone's *Commentaries on the Laws of England* (1765–69), which proposes that property begins with "occupation," a term that refers not only to discovery but also to the transformation of the discovered land through labor. For Blackstone, this conjecture about the origin of property fit into a general theory of world history that was divided into four stages, the first of which was based on hunting and gathering. In this savage stage, humans did not see property except in a few movable objects, like tools and clothing, but as they developed agriculture and commerce, their ideas of property changed, and they began to stake their claims to land and other sequestered goods.[33]

This line of thought was often invoked to justify the conquest of territory in colonialism. Take, for example, the tenet of natural reason known as *res nullius*, a Latin term ("things without owners") derived from Roman jurisprudence that refers to the process by which unowned things are acquired as property. According to Henry Sumner Maine, *res nullius* is a category that encompasses "wild animals, fishes, wild fowl, jewels disinterred for the first time, and lands newly discovered or never before cultivated." In addition, Maine states that *res nullius* is the ancient source standing behind international laws on territorial acquisition, captivity, and enslavement. Following Maine's interpretation, the principle of *res nullius* and its derivative *terra nullius* ("land without owners") played an important role in early modern debates among European powers concerning the legitimacy of overseas settlement. The assumption was that land remained unowned until it was occupied and used for some purpose, such as the cultivation of crops. In this scenario, the settler's right to appropriate land was justified on the same principle as the wolf's right to his well, his field, or his vegetable garden. Nature, as Locke had affirmed, did not belong to everyone. It belonged by right not to those (like the rabbit) who would live idly off its bounty but to those (like the fox and wolf) who were willing to improve (and thereby "occupy") the land. What counted as occupation and what counted as a legitimate purpose were questions that were resolved differently at different times in the debate over *res nullius*. It is also unclear whether *res nullius* was working as a doctrine with the power to guide policy or as a convenience occasionally or imprecisely cited as circumstances warranted. Although we may not be able to generalize about the practical application of *res nullius*, we can say for certain that these ancient ideas about "things without owners" underwent a global diffusion that was comparable in scale to the tar baby. No less than the tar baby, these rudiments of natural reason were early and indispensable artifacts of global culture.[34]

Neither element in the *res nullius* equation, however—neither land nor labor—is indispensable to the tar baby story, no matter what the wolf says. There are versions of the story where labor precedes the property claim, but as we have also seen, there are other stories in which the resource under dispute is available in nature: a spring, for instance, rather than a well, a grove, a blackberry bush, or a wild patch of peas rather than a planted field. In other cases, the story simply forgets about land and labor. Rather than starting with the individual mixing labor with nature, the story places us at the scene of a crime from which relevant details, concerning status and possession, are established only in retrospect. Indeed, it is crime that comes closest to the condition of a constant in the story—as Parsons notes, it is "almost always" there—or at the very least closer to one of the "fundamental elements" in Espinosa's calculus than either labor (which often enough disappears) or the untouched land (a dream that turns out to be no more substantial than the dew on the grass). When we approach the tar baby as a story that originates not in labor but in crime, we confront some interesting implications, including the possibility that the rabbit has to steal the peas, oranges, or turnips before they can be counted as property belonging to his rivals. If this proposition sounds counterintuitive, it also speaks directly to the situations in which the story was being told—situations where land and resources were appropriated based not on the doctrine of *res nullius* but on the rules governing forfeiture and confiscation in a time of warfare.[35]

In the law of nations, no less than in the tar baby story, it can be difficult to understand the relationship between labor and property. Mixing your labor with nature may give you a right to the fruit or grain that you have cultivated, but it is not clear how it can give you permanent title to the land you happened to have worked for a season, or why that title should be transferable to heirs by inheritance or strangers by trade. Among the colonial powers, there was a longstanding debate over whether things in the world that on first glance seemed untouched or inefficiently used, should be counted as *res nullius*, or whether it was more appropriate to assume to the contrary that they belonged to someone. We know that there were some cases in which philosophers and governments rationalized expropriation by imagining a world that was empty and unowned, as Locke does with his acorns, but we also know there were many cases in which settlers, merchants, governors, and slave traders recognized that the resources they wanted were owned by other people—the lands inhabited, the bodies self-possessed—and in consequence, they came to justify their designs not through *res nullius* but instead by imagining that these prior claims could be disqualified on moral grounds. They admitted that other people might have a claim on the world, but they also suggested that these people had forfeited their claim by committing a crime against nature. The justification for expropriation begins in these cases not with the fox digging his well or the wolf weeding his garden but with the crime committed when the rabbit takes the fox's water or the wolf's produce.[36]

Based on this reasoning, colonial philosophers, including Francisco de Vitoria and Hugo Grotius, wrote a series of major treatises and policy statements during the sixteenth and seventeenth centuries that specified the crimes against nature committed by Africans and American Indians that had caused them to forfeit their natural rights to their possessions and their territories, leaving them vulnerable to countervailing claims made by would-be colonizers. In *Relectio de Indis* (1539), Vitoria argued barbarians overseas were neither natural slaves nor brutes without "true dominion" over their territories. Until proven otherwise, they were to be considered reasonable creatures and permitted the same rights accorded to civilized people. Vitoria also argued, however, that responsibilities came with these rights and that barbarians, no less than civilized people, were to be called to account when they violated the laws of nature. Barbarians were charged with crimes that were unspeakable, like cannibalism or blasphemy, but more often the crime occurred in the course of ordinary interaction. When settlers were not welcomed with open arms, when the terms of commerce were misconstrued, when there was confusion over access to resources, it was possible to accuse the barbarians of infringing the law of nature and to determine in consequence that they had no rights that had to be respected.[37]

Unlike *res nullius*, this approach justifies expropriation based not on positive actions taken by property owners but instead on crimes committed by the conquered population. If the safety of traders or settlers was in some way endangered by the hostility of the resident population, Vitoria proposed that it was right to wage "defensive war or even if necessary offensive war" against the natives. These ideas were commonplace in the law of nations. They were extended, for instance, by Hugo Grotius. "War is lawful," Grotius writes, "against those who offend against Nature." Like Vitoria, Grotius suggests that "making war" is justifiable when you are "prevented" by a resident population from "traveling or sojourning" on their land or when you are "debarred from trade." Writing in 1758, Emer de Vattel would agree that when a people commits a "breach" against the "law of nations," it is legitimate to extinguish the threat they pose by whatever means necessary. Under these circumstances, Vattel says, "refusal of quarter" is acceptable. In the final book in his *Commentaries on the Laws of England*, Blackstone imagines a case where a "robbery" or "depredation" is committed against an ambassador in a foreign territory and or a trading vessel at sea, observing that such a crime is sufficient to reduce its perpetrator to a "savage state of nature" in which he loses "all the benefits of society." Every society, Blackstone finds, has the right to punish such criminals for the same reason that every individual in the state of nature can punish the "invasion of his person or personal property."[38]

Crime against nature was supposed to warrant not only conquest but also enslavement. Vitoria emphasized that the measures taken in punitive or preemptive warfare should not be disproportionate to the crimes committed by the natives, but if the natives persisted in their resistance, it was valid to proceed to "extremities" including "seizing their cities and reducing them to subjection." Remarking that the same principles were enforced in cases where the enemy was civilized, Vitoria observed that it was a "universal rule" in the "law of nations" that "whatever is captured in war becomes the property of the conqueror." Following on these precedents, which were in turn based on Greek and Roman jurisprudence, Vitoria insists the rights of conquest apply not only to territory and treasure but also to the conquered population, as it was acknowledged that "men may be brought into slavery" in the course of just war. These ancient ideas about slavery were also adapted by other early modern philosophers, including Locke, who defines slavery along the same lines as Vitoria in the third ("Of the State of War") and fourth ("Of Slavery") chapters of the *Second Treatise*. According to Locke, slavery is "the state of war continued, between a lawful conqueror and a captive." He proposes that slavery is justifiable when it is associated with legitimate warfare carried out against enemies, such as the rabbit, who have sinned against nature and so "forfeited their lives . . . and lost their estates." Reduced, by virtue of the crimes they have committed, to a condition where they have no rights others are bound to respect, it is proper according to Locke that criminals are robbed, killed, or enslaved as punishment for their actions. Banned from familiar associations and rituals of recognition, captives in a just war are consigned to social death, a term that the sociologist Orlando Patterson uses to describe the dishonor and alienation that marks the transition into slavery.[39]

In reflecting on the situation of the outlaw banished to the wasteland as punishment for committing a crime against nature, Blackstone draws a similar analogy to racial slavery. "For when it is now clear beyond all dispute," Blackstone writes, "that the criminal is no longer fit to live upon the earth, but is to be exterminated as a monster and a bane to society, the law sets a note of infamy upon him, puts him out of its protection, and takes no further care of him than barely to see him executed. He is then called attaint, *attinctus*, stained or blackened." The outlaw is blackened by his crime. Like the slave, condemned by his blackness, the outlaw "is no longer of any credit or reputation . . . for, by an anticipation of his punishment he is already dead in law."[40]

There are certainly versions of the tar baby story that make this explicit connection, concluding with the trickster enslaved by his enemy. In the story taken from the Philippines by Millington and Maxfield, Masoy finds that he has trapped the thief, and announces: "So you are the robber who has stolen my fruit! Now you will pay for it with your life." "Oh, spare my life," the thief replies, "and I will be your slave forever!" Masoy asks the thief if he will promise not to steal from his garden again. "I do," the thief pledges, "and I will serve you faithfully all my life." After further adventures, the story ends with Masoy living in a palace with the thief and other "slaves to serve him." Choosing bondage over death, the trickster moves through each stage in the classical narrative in which legitimate slavery derives from captivity in warfare. We see this same sequence presented in a version recorded by Dean Fansler in which a thieving monkey's life is spared for promised service, and in a version collected by Melville and Frances Herskovits where a king spares a tortoise in order to sell him into slavery.[41]

In other versions of the tar baby story, this sequence comes to another ending. Following from the first scene, where the trickster commits a crime against nature, and extending through the second scene, where the rabbit is held captive in a justified war of retribution, we arrive at the point where the rabbit is held by the tar baby, and the wolf has a decision to make. The wolf has the prerogative to kill the rabbit as punishment for his crime, a prerogative that he invokes, for example, in a story told by Mary Kindred in Texas in 1937, which ends with the rabbit burned at the stake. Another choice would be to mitigate this punishment: for instance, by allowing the thief to remain alive as a slave, as Masoy does, or else by exiling the thief to the wasteland outside civilization, which is what the wolf thinks he is doing when he banishes the rabbit to the briar patch. When the wolf flings the rabbit into this barren landscape, he continues to follow the script introduced at the beginning of the story. Liberating the captive in order to banish him to the inhospitable reaches of some adjacent swamp or desert was an entirely expected and predictable outcome in the narratives of crime and captivity imagined by Locke, Vitoria, and Grotius. Following their banishment, outlaws exiled to the backcountry were understood to belong nowhere and to nobody. They were without lord, tribe, kin, or caste. If they were robbed, assaulted, or otherwise abused, they had no right to appeal for justice. Forced beyond the outer boundary of society, the outlaw suffered a loss of standing comparable to the slave.[42]

Blackstone makes an important point when he describes the loss of credit that comes with outlawry. The outlaw has no perspective that counts as far as law is concerned. All consideration of intentions, experiences, attitudes, and tendencies is irrelevant after the crime against nature has been committed. Marx makes a similar point about the lazy rascals who serve as negative examples in political economy. Defined by their moral failure, lazy rascals are disqualified from consideration as rational actors in civil society, leaving no opportunity to ask about the nature of their intentions. How these allegedly dull and indolent individuals saw themselves and their place in the world; how they understood their relationship to the earth before someone else staked an exclusive claim to its produce; how they would have described the customary rights to water, wood, fish, and game that existed before the new regime of property; how they organized themselves and negotiated with their neighbors before they were arraigned, kidnapped, colonized, and enslaved—these are questions we are not permitted to ask.[43]

As we have seen, the same is true for the rabbit. Given the rabbit's crimes, it seems that the wolf has the right to expropriate everything that belongs to the rabbit and his family—their lands, their possessions, even their bodies. The story's opening scene is structured, moreover, to erase the rabbit's perspective on the world. Casting the rabbit as a selfish hustler who scams his hardworking neighbors, or as a free rider who sacrifices the good of the community whenever it serves his own interests, the story adapts a narrative conceit that is designed to make identification with the rabbit as difficult as possible.

This leaves us with an acute problem of interpretation. How do we explain the identification we are supposed to have with the rabbit? What are we to make of the fact that the most longstanding assumption about the story—its identification with the trickster—appears unwarranted when the story's opening scene is taken on its own terms? At the very least, it seems that identification is not something that we should take for granted. The standard approach to the story is not wrong in this respect, but it is too hasty in presuming something that develops only incrementally in the story, as the crime against nature gives way to the ensuing scenes of captivity and escape. One of the major weaknesses in this standard approach, then, is its failure to recognize the complexity of the challenge the story sets for itself. The story seeks a basis for identification from within a conventional situation where identification seems impossible. Responding to this challenge, the tar baby tells more than one story at once. It tells a story about the rabbit's struggle for material resources, and at the same time, it tells another story about the composition of the rabbit's perspective on the world.[44]

Chapter Three
STICKING FAST

Circumscribed from the start of the story by his crime against nature, the rabbit stands at once as slave to master, native to settler, lazy rascal to frugal elite—stands, furthermore, in these positions as they were defined in the jurisprudence written by his enemies. When we attempt to account for this introductory sequence, rather than factoring it out of the story, we are left with several problems, one of which is how to explain the identification that we are supposed to have with the rabbit. This identification is plausible, and there is testimony supporting the idea that the people who were telling and hearing the tar baby story felt a strong affinity with the rabbit, but it is hard to square this assumption with the opening gambit that frames the conflict between the animals. Christensen, for example, offers a theory about the identification experienced by her informants that is difficult to reconcile with the story she records from them, which starts with the rabbit stealing the wolf's corn and peanuts. Truth be told, it is easier to imagine that slaves would identify not with the rabbit in this case but with the wolf, who has the fruit of his labor stolen by someone who does no work himself. Christensen's story, like many others, gives us reason to question the one-to-one identification with the rabbit that is supposed to exist automatically in the tar baby. The justice of the wolf's actions can be deduced from his honest labor and his good-faith efforts at cooperation, but the story provides no means by which to gauge the legitimacy of the rabbit's competing claim.[1]

The rabbit, in other words, occupies a subaltern position not only in the story's reception, where he is associated with subsistence workers and slaves, but also within the story itself, where he is representable only to the extent that he is excluded from the society to which the other animals belong. The rabbit's values are only portrayed from the standpoint of their criminal nature, leaving us with no way to understand them in positive terms. The rabbit may be motivated by a subsistence ethic or some inherited sense of customary entitlement, but the story's opening is structured to prevent these logical possibilities from even becoming a matter for conjecture. The rabbit's perspective manifests inside the story only negatively. It is only by thinking slowly and persistently through this negative characterization that we are likely to arrive at a worthwhile account of what we are doing when we root for the rabbit, not to mention what we are doing when we claim the rabbit's crime as a representative example of political activity.

No matter the specifics of the situation, the story is committed at its outset to this negative depiction of the rabbit. One thing we can say for sure is that the rabbit is guilty of the crime he is accused of committing. Again, as Parsons explains, the story is "almost always" about catching a thief. Crime against property is one of the story's "fundamental elements," Espinosa agrees; but like Parsons, Espinosa fails to note that the fundamental fact about this fundamental element is that its effect upon the story is to make the rabbit inaccessible to identification. Given the facts of the case, how can we root for the rabbit? He refuses a partnership when it is offered to him. He does no work. What reason does he have to complain, or even worse, what right does he have to treat the spring or garden as if it were his own? The story makes it seem as though these questions have no positive answers.

Barred from consideration is the possibility that the rabbit has his own incommensurate set of values, or his own sense of entitlement to the resource, based on reasoning that others would recognize as legitimate. No allowance is made for the possibility that there is more than one way to see the situation. The rabbit is simply out to get what he can. Often he does not even bother to give an excuse. When he tries to explain himself, he does not give a convincing account. The story refuses the rabbit the chance to justify his actions based on any principle that would be acceptable to a community. His actions have no basis in custom, and the story's certainty on this point is reinforced by the structure of its opening scene, which associates the rabbit with the inevitable lying, cheating, and stealing that is supposed to undermine communities that attempt to organize themselves.[2]

If the story's opening scene poses the problem of the rabbit's point of view, the solution to this problem is given in the ensuing episodes. The key is the intermediate sequence in which the trickster is trapped by his enemy—the so-called stickfast sequence—seen by many critics as the story's essence. In some versions, as we have already noted, the stickfast sequence follows several failed attempts to catch the rabbit, involving scarecrows or armed guards, before the property owner eventually figures out how to build a trap that works. Typically, the successful trap is made from tar, pitch, bird lime, tree gum, rubber, glue, beeswax, resin mixed with ashes, or some other sticky, dark, viscous material, and is fashioned to resemble a sentient creature. The tar baby is sometimes given a hat and clothes to make it seem more lifelike. There are also versions of the story where the tar is not shaped to resemble a sentient creature but is spread on an object such as a gate, stool, barrel, bucket, or stone. In other stories, the trap is organic, not artificially constructed: it can be an octopus, an ogre with unwashed hair, a rotted stump, or a sticky substance oozing from the ground. Other times the trap involves a supernatural agency like a magical amulet, vodou doll, or an ornament that is cursed by a witch. There are also more surreal variations, including a version taken from the Amazon Basin where the trickster touches a painting of an armadillo and is caught when the armadillo, and its tarred tail, come to life.[3]

FIG. 3.1. A. B. Frost, "[The Fox Builds the Tar Baby]." Pen and ink. From Joel Chandler Harris, *Uncle Remus: His Songs and His Sayings, with One Hundred and Twelve Illustrations by A. B. Frost* (New York: D. Appleton and Company, 1915), 8.

The trap can be made from beeswax, tree gum, bird lime, body fluid, or decayed wood, but it is arguably the eponymous tar—specifically pine tar—that serves as the story's most revealing symbol. A combination of hydrocarbons and free carbon produced by destructive distillation, tar is treated in the story both as an industrial commodity and as material cause, with plot implications hinging on its viscosity, its pliability, its tenacity, and its blackness. Because it was an organic compound requiring only the most rudimentary processing, it could be hard to tell if pine tar was a natural resource or a human innovation. In account books and trade policies, pine tar was indexed somewhere between nature and culture, an ambiguity that frequently caused confusion in colonial record keeping, as in the notoriously inconsistent shipping registers in the eighteenth and nineteenth centuries that sometimes classed pine tar with agriculture and other times with manufactures.[4]

If this elementary equation between raw material and human technology confounded the statisticians, it also made tar into a substance that was oddly suited to symbolic interpretation in a manner distinguishable from other sticky substances, like gum or beeswax, which had only to be gathered before they were put to use. Because tar was a manufactured product only a step or two removed from its uncultivated state, it embodied the equation between labor and nature in a way that was exceptionally legible, and it was used accordingly by settlers to distinguish themselves from natives who were not able to recognize the value locked in the pine trees, which only became accessible through human labor. "The Indians," John Brickell writes in *The Natural History of North Carolina* (1737), "never make either Pitch, Tar or Turpentine," because "ranging and hunting continually through the Woods" is "all the Industry they are given to." By supplementing their hunting and foraging with a "small quantity" of maize grown indiscriminately, Brickell held that the native population was "as well satisfied with this way of living as any among us who by his Industry has acquired immense Treasure." The difference between settlers and natives, according to this formula, is like the difference between the wolf and rabbit. Like the wolf, settlers secure their long-term prosperity by mixing their labor with the land, whether by working in a pasture or in a pine barren, while the natives, like the rabbit, remain idle, sinking ever deeper into their poverty, becoming less contented by the day, sooner or later turning to crime.[5]

As a weapon in the war against the rabbit, tar indexes aspects of the wolf's mentality, but it also has other implications in the story that follow from its historical and physical attributes. Whether in production or exchange, pine tar and its by-products were important to modern slavery, in particular to the development of the triangle trade that crisscrossed the Atlantic between the sixteenth and nineteenth centuries, facilitating the exchange of export commodities between Europe, America, and Africa. One reason the British colonized North America was that it needed a new source from which to import pine tar, which was used to insulate wooden ships, including those in the Royal Navy, to keep them from rotting. The problem was that Britain bought its tar from Sweden, creating a trade imbalance that was unacceptable under the prevailing doctrine of mercantilism. Documentation from explorers, dating all the way back to Thomas Hariot's *A Briefe and True Report of the New Found Land of Virginia* (1586), suggested that there were longleaf pine barrens up and down the Atlantic seaboard of North America that were ready to be processed into tar, pitch, rosin, and turpentine. The North American trade in tar would not commence in earnest for another century, but these early statements anticipate its importance not only to maritime commercial infrastructure but also to the international trade in cotton, sugar, and slaves. For a time, tar was treated as a universal equivalent, as Thomas Gamble explains in 1921 in his history of the naval stores industry. "As with wool in England in the middle ages," Gamble writes, "tar and pitch became the recognized staples and standards of value." Tar was used in places like North Carolina to pay debts and rent, and it was also used in the Atlantic trade network by people like Edward Salter, a merchant in Bath who in 1734 had his brigantine packed with tar to be exchanged directly for a cargo of "young negroes."[6]

The tar baby story understands all these things. It is no accident that the wolf so often chooses tar as the medium for the trap. As an example of tar's symbolism in the story, consider the following passage, which appears in an early version of the story that was transcribed by Mary Hose and then published in *Harper's Weekly* in 1867:

> B'r Rabbit . . . seed der Tar Baby, a standin' up, so impident like—so him say, berry perlite, "Good-mornin' ter yer, ma'am!" De Baby no anser. B'r Rabbit say—"Eh! eh!" ter heself; he look um straight een e yeye an ax um a'gin, "Good-mornin ter yer, ma'am!" De Baby no anser. B'r Rab-

bit . . . him say, "Who'se yer pappy an' yer mammy dat larnt you yer no-manners, Miss?" De Baby no anser. B'r Rabbit say, "Look 'e yer gal! you dunno me! You no talk ter me, me larn you wat manners is!" De Baby *no anser*! B'r Rabbit him draw off en hit um a slap. He han fassen ter der Tar Baby face! "Nebber mine, yer imp!" ee say, "I got nudder han', eff I hit yer wid dat I meck you laff t'udder side yer mout!" He hit um wid de odder han; de odder han' fassen. He hit um wid de right foot; de right foot fassen. He hit um wid de leff foot; de leff foot fassen! B'r Rabbit him dunno wuffer do, but ee tought ee would do dee bess ee could; so he say, "Look yer gal at dis yer head ob mine, wot you tink would cum ub you eff I was ter *butt* yer wid it? I tell yer dis fur wunce, now, yer better lem'me go!" De Baby no answer. He butt um wid de head, an' he head fassen!

Espinosa describes this scene as the "multiple-attack and stickfast episode," which in this case also includes the "no-reply formula," a dramatic monologue that devolves from greeting ("Good-mornin' ter yer, ma'am!") into threat ("You no talk ter me, me larn you wat manners is!") into the signature five-fold sequence in which the rabbit is caught by one hand, the other hand, one foot, the other foot, and by the head.[7]

Variations on this stickfast sequence have been recorded throughout Africa, North America, South America, Asia, and Europe. A Cherokee story collected in 1845 by James Wofford, for instance, begins conventionally with the animals holding a council and working together to dig their well. The rabbit, a "lazy fellow," refuses to work, offering the familiar excuse that the dew is enough for him. Noticing that the rabbit stays "sleek and lively" in spite of the drought, the animals are suspicious and construct a tar wolf, leaving the trap on the road to the well, setting the scene for the no-reply sequence, the escalating threats ("Get out of my way or I'll strike you!"), and the rabbit's discovery that he has been caught. Another example, collected by Melville Herskovits in Dutch Guiana, concerns a king who sets a "tar-baby" in his yard to catch a thief who has been stealing his plantains, leading again to the sequence where the thief, in this case Anansi the spider, addresses the tar baby ("Father, how are you?"), receives no reply, threatens the tar baby ("If you don't speak to me, I'll slap you"), strikes and then strikes again ("If you don't release me, I'll give you another with my other hand"), with the routine repeating until he is stuck at five points with "his head, his hands, and his feet" caught by the tar baby.[8]

Another example of this sequence was published by Père Capus, a member of the Catholic missionary organization known as the White Fathers, who transcribed a version of the tar baby from the Basumbwa, a tribe in German East Africa, in which a rabbit steals produce from a garden, and the owner cuts a log into the shape of a human, adorning it with cloth and beads and smearing it with gum. The rabbit salutes the figure ("*Mpola!*"), but it gives "no answer." The rabbit takes offense: "Do you hate your neighbours then? They salute you, and you say nothing." The rabbit then strikes again and again, and is stuck fast. Yet another version of the stickfast sequence appears in a story taken from the Ronga-speaking people in Mozambique. In this case, the conflict concerns the theft of groundnuts from a village. In an effort to trap the thief, the inhabitants build a figure from the gum of the myombo tree, a substance named in the French translation as "la glu noire." The meeting with this sticky black figure in the groundnut patch once again follows convention, leaving the hare trapped at five points. It would be easy to multiply these examples, as the stickfast episode remains remarkably consistent across the global tradition of the tar baby. In each case, our anticipation reaches its climax as the trickster speaks and is rebuffed, speaks again and is rebuffed, before issuing his final warning and ordering the tar baby to say hello or suffer the consequences.[9]

In this scene, the joke comes at the rabbit's expense. When the rabbit greets the tar baby expecting a response, we know that he is making a mistake, because we know tar cannot speak even when it is molded to resemble a sentient creature. The rabbit strikes the tar baby, and traps himself, because he feels that he has been insulted. If the rabbit only knew better, the story implies, then he would be able to evade the fox's trap, as he would recognize that objects, like volcanoes or amulets or tar babies, are incapable of malice. The rabbit's ignorance on this point sets him in contrast to his knowing enemy, who unlike the rabbit realizes that tar is not a potential interlocutor but a processed material, already one step removed from nature, that can be molded to serve as a technology (or what Uncle Remus calls a "contrapshun"). The dramatic irony here is both stable and continuous with the rabbit's characterization in the opening scene: it prevents us from understanding the encounter from the rabbit's point of view, pulling our seemingly objective vantage, whether we like it or not, into alignment with the wolf, based on the knowledge we share with him. Across the story, the rabbit is defined by his failure to grasp the instrumental approach to nature that the wolf displays at the start (where the wolf extracts resources from nature to meet his annual subsistence needs) and in the encounter with the tar baby (where the wolf collects a raw material, sometimes a substance available in nature like tree gum and other times an industrial product like tar, and shapes it into a tool). The ignorance the rabbit exhibits at the outset is compounded when the wolf reveals not only his superior scientific knowledge of the world but also his capacity to take advantage of the rabbit's superstition.[10]

It is important that the rabbit's mistaken address to the tar baby is allowed to stand in the story as a sign of his mentality. The rabbit's mistake is not only foolish but also predictable and socially representative. After all, the only reason that the fox is able to trick the rabbit is that he knows something about the rabbit, and what he knows about the rabbit is that the rabbit is inclined, to some extent, to attribute intent to inanimate objects. When the fox goes to the trouble to build the tar baby, he banks on the fact that the rabbit is likely to mistake the tar baby for a sentient creature and thus to misconstrue its silence for a slight. The fox succeeds in trapping the rabbit only when he abandons his efforts at around-the-clock surveillance and adopts a premeditated strategy of deception based on the rabbit's predictable confusion about the relationship between subjects and objects in the natural environment.[11]

The rabbit's confusion is intelligible in the story as an example of fetishism, a fact that was not lost on collectors who saw this mistake in connection with other versions in which the trap in question is not a tar baby but a wooden totem with the power to immobilize its victim. In some early cases identified by collectors as precedents to the tar baby, the enchanted object actually speaks to the rabbit, as in the version collected in West Africa by Robert Nassau, where the fetish, a "little image of a man," replies "No!" when the trickster asks to be let go. At times, the substitution of tar baby for totem has even been seen as a symptom of secularization, marking the transition into a world that has lost its faith in magic, a world in which some characters (like the rabbit) continue to believe in the magical animation of inanimate objects (like the tar baby) even as the story does not. Tracking the fetish's transformation into a technology, collectors marked the changes in consciousness that were supposed to have occurred as Africans came into contact with other cultures.[12]

In *Congo Life and Folklore* (1911), John Weeks provides the following assessment of the story's secularization:

> About three generations ago the Congo natives were transported in large numbers as slaves to America, and naturally they carried with them their language and their stories. The goobah in Uncle Remus is a corruption of nguba, the Lower Congo word for peanut; and Brer Rabbit is the gazelle, Brer Fox is the leopard, and the Tar-baby is the fetish called Nkondi; but in the Tar-baby a concession is made to civilization, for in Uncle Remus's account the image is cov-

ered with tar to account for Brer Rabbit sticking to it, whereas in what I believe to be the original story the Nkondi image causes the victim to stick by its own inherent fetish power. . . . All raw natives would believe that a fetish by its own magical powers could hold tightly its victim without the aid of such extraneous things as tar and wax. It is apparent that the narrators have lost faith in the magical powers of their fetish, and have introduced the wax and the tar to render their stories a little more reasonable to themselves.

As the story travels from Africa to America, ngubas become peanuts, gazelles become rabbits, and leopards become foxes, but the symptomatic adaptation, according to Weeks, is Nkondi's metamorphosis into the tar baby. Interested in change over time, Weeks is still committed to seeing the tar baby as a "cultural survival," a catch-all term introduced by E. B. Tylor in 1871 to refer to customs carried into "a new state of society different from that in which they had their original home." For Weeks, it follows that the story preserves not only a plotline but also a set of values and assumptions from its native culture. Stories like the tar baby, John MacCulloch agrees, are not mere "products of the imagination" but "reflections of the ideas which governed the minds of the people with whom these tales arose."[13]

It matters to the story that fetishism is an idea that originated at a specific time and place. The stickfast sequence draws with remarkable self-consciousness from the discourse on fetishism that was developed in the seventeenth century by Portuguese and Dutch merchants trying to explain what they saw as the distorted sense of value among the people who lived along the Gold and Slave Coasts in West Africa. As defined in travel writings such as Willem Bosman's *A New and Accurate Description of the Coast of Guinea* (1703), fetishism refers to the tendency to interact with objects as if they had purposes, thoughts, and intentions. For Bosman, it was this mental confusion that led "the

Negroes" to invest power and significance in trifles that they had collected by chance, whether a "Bird's Feather" or a "Pebble," a "Lion's Tail" or a "Bit of Rag." Fetishism came into the world, in other words, to explain irrationality at the site of trade. When travelers like Bosman or lay intellectuals like Charles de Brosses tried to explain the perverse miscalculation that made Africans willing to exchange precious commodities for trifles, they speculated that this irrationality was a general feature of the black mind, which was predisposed to attribute inordinate powers to objects chosen indiscriminately. By the conclusion of the eighteenth century, fetishism had become an indispensable concept in the comparative study of religion. Although it was applied broadly to primitive races throughout the world, the concept of fetishism retained its special connection to the continent that was its source. Fetishism, as William Pietz notes, was "taken . . . to characterize the essence of the African mentality." It was understood as the "central institution in African culture and society and the one most responsible for its perceived perversity." Fetishism explained why Africans had developed neither science nor a properly political sphere, as its prominence in their thoughts had warped their orientation to nature (the realm of objects) and society (the realm of subjects).[14]

This is a discourse whose influence is most often associated with Hegel's *Lectures on the Philosophy of History* (1837), which assembles second-hand observations about fetishism into an argument about Africa's distinctiveness in relation to other civilizations in the world. Hegel follows the thinking of previous generations of merchants, explorers, missionaries, and slave traders in his assumption that Africans are inclined to "exalt" the "first thing that comes in their way," whether "an animal, a tree, a stone, or a wooden figure." For Hegel, the most important thing about African fetishism is that it is a religion without any relationship to universality. Unlike idols, which at least have some iconic reference, fetishes do not signify anything beyond themselves. By definition, they lack the capacity to transcend the medium of their concrete and sensuous existence, meaning that they are blocked from attaining the categorical universality that is the prerequisite to participation in world history. According to Hegel, if you want to know why Africans are a people without politics, why they remain a people outside history, you need to look no further than this mistaken approach to material objects, an approach expressed perhaps nowhere more anxiously in the canon of world culture than in the rabbit's address to the tar baby.[15]

The story links the idea of fetishism to Africa not through the rabbit (a species that is native to several continents) but through the magical object (the tar baby) that is animated by the rabbit's expectations, an object whose racial status is marked in its extreme pigmentation and distorted countenance. In some cases, this status is made explicit. The tar baby's racial denotation is specified when it is glossed as a "queer black thing" or is said to be "as black as a Guinea negro." In Corsica, the tar baby is even described as a "little Congo." On the Cape Verde Islands, the tar baby is seen as a "little black boy." In Sierra Leone, it is characterized as a "black police." In Venezuela, Uncle Rabbit addresses the tar baby: "You black man!" In Mexico, he announces, "Good day to you, old blackie!"[16]

The tar baby's racial status is communicated as well in the illustrations that accompany the earliest published versions of the story, including the line drawing by Frederick S. Church in the original edition of *Uncle Remus: His Songs and His Sayings*, which reinforces something that everyone in 1880 was already supposed to know: the tar baby is an image of a slave. In Church's picture, the tar baby's complexion, no less saturated than the darkened forest in the background, is matched with morphological traits, including an arching nasal bridge and projection in the mouth and jaw, that were associated with the so-called Negroid feature set in the racial typology favored at the time by physical and forensic anthropologists. These characteristics only became more stylized in the blackface iconography that was adopted in

FIG. 3.2. G. Robert Kemp, "[The Tar Baby]." Pen and ink. From Jean-Baptiste Frédéric Ortoli, *Les Contes de la Veillée* (Paris: Librairie d'Éducation, 1886), 19.

newspaper cartoons, illustrated children's books, and advertisements used to promote products like Tar Baby Toilet Soap. If blackness is insinuated into the story first as criminality, second as the threat of captivity and enslavement, and third as the primitive mentality associated with fetishism, it is finally materialized and projected onto the face of the tar baby, an object that condenses the preceding threats to the rabbit's subjectivity. The stereotype ("thief") that blocks the rabbit's perspective at the start reappears in this case as an externalized object ("tar baby") whose disconcerting impassivity again destroys the possibility of the rabbit's connection to the social world.[17]

Given the longstanding controversy over the tar baby's relationship to the African continent, it is intriguing to discover that there is in fact something intrinsically and undeniably *black* about the rabbit and the tar baby—the subject and object of fetishism—as they are represented in the story. There are good reasons to balk at this characterization, which is inextricably tied, if not reducible, to colonial fantasy, but nevertheless it needs to be taken seriously if we are to engage the story on its own terms before shifting attention to the imagined circumstances of its reception. Critics have tended to believe that the story's significance under slavery derives from the slave's immediate identification with the rabbit, but in the story, this identification is reversed. Rather than the slave discovering agency by identifying with his or her image as reflected in the character of the rabbit, we witness the rabbit trying and failing abjectly to identify with a stereotyped likeness of a slave. Retaining the choreography of identification in the face-to-face encounter between the rabbit and the tar baby, the story is nevertheless explicit that we are witnessing not dialogue but dramatic monologue, not identification between two creatures (slave and rabbit) but instead a single creature (at once rabbit and slave) staring in disbelief at its own mirror image, an image whose grotesque distortion makes a mockery of the attempt to achieve self-mastery by identifying with your reflection in the world.[18]

FIG. 3.3. Frederick S. Church, "[The Rabbit and the Tar Baby]." Pen and ink. From Joel Chandler Harris, *Uncle Remus: His Songs and His Sayings: The Folk-Lore of the Old Plantation* (New York: D. Appleton and Company, 1881), 23.

It turns out that identification in the tar baby is more complicated than we have assumed. Indeed, it would appear that identification in this case has to refer to at least two things at once. It refers to the slave (as storyteller) identifying with the rabbit, and it refers to the rabbit (as character) encountering a sculpted image of a slave and acting out a farce about the withholding of recognition. As rivalry between the rabbit and the tar baby gives way to the possibility of an identification that would form the ego of the rabbit in the image of the slave, we cannot help but remain skeptical, as the story has already told us that it is an error to relate to an inanimate object in this way. At this point, the story's irony forces us into line with the perspective of the rabbit's adversary, a perspective shared by most of the story's collectors. We know what the fox knows, and what the rabbit seemingly does not know, about the tar baby, in the same way that we also know what the collector is supposed to know, what the story's original narrators seemingly did not know, about the fetish.[19]

From this point, the sequence continues to accrue associations. The rabbit's fetishism, staged in his apostrophe to the tar baby, is presented specifically as a tendency to treat objects as if they were persons, but it also reflects the corollary tendency to treat persons as if they were objects, anticipating the potential outcome of the rabbit's captivity in slavery. In some cases, this reversal is anticipated by the rabbit's initial response to the tar baby. "Brer Rabbit come prancin' 'long twel he spy de Tar-Baby," Harris describes, and "den he fotch up on his behime legs like he wuz 'stonished." Astonishment is an idea that repeats in other versions, including one transcribed by Charles Colcock Jones Jr. from the Georgia coast (where the rabbit is "stonish" by the tar baby) and another reported by Frédéric Ortoli from Corsica (where the rabbit gazes at the tar baby "with astonishment" before recovering his wits and saying hello). If the rabbit's astonishment conveys the novelty of the tar baby as a strange creature the rabbit has not seen before, it also suggests that the tar baby poses a threat to the rabbit's subjective existence in the world. Astonishment results from an encounter with something that cannot be assimilated to your existing sense of the world, an encounter that shocks the system, leaving you paralyzed, deadened, or literally, as the etymology implies, turned to stone. If the rabbit's apostrophe to the tar baby evokes the possibility of transforming an object into a subject through the magic of direct address, his astonishment, which precedes and exceeds the address, suggests the opposite, marking his alienation.[20]

As the scene develops, the rabbit is unsure what is happening. He does not have the clarity needed to make a plan. When he hails the tar baby, he is rebuffed. When he attacks, he is immobilized. With each blow he strikes for his freedom, he finds himself worse off than he was before, with the cycle repeating until he is left to the mercy of his enemy. "His fis' stuck, en he can't pull loose," Harris describes. The rabbit repeats his threat: " 'Ef you don't lemme loose, I'll knock you agin.'" He strikes with his other hand, and finds that it also becomes caught. Then the rabbit "lose de use er his feet in de same way" and "squall out dat ef de Tar-Baby don't tu'n 'im loose he butt 'er cranksided." The rabbit head-butts the tar baby, and the battle is complete. The fox reveals himself and jokes that the rabbit looks "sorter stuck up," a pun that glosses the rabbit's current predicament in relation to his fetishism, playing on the rabbit's mistaken belief that the tar baby was being pompous. The stakes of this ongoing struggle for recognition have now been made literal, as the rabbit is prostrate, leaving him without any choices to make. At this point, the threat of death is real. Left defenseless, the rabbit confronts the possibility that his story will end badly, when he is killed (and thereby turned to nothing) or enslaved (and thereby reduced to a degree of consciousness where his personality is destroyed and initiative is impossible).[21]

This existential dilemma provides the crux for some of the most perceptive interpretations of the tar baby story, including Ralph Ellison's meditation in "Hidden Name and Complex Fate" (1964). Ellison reads the rabbit's "fearful struggle" with the tar baby as an emblem for the individual's struggle with circumstance. In Ellison's account, the tar baby is a metaphor for "the world," signifying the facticity that threatens to make a mockery of our best intentions. Ellison takes his cue from the pessimistic interpretation of the struggle for recognition that was developed most influentially in Jean-Paul Sartre's *Being and Nothingness* (1943), an interpretation that also shaped the analysis of the colonial situation in Frantz Fanon's *Black Skin, White Masks* (1952). Fanon depicts an encounter in which he seeks recognition from another only to find he has already been trapped into embodying an identity that is "already there, waiting" for him. Like the rabbit caught by the tar baby, Fanon finds himself stuck. For Fanon, this stage in the struggle for recognition ends in a deadlock. The tar baby will never recognize the rabbit, and the master will never recognize the slave.[22]

The existential impasse explored by Fanon and Ellison is also preserved in modern colloquial usage, in which the term "tar baby" refers to a problem that gets worse the harder you try to solve it. Denoting blocked agency and misalignment of intentions and outcomes, "tar baby" was accepted as a term of art in discussions concerning domestic politics, most notably in the United States, where it was applied to situations ranging from the Watergate hearings to the Savings and Loan scandal, from corporate taxation to the separation of church and state. The term was used with even greater frequency in foreign policy circles to describe diplomatic and military engagements in places such as Vietnam, Nicaragua, Tibet, China, Yugoslavia, South Africa, and Iraq.[23]

The term "tar baby" functions in a similar manner when used as a racial epithet. In such cases, the threat to the rabbit is preserved in the term's racism. Some say that this derogatory usage departs from the term's meaning in the story. Lucinda MacKethan writes, for example, that anyone who objects to the term's racism would "benefit from knowing more about the allusion and its origins." Instead of "being insulted," she suggests that "people of color" should "take pride" in the rabbit's perseverance. John McWhorter draws a similar distinction between the term's "basic" meaning, which is "folkloric," and its "secondary" meaning, which he believes was derived relatively recently not from the story but from "the fact that it sounds like a racial slur, because tar is black and baby sounds dismissive."[24]

Such claims are belied by evidence showing that "tar baby" was already being used as an epithet before Harris began publishing his Uncle Remus stories. The term appears in print as a racial slur as early as 1839 in a blackface sketch in the *Saturday Evening Post* in which a character addresses his rival: "Look heaw . . . you tar-baby." The term is used in this way with increasing regularity across the nineteenth century. For example, a column in the *Atlanta Constitution* from the year after Harris published *Uncle Remus: His Songs and His Sayings* complains about the ruckus caused by a "young 'Tar Baby' about six years old . . . yelling at the top of his voice." The *Constitution* freely used the term as an epithet ("as black as a tar baby") to describe character and complexion, and other publications followed suit. Harris himself turned the term's racial denotation into a joke in a later story in which the rabbit encounters a black servant named Drusilla and mistakes her for the tar baby. "I see you've brought the Tar Baby," the rabbit says. "She's grown some since I saw her last. . . . I hope she's not as sticky as she used to be." Drusilla's reply works through the term's dual meaning as epithet and as cultural tradition. "Huh," she says, "I ain't no Tar Baby. I may be a nigger, an I speck I is, but I ain't no Tar Baby. My mammy done tol me bout de Tar Baby in de tale, an she got it fum her gran daddy. Ef I de Tar Baby, I'm older dan my mammy's grandaddy." All of which shows that it is impossible to separate the term's racism from what William Safire calls its "original intent" in the story. Nor should we try to divorce the term from its racism given that its meaning as a threat to the rabbit's identity is not only preserved but compressed and intensified over the history of its colloquial adaptation.[25]

Given that the problem of consciousness represented in the encounter with the tar baby leaves little or no cause for optimism, it is interesting and somewhat surprising to recall that collectors believed they had discovered a tacit solution to this problem as early as the turn of the twentieth century, a solution based not on the substitution or deception that typically propels the story but instead on the story's free-ranging circulation in the world. When influential studies such as Stanley Elkins's *Slavery* (1959) began to ask whether anyone could preserve a sense of autonomy under extreme conditions of oppression, it was possible to respond by picking up on this tradition of thought and pointing to stories like the tar baby as evidence that slaves had retained their cultural traditions in spite of their dispossession. If the tar baby seems circumspect about the very problem—the loss of subjectivity—that Elkins transforms into a historiographical trope, this reticence has never fazed the advocates who have counted the story's circulation as confirmation of an enduring individual and collective agency among slaves, practiced as cultural politics.[26]

Discovering freedom in captivity, this argument is surprising not least because it depends on the strong precedence granted to the stickfast sequence in the analysis of the tar baby story following the publication of Joseph Jacobs's *Indian Fairy Tales* (1892). This precedence was warranted based on an assumption that was common to early studies of cultural diffusion, which held that "oddness or complexity" was sufficient reason to suspect that analogous stories from seemingly disparate cultures were causally connected. It seemed plausible to assume that relatively simple or conventional aspects of a story might have been invented independently in distant locations, but in cases where the elements in question were curious or complicated, it seemed that their geographical distribution was more likely attributable to diffusion from a common source. Accordingly, it made sense that collectors would seek to chart the course of the tar baby's global migration by focusing on the story's most unusual episode. It was left to Jacobs to turn this hunch into the foundation for future research. After Jacobs, it was widely accepted that the fivefold attack, which critics would classify as the "stickfast motif," was the story's "outstanding characteristic." Other stages in the story might be cut or transformed beyond recognition, but the multiple attack and catch had to be there if the story in question was to qualify as a version of the tar baby. In some versions, the rabbit might be driven by motives other than hunger and might escape to remote locations other than the briar patch by means other than deception. The rabbit, again, might not even be a rabbit, and the tar baby might not even be a tar baby. Any story lacking the stickfast motif, however, was not a version of the tar baby. In such cases, the story was no longer recognizably itself. In 1930, Ruth Cline encapsulated this insight. The tar baby, she held, "would be pointless were nobody to stick to it."[27]

Sticking fast is the story's essence. More than anything else, it was the consensus on this point that led to increased speculation about the story's circulation. Once the story was reduced to this one essential element, it became possible to establish connections between variants that otherwise seemed unrelated to one another. It had always been easy to follow a simple chain of substitution, in which the tortoise takes the rabbit's place, or the story begins with the theft of water rather than the theft of produce, but once one element, rather than the story as a whole, became the object of analysis, the range of potential connections increased exponentially. Critics could be more creative in finding links between stories, and this increased flexibility proved useful not only to scholars arguing for the story's diffusion across cultures but also to those who continued to make the case for the decisiveness of its African provenance. From Hausaland to Haiti and from Lithuania to the Philippines, collectors discovered tales that were connected to one another through the trope of sticking fast. The sticky medium was sometimes a tar baby, but other times it was a gate smeared with bird lime, or a decayed stump, or someone's sticky unwashed hair.[28]

Jacobs and his followers reduced the story to this core sequence in an attempt to track its movement in the world. This strategic decision has also shaped interpretation of the story. It was the precedence given to the stickfast sequence that widened the story's range of association to the point where it could be conceived as a truly global phenomenon, making it possible for scholars to claim the story as evidence against the argument that slaves had no capacity to retain or produce culture.

As we have observed, this interpretation involves some sleight of hand: it invokes the story's global diffusion to solve the problem posed in the story when the rabbit is trapped by the tar baby. In this interpretation, the agency that is nearly extinguished inside the story reappears in the story's mobility, its amazing capacity to overcome the friction of time and space, which restores the freedom that is denied to the rabbit when he is caught in the trap. The stickfast sequence, in other words, is the point in the story at which agency is most in doubt, and it is also the point from which agency is recovered through the story's global diffusion. This interpretation is too easy, of course: it takes the psychic impasse represented in the rabbit's encounter with the tar baby and turns it into a cultural problem that can be dispatched with relative ease by citing the mere fact of the story's transmissibility. A better interpretation becomes possible when we refuse this consolation and instead concentrate our critical attention on the problem of consciousness as it is represented in the story.

Chapter Four
SAY MY NAME

In most cases on record, the tar baby story has a three-part narrative structure: a problem statement, concerning the competition for resources between two representative characters, or between one character and a community; an intermediate sequence in which the struggle intensifies through a scene of captivity, in which the fight between enemies becomes a struggle for recognition; and a solution, which sometimes involves punishment but more often involves an escape that resolves the problems, both material and metaphysical, dramatized in the previous scenes. By reducing this tripartite sequence to the central episode where the trickster is stuck fast to the tar baby, critics have resolved the problems presented inside the story, looking away from the story to the history of its global diffusion. In this interpretation, the story is not only an example of culture but a metaphor for culture's capacity to provide sustenance under dire conditions of oppression.

A better interpretation becomes possible when we approach the stickfast sequence not in the secondary context of its cultural diffusion but instead in the primary context presented in the story. The alienation the rabbit experiences in his captivity is treated in the story as a psychic and indeed metaphysical problem, but at the same time, this alienation is cast in terms of the struggle for resources represented in the opening scene. If, at first glance, the stickfast sequence poses the problem of alienation in a way that seems not only unresolved but also unresolvable, the story finally suggests there is a way out. Doubling back on its own skepticism, the story anticipates this positive resolution in its oblique references to the rabbit's belief in custom.

From the beginning, the story refuses the rabbit the chance to justify his actions through any principle that would be acceptable to a community. The rabbit's actions, in other words, appear to have no basis in custom, and the story reinforces this point in the opening scene: custom fails to provide a sustainable moral orientation not only in the individual case of the rabbit but also in the generic case of society at large. If the opening sequence treats the customary justification for the rabbit's criminal activities as something inconceivable, something impossible to factor into the storyline, the ensuing encounter with the tar baby represents the rabbit as a character guided by traditional assumptions, but it acknowledges the existence of these assumptions only to reduce them to superstition. At this intermediate stage in the story, the distinction between the rabbit's superstition and his enemy's science only strengthens the negative orientation to custom established in the opening sequence by recapitulating the conventional terms in which traders, colonizers, missionaries, and other outsiders represented primitive cultures. Custom was the familiar classification used in ethnography to designate institutions and practices represented as brutish. Custom's irrationality was posed in opposition to the reasoned critique brought by enlightenment, and its tyrannical capacity to reduce adherents to intellectual servitude was similarly cast in opposition to the liberty afforded by critical self-reflection. At first criminalized, custom is associated, at this intermediate stage in the tar baby story, with archaic cultures immoral in their disrespect for property and incompetent in their efforts to navigate the modern world using outmoded norms that were, at best, an unreliable guide to the laws of nature. The rabbit discovers this weakness soon

FIG. 4.1. A. B. Frost, "[The Fox Laughs at the Stuck Rabbit]." Pen and ink. From Joel Chandler Harris, *Uncle Remus: His Songs and His Sayings, with One Hundred and Twelve Illustrations by A. B. Frost* (New York: D. Appleton and Company, 1915), 10.

enough when he learns the tar baby is not a sentient creature, as he had previously believed, but instead a "contrapshun" fabricated by his enemy.[1]

While the story makes its skepticism about custom seem natural and inevitable, it is important to remember that this skepticism would have been unfamiliar to many of the people hearing the story. Given their own first-hand experience with subsistence arrangements that had proven successful over the long term, they would have experienced the moral situation established in the opening scene not only as counterintuitive but also as counterfactual. The story's skepticism about the capacity for sustainable self-organization would have seemed far-fetched in a situation where there was so much evidence to the contrary. The story, in other words, begins by positing the falsehood of something that

Chapter Four

many people hearing the story would have experienced to be true, leaving us to wonder how these people would have squared the story's negative assumptions with facts on the ground that presumably could not be denied.[2]

As an example, consider the Visayan story about the theft of Masoy's fruits and vegetables. Subsistence producers on Panay and nearby islands were bound to one another by customs that were developed over time to address ordinary problems, and these customs persisted both during and after colonial rule. In the Philippines, as in many other locations in the Asian-Pacific Monsoon Belt, the biggest obstacles to agriculture were presented by seasonal rainfall, which communities addressed by entering into small-scale irrigation cooperatives known as zanjeras, encompassing both tenant farmers and landowners, all of whom had a right to participate in self-governance and a duty to contribute to construction and maintenance of dams, cisterns, and channels. The zanjeras allocated access to the irrigated land. Access was predicated on a farmer's continuing contribution to the irrigation network, and it was typically divided to ensure that everyone had not only an equal portion of land but equal access to a portion of the best land nearest to the source of the irrigation. Because everyone typically had some land near the source and another parcel in the less desirable bottoms, it was possible to make quick decisions about limiting irrigation in years when there was not sufficient rainfall to supply water to the entire system. By cutting off irrigation to the bottoms, the prime land could be saved and the poor land sacrificed, guaranteeing that all farmers were treated equitably. The zanjeras are only one example of how self-organized communities have managed to solve a social dilemma that would spell disaster for the society of the animals in the tar baby. Again, this does not mean there were no cheaters, thieves, or would-be tycoons in the Philippines. Rather, it means Masoy would have dealt with the theft of his property according to norms that linked him to an established network that existed to solve such dilemmas. A scene in which Masoy stands alone, mixing his labor with nature and defending the fruits of his labor in isolation, is a scene different in kind from the setting where fruits and vegetables were typically grown in the Philippines.[3]

This situation existed not only on Panay but also in many of the other places where the story was told. We now have extensive documentation showing the long-term durability of subsistence arrangements in a variety of circumstances throughout the world. The evidence assembled by Elinor Ostrom in particular has undercut the earlier claims made by Garrett Hardin about the unsustainability of common pool resources like springs, fisheries, pastures, and forests. Ostrom admits that these arrangements have not always worked, but she also notes that the market-based and state-based alternatives preferred by critics like Hardin have also often failed. Looking to examples from the allocation of timber harvesting in the Japanese mountains to the system governing sea tenure among black raft fishers off Bahia, Ostrom has specified the design principles that have made for successful commons arrangements, which include well-defined boundaries, open participation in rule-making, mutual monitoring, graduated sanctions, and opportunities for low-cost conflict resolution. Again, this is not to say there were no free riders in these places. The success of these voluntary arrangements hinged on whether participants could develop norms forceful enough to constrain individual behavior when cheating became a problem, while remaining flexible enough to encourage members to take the needs of others into consideration. They did not always work, but when they did, it was due to rules that participants made for themselves.[4]

When people have confronted the social dilemmas faced by the characters in the tar baby story, they have responded in creative ways that have enabled them to govern themselves without privatizing resources or ceding authority to a government. In a general sense, communities have sustained themselves in this manner by drawing from the commons, a term that refers to shared resources, like the rainfall on Panay, in which all stakeholders have an equal interest. "Disparaged . . . as a source of laziness and disorder," Sylvia Federici explains, the commons were "essential" for peasants, serfs, slaves, artisans and smallholders who were able to survive "only because they had access to meadows in which to keep cows, or woods in which to gather timber, wild berries and herbs, or quarries, fish-ponds, and open spaces in which to meet." The commons, Federici continues, encouraged "collective decision-making and work cooperation," and they provided the "material foundation" for "solidarity." By embedding production and exchange in institutions and relationships defined by noneconomic factors like kinship and religion, people have done what thinkers like Garrett Hardin say is impossible by making their existence into something other than a zero-sum game.[5]

Commons institutions, however, are not always positively focused on communal solidarity. More often, as Ostrom has emphasized, they are focused on setting boundaries and resolving problems, like free riding and theft, which inevitably arise in self-organized communities. The difference between successful and unsuccessful commons arrangements comes down to how boundaries are drawn and rules are enforced. The key is to establish an arrangement where individuals are required to consider the needs of others when making their own decisions. "If one fisher occupies a good fishing site," Ostrom explains, "a second fisher arriving at the same location must invest more resources to travel to another site." "If one irrigator allocates time and minerals to repairing a broken control gate in an irrigation canal," she adds, "all other irrigators using that canal are affected by that action, whether or not they want the control gate fixed and whether or not they contribute anything to the repair." According to Ostrom, the "key fact of life" for participants in such a system is that they are connected in a "lattice of interdependence" that breaks down when individuals strike out on their own without considering the consequences for others.[6]

It is hard to imagine how these commons institutions could exist in the world of the tar baby. The fact that these institutions were constructed and maintained over generations is something unimaginable in a setting where the fantasy of open access (living off "de jew on de grass") is the only alternative to the current state of chaos. Nevertheless, evidence showing the success of commons institutions has altered how we see places like the Bight of Benin, the Amazon Basin, the Georgia Low Country, and the Visayan region of the Philippines, and it is only fitting that this evidence is factored into the interpretation of the stories told in these places, the tar baby among them.[7]

The reason it is so hard to reconstruct the relationship between the tar baby story and these commons institutions is that the story is geared to a moment in time when these institutions were under attack. When individuals began to claim natural resources previously held in common as their own private property, communal access to these resources was blocked. People who were used to hunting in the nearby forest, or fishing in a familiar stream, or gathering peat from the bog behind their house, found that their customary rights had been turned into crimes. Merely setting foot in the woods you had known since your youth became criminal trespass. The consequence was that the world became suddenly and inalterably foreign. "Enclosure," E. P. Thompson explains, "in taking the commons away from the poor, made them strangers in their own land." In the historiographical tradition that Thompson helped to establish, there is a strong emphasis on the alienation that results from expropriation, an alienation that is also expressed in the tar baby.[8]

In the story, this alienation results in the wholesale assimilation of intellectual dilemmas, such as zero contribution and original appropriation, that have been used by thinkers like Locke and Blackstone to demonstrate the necessity of the regime of absolute property. The reason we are barred at the outset from thinking that the rabbit may have his own claim to the water in the well or the peas in the patch is that the story represents his theft from the same perspective that is adopted in Locke and Blackstone, a perspective from which customary right has already been turned into crime. From this perspective, custom appears only as crime, and traditional labor routines appear only as laziness.

The rabbit appears to be depraved and unethical from the outset, because he is criminalized before the story begins. In some versions, this negative characterization continues into the next episode in which the rabbit is trapped by the tar baby. The rabbit's approach to the tar baby in these cases is motivated by the same selfish desire that led the rabbit to steal from his neighbors. In some cases, the tar baby is made to look like an attractive woman to provoke the rabbit's sexual desire. In other cases, the tar baby holds a cake, a bottle of whiskey, or a deck of cards to tempt the rabbit. The implication in these stories is that the rabbit is polite to the tar baby only because he wants something from the tar baby—whether food, or sex, or the chance to cheat at blackjack. Characterization is continuous with the preceding scene. First, the rabbit lies to get corn or papayas from his neighbors, and then he feigns politeness to get what he wants from the tar baby. Following this sequence, the rabbit's frustration with the tar baby's nonresponsiveness seems like harassment and his attack on the tar baby like an attempted mugging or sexual assault. In both cases, the rabbit's most "salient trait," in Charles Joyner's words, is his "utter disdain for ethical and other norms." The rabbit is a "monument to amorality," a self-centered creature motivated only by his own appetite.[9]

In most versions on record, however, the rabbit's approach to the tar baby is unmotivated. Meeting the tar baby for the first time, the rabbit approaches the figure with all of the energy, generosity, and goodwill that he withheld from his neighbors during the story's opening sequence. The rabbit is inclined to presume the best about this stranger, answering the question raised by the encounter (Who is this creature? A friend or an enemy?) in the affirmative ("Hey friend!") without waiting for a sign from the tar baby. Whatever differences may exist between them, the rabbit assumes that these differences can be bridged by staying true to the established norms that are supposed to govern relationships between individuals even under uncertain circumstances. If the backstory presents social dilemmas as insuperable, as stumbling blocks that will inevitably lead to society's undoing, the rabbit's approach to the tar baby presumes, to the contrary, that interpersonal problems inevitably arise in the course of social interaction, but that such problems can and should be solved. In this scene, the rabbit is happy to give this stranger the benefit of the doubt, greeting the tar baby as a friend, taking it for granted that the tar baby will do the same.[10]

In the versions where the rabbit's approach is driven by appetite, his self-interested approach to the tar baby is predictable and therefore easy to explain. More often, however, his motives are mysterious. He greets the tar baby, because greeting strangers in the road is the polite thing to do. The rabbit's commitment to an ethics of interpersonal recognition, encoded as a point of etiquette, represents a complete break from his characterization in the preceding scene, and as such, it demands some explanation. Coming upon a stranger in the road, the rabbit recognizes the tar baby with the expectation that his recognition will be reciprocated. As far as the rabbit is concerned, this expectation is socially established. It seems there is nothing unusual about this expectation, which is why the rabbit so quickly construes the tar baby's nonresponsiveness as a swerve away from customary practice, or more pointedly, as an insult that is intended to communicate disregard.[11]

Our sense of the story as a whole changes when we take into account the rabbit's disappointment during the encounter with the tar baby. This brief and admittedly incongruous display of decorum may seem at first like a slight basis from which to reconsider the rabbit's character, especially as it stands as a prelude to violence, but it is important to remember that from the rabbit's perspective, the violence between the rabbit and the tar baby is not an inevitable fact of existence but instead the result of a breakdown in an established etiquette that otherwise serves as a reliable basis for civil interaction. Shocked at the tar baby's boorish indifference to social convention, the rabbit replies: "Do you hate your neighbours then? They salute you, and you say nothing." From Nigeria to Mexico, from South Carolina to the Philippines, the trickster expresses dismay at the tar baby's breach of social etiquette. He instructs: "One must say something when he meets one." He scolds: "Who'se yer pappy an' yer mammy dat larnt you no manners?" He enforces norms: "Behave you'self!" If the rabbit begins the story as an antisocial character whose self-centered actions expose the weakness of customary norms, he has already become something else by this middle episode. Indeed, he turns into something like his own opposite. During the meeting with the tar baby, the rabbit exemplifies the ethics of the community that he had previously spurned.[12]

If the story starts by rehearsing the distinction between those who work and those who play in its contrasting treatment of its characters, it also circles back on this moralism, providing a critical second take in the rabbit's encounter with the tar baby. In many ways, this scene functions like a dream in which the rabbit revisits the wolf's original claim on the land. If the legitimacy of the wolf's claim is something that is established in the opening scene, it is also something repeated in the storyline, albeit in a peculiar pantomime, in which the wolf is replaced by a proxy, a tar baby, whom the rabbit attempts to greet on the road, mistaking the lifeless pitch for an animate creature who should be able to respond when addressed. From this point, we can look back to the story's opening and find something that should not be there: a basis for identification with the rabbit. If the structure of the story's opening makes it impossible to see the struggle from the rabbit's point of view, in the ensuing encounter his perspective emerges into an objective situation where, by all rights, it should not exist.

When we suspend our judgment long enough to consider this sequence from the rabbit's perspective, something we can see is how the rabbit's disappointment in the encounter with the tar baby replays the story's inaugural event when the rabbit finds that he has been excluded from the resource claimed by the wolf. In both cases, the rabbit's established expectations are dashed when a potential partner deviates from custom. The tar baby's passive aggression resembles the wolf's property claim to the extent that both acts break with existing social norms. When the tar baby refuses to respond, it breaches an etiquette the rabbit takes for granted, and when the wolf asserts his proprietary rights, he violates the set of customs used to regulate access to the resource he would now claim as his own. If the pretext treats the wolf's claim as already accomplished, as a past action whose moral justification occurs in retrospect, in the next scene it is possible to imagine the seizure of property as a disruption to an existing network of relationships.[13]

This dreamlike repetition of the story's opening scene is fundamental, for example, to Frédéric Ortoli's version from Corsica, where the greeting ("Hey friend! Who are you?") is anticipated by the theft of water from the goat; Millington and Maxfield's version from the Philippines, where the greeting ("Good morning") is anticipated by the theft of fruit and vegetables from Masoy's garden; Abigail Christensen's version from South Carolina, where the greeting ("Gal, what you name?") is anticipated by the theft of corn and peanuts from the wolf; Père Capus's version from the Basumbwa, where the greeting ("*Mpola!*") is anticipated by the theft from a ripened field of *bukonzo* (a species of sorghum); Arthur Huff Fauset's Jamaican-derived version from Nova Scotia, where the greeting ("Hello, there") is anticipated by the theft of corn from Brer Tacoma's field; Mary Hose's version from the interior of Georgia, where the greeting ("Good-mornin' ter yer, ma'am!") is anticipated by the theft of peas from the old man's patch; Katherine Judson's version from the Biloxi Indians, where the greeting ("Friend, what is the matter? Are you angry?") is anticipated by the theft of potatoes; Richard Dennett's version from French Congo, where the greeting ("And what may you be doing here, Sir?") is anticipated by the theft of water from a well belonging to the antelope; Elsie Clews Parsons's version from the Bahamas, where the greeting ("How you do?") is anticipated by the theft of unspecified produce from a garden; and William Mechling's version from Oaxaca, where the greeting ("Friend, give me room to pass") is anticipated by the theft of beans from a field belonging to a boy and his mother.[14]

During the encounter with the tar baby, the wolf's claim becomes imaginable in the present tense from the rabbit's perspective: first as incomprehensible, then as inconsiderate, and finally as threatening, a sequence that restores the context of expectation suppressed in the opening scene by the framework that criminalizes the trickster's established right of access to a resource claimed by his enemies. When he addresses the tar baby as if it were a sentient creature, the rabbit revisits the alienation that he feels when he discovers his exclusion from the commons. In this original experience, the rabbit is alienated or objectified by the wolf's refusal to recognize him as a partner in an established context of social interaction. The wolf treats the rabbit's expectations at best as if the rabbit were trying to get something for nothing, or at worst as if they were nonsense. The wolf claims the resource in a way that suggests he sees no reason to take the rabbit into consideration, and the disrespect conveyed by his claim returns when the tar baby fails to respond to the rabbit's gestures of recognition. What the rabbit wants from the tar baby, in other words, is the recognition he is denied in the story's opening scene.[15]

The problem of recognition is elaborated in the canonical version of the story given by Joel Chandler Harris, in which the rabbit greets his would-be interlocutor with the usual courtesy. "Mawnin'!" the rabbit says to the tar baby. When the tar baby says nothing in response, the rabbit tries again: "How duz yo' sym'tums seem ter segashuate?" When the tar baby does not respond, the rabbit persists in his folly. Rather than realize his mistake, he interprets the tar baby's silence as if it were intended to insult him. He considers various possibilities. He wonders if the tar baby could be a snob. He wonders if the tar baby is hard of hearing. He wonders if the tar baby could be gaslighting him, or taunting him, or challenging him to a fight. In Millington and Maxfield's story from the Philippines, the trickster explicitly states the question on his mind: "Why," he says, "do you not answer me?" Of course, this question only compounds the irony at this point in the story by revealing the rabbit's continuing conviction that the tar baby's silence is an intentional act. Despite mounting evidence to the contrary, the rabbit remains committed to the idea that the tar baby is choosing to remain silent. The tar baby can respond to him, but for some reason, the tar baby will not respond to him, and the only question is how to interpret its silence—as snub or rebuke, as dare or defiance.[16]

The rabbit's salutation ("Mawnin'!") in this scene also functions like a solicitation, with the tacit understanding that it will receive a response. The rabbit is acting on a customary agreement that says, "I will recognize you, and you will recognize me in return." This custom is broken, however, by the tar baby, whose silence is matched by its blank visage, which offers "no sign of recognition." The tar baby returns the rabbit's gaze with a vacant stare that does not, that cannot, supply the recognition that the rabbit needs to orient himself in the world. At this point, the struggle escalates, as the rabbit abandons all pretense to courtesy and demands the recognition he was denied, a demand that leads to an imagined battle of wills in which the potential resolution involves not the softening of the eyes, the nod, or the sardonic cracking of a smile but the surrender that comes when one or the other blinks or looks away. "'I'm gwine ter larn you how ter talk ter 'spectubble folks ef hit's de las' ack,'" the rabbit says to the tar baby in Remus's version of the story. "'Ef you don't take off dat hat en tell me howdy," the rabbit concludes, "I'm gwine ter bus' you wide open.'" The rabbit "keep on axin' 'im," and the tar baby "keep on sayin' nothin'" until finally the rabbit "draw back wid his fis' . . . en blip he tuck 'er side er de head." Having addressed the tar baby as a friend, the rabbit now tries his hardest to make the tar baby into an enemy who can be forced to recognize him against its will. Having experienced the tar baby's silence as a violation, the rabbit abandons his faith in reciprocity, deciding instead to claim his freedom by turning the tables, imposing his will, and killing or wounding the tar baby, a deed he will perform even if it is his "las' ack," resulting in his own demise.[17]

In this scene, the story spirals inward as the rabbit internalizes the battle for resources as a struggle for recognition. What the rabbit wants from the tar baby is the recognition that he believes will restore his subjective standpoint in the world. The rabbit's consciousness at this stage is shaped by his dispossession, but he is convinced that he may still receive a reprieve from this psychic confinement if he can somehow convince, cajole, or threaten the tar baby into acknowledging his existence. Like the enslaved captive in a war of retribution, the rabbit struggles to free himself by winning back recognition from the tar baby. When this recognition is not forthcoming, the rabbit threatens to turn the tables and kill the tar baby, using violence to break through his alienation. "By God, I'll make you know who I am," the trickster threatens the tar baby during their encounter in a Nova Scotian version of the story. As he becomes increasingly desperate, the rabbit gets explicit about these options. The tar baby can reply to his greetings, allowing their interaction to proceed on familiar terms, or the tar baby can relent and recognize him in response to his threats of violence, or else the tar baby can persist in his stubborn silence and suffer the consequences, an outcome in which the rabbit would secure his freedom by avenging his dishonor.[18]

In all cases, the stakes are the same for the rabbit. What the rabbit wants from the tar baby is a properly formed response— "I'm very well. And how are you this morning?"—that would shore up his place in the world while also confirming the authority of customary procedures, abbreviated here as a point of etiquette, that he had previously taken for granted. Failing that outcome, he will settle for beating the tar baby until it relents, even killing the tar baby, if it persists in its passive aggression. It is difficult at first to say why the rabbit is unable to see what should be obvious about the tar baby, why he becomes so upset with the tar baby, why he is unable to walk away from the tar baby while he still can, but we can begin to understand the reasons for his persistence once we appreciate what is ultimately at stake for him in this awkward encounter, in which absolutely everything, including his very existence, is hanging in the balance.

Again, the problem here is that the rabbit's customary requests for recognition seem implausible and even ridiculous. The rabbit's courtesy brings with it only the ghost of an expectation, an expectation that is out of sync, as it is detached from any context in which it would appear reasonable. We see what the rabbit wants, and we see why the rabbit wants what he wants, but we also see that the rabbit will never get what he wants, because unlike the rabbit, we can see the tar baby for what it really is. None of the outcomes the rabbit imagines are possible given the objective structure of the situation. We know the rabbit will never receive the recognition he desires, because we know the tar baby is an inanimate object lacking the ability to recognize anyone. It is equally difficult to say how the rabbit's attack on the tar baby could accomplish the intended result of either injuring or killing the tar baby, as the story never entertains the possibility that an inanimate object can be injured or killed. All of which is to say that the encounter with the tar baby is presented in a way that blocks every resolution tendered in the story. The story stages the problem of the rabbit's subjectivity with reference to these resolutions, but they are promised only to be withheld, making the rabbit's perspective seem once again not only unresolved but unresolvable.[19]

Seemingly against the odds, although not in every instance, the rabbit discovers a way to liberate himself from the tar baby and, by implication, from the intractable problems of action and identification that are staged in the scene of his captivity. Different versions of the story end in different ways, but the most famous ending—the escape to the briar patch—builds upon the commitment to custom that appears, albeit obliquely, in the rabbit's conventional address to the tar baby. If the stickfast sequence suggests that there may be more to the rabbit's worldview than we were previously able to surmise, including a commitment to inherited customs, the briar patch grounds these customs in the world, demonstrating that the institutions supported by the commons were not unsustainable or doomed to obsolescence in the way that thinkers from Locke to Hardin have assumed. It turns out that the commons is still right where it was all along, on the unenclosed lands to the side of the road where the wolf has laid his trap. The briar patch has been there all along, but it does not appear in the story until the very last minute.

Chapter Five
THE BRIAR PATCH

For anyone interested in deriving a theory of politics from the rabbit's tactical intelligence, the most important moment in the story comes at the very end. As with every other stage, the conclusion varies according to version. Sometimes the rabbit escapes from the trap by persuading some other animal to take his place. In one case, the wolf demands that the rabbit abandon his lazy ways ("Brudder Rabbit, ef we turns you loose, is you gwine work?") and the rabbit assents before making his escape. Other times, as we have seen, the story ends with the trickster suffering punishment, whether slavery or death, at the hands of his enemy. Most celebrated, however, are the versions of the story in which the rabbit escapes from the trap by convincing his captor to release him into a briar patch, bramble, thicket, wilderness, or some other forbidding wasteland. During the escape, constriction and claustrophobia give way to the exhilaration and freedom that come as the rabbit returns to the unenclosed landscape that he calls home.[1]

According to the most common interpretation, the briar patch stands as a metaphor for culture, sometimes a subculture sustained by either *de facto* or *de jure* segregation. Some critics, including Larry Neal, suggest that the rabbit's escape proves the problem of subjectivity posed in the encounter with the tar baby was never as difficult as other critics, including Ralph Ellison, have believed. According to Neal, the recognition denied first by the property owner and then by the tar baby is consistently available to the rabbit in the briar patch. The "confusion and absurdity" dramatized when the rabbit believes the tar baby will talk back to him is not an example of the existential quandary of blackness. On the contrary, it is evidence that the rabbit has lost touch with the community that is the only source of the recognition he desires. Neal's claim about the rabbit's entrapment and escape is echoed by other critics, including Albert Murray, whose interpretation takes implicit aim at Daniel Patrick Moynihan, a sociologist and political advisor to U. S. President Lyndon Johnson, who argued that African Americans were alienated by their oppression to a degree that made it hard to sustain social and familial relationships. "Down-home boy that I am," Murray writes, "I have never been so unhip, so unbelievably square, as to mistake a tar baby for the me I think I should be, certainly not because some social science head-counting racial one-upman decides that a tar baby stands for all rabbits."[2]

This cultural interpretation of the tar baby became a warrant for the new social history. For scholars like George Rawick and John Blassingame, the briar patch symbolizes the heritage of songs, stories, beliefs, and rituals that formed the slave community. Based on this interpretation, the tar baby is cited as *prime facie* evidence against the argument, most strongly associated at the time with Stanley Elkins, that slaves lacked the common culture and family structure that was needed to foster independence. Focusing on the United States, Elkins claims that slavery was a closed system whose brutality destroyed the "personalities" of its victims, leaving them without the capacity to establish durable relationships or stable family structures. Writing against this scholarship, Rawick for instance looks to the tar baby to show that slaves had an "independent community" that "molded the slave personality." According to Rawick, slaves experienced extreme and even soul-crushing oppression, but they were "kept whole" by the "day-to-day and night-to-night life of the slave quarters." Rawick suggests that "the essence of the slave personality produced by this community is contained in the Br'er Rabbit stories . . . as they were carried from Africa in the oral traditions of black people." By telling these stories, slaves found the "footing" to think and act for themselves. This claim has accompanied the story almost from the time it was first transcribed. Over time, it has been compounded by assumptions about the character and composition of subaltern politics that have kept us from seeing the briar patch as anything other than a sign of culture in the most abstract sense. John Callahan encapsulates this approach to the story by posing a rhetorical question. "What," he asks, "is the briar patch but a figure for the milieu of slavery?"[3]

This cultural interpretation of the briar patch is extended and eloquently expressed in Toni Morrison's fourth novel, *Tar Baby* (1981). Morrison's novel concerns the tortured romance between two central characters, Jadine and Son. Jadine is worldly, materialistic, educated at the Sorbonne. Standing as a case in point for the arguments made by Larry Neal and Albert Murray, Jadine's problem is that she has lost touch with her cultural heritage. "She has forgotten her ancient properties," we are told near the novel's end. By contrast, Son is a fugitive who sneaks onto Isle de Chevaliers, a small Caribbean island that is home to Jadine's wealthy aunt and uncle. Through this romance, Morrison transforms the story of the tar baby into an allegory about cultural assimilation. In this allegory, Son is the rabbit, and Jadine is the tar baby. Like the rabbit, Son is described as a "thieving" and "no-count" rascal. In contrast, Jadine is depicted as the tar baby, an "inauthentic" parvenu who has chosen to abandon her culture. As such, Jadine represents a temptation to Son, an invitation to forget his own past.[4]

Once established, this allegory becomes increasingly complex. Tar stands not only for the temptation Jadine presents to Son but also for the black culture that Son embodies. Son's attempt to reconnect Jadine to her heritage is figured in a sexual encounter as "[breathing] into her the smell of tar and its shiny consistency." The identification with Son is complicated, moreover, as he turns violent. "I got a story for you," he tells Jadine, as he is about to assault her. "Once upon a time there was a farmer," Son begins, "a white farmer. . . . A rabbit came along and ate a couple of his . . . cabbages." In the end, Son's attempt to reform Jadine fails. Like the rabbit, he escapes back to the unenclosed landscape where he belongs, in this case the foggy far side of the island, where the "champion daisy trees still grow." The novel ends with Son escaping to his own briar patch, "lickety-split," to join the wild horsemen who live "up in the hills" away from the city.[5]

From Larry Neal to John Blassingame, from Albert Murray to Toni Morrison, the briar patch has been understood as a symbol for culture and as an antidote to alienation. As we have seen, this interpretation builds on the longstanding interest in the story's diffusion. We know that the story of the tar baby was useful to people as a guide to life, because they kept telling it. It was a survival adaptation. At the same time, there is more to say about the briar patch. It is certainly true that the briar patch suggests something like "rootedness," but this interpretation can be made more concrete and exacting when the story is reconnected to the contexts in which it was originally told.[6]

As a start, we need to think more precisely about the backcountry to which the rabbit escapes. Sometimes he flees to a "briar patch," other times a "brier-bush," other times a "brier thicket," a "bramble," the "fine grass," or a "berry patch." In a Texan version of the story the rabbit is thrown onto the prairie, where he tells his captor that he is afraid some animal will eat him. Running into the distance, the rabbit taunts his captor: "This is my father's land." In Nova Scotia, the rabbit is tossed out in the freezing cold. "Ho, ho," he announces, "I was bred an' born in de snow, didn' you know dat?" There are also several ways of extending the plea to milk the tension, as we see in a version by the Biloxi Indians. "If you are so afraid of a brier patch, I will throw you into one," says the Frenchman. "Oh, no, no!" says the rabbit. "I will throw you into the brier patch," repeats the Frenchman. "I am much afraid of it," says the rabbit.

"Since you are in such dread of it, I will throw you into it," says the Frenchman. In contrast, two versions from South Africa collected by James Honeÿ improvise on the means of escape, as the jackal shaves and greases his tail and then convinces the lion that he should be swung in circles before being put to death.[7]

Regardless of the specific details, the escape always involves some deception. Frequently the deception is framed by what Espinosa calls the "mock plea," in which the trickster beseeches his captor to do anything—torture him, burn him, roast him, boil him, drown him, extract his eyeballs, tear out his ears, cut off his legs—except banish him to the place where, unbeknownst to his captor, he will be safe. "Please," the rabbit implores the fox in one story, "don't fling me in dat brier-patch." "Trow me in de fire," the rabbit begs the wolf in another story, "'cause if you trow me in de brier-bush I'm done." In Christensen's story from the South Carolina Sea Islands, the rabbit begins by asking for clemency: "Oh, Maussa Wolf, do le' me go, an' I nebber tief groun'-nut no mo'." The wolf refuses: "No, Brudder Rabbit, you ben a tief my corn las' 'ear an' you ben a tief groun'-nut dis 'ear, an' now I gwine eat you up." The rabbit then pitches into his reverse psychology, drawing an analogy between his own body and the corn that is the object of his dispute with the wolf. "Oh, Maussa Wolf," he begs, "You ma' roas' me, you ma' toas' me, you ma' cut me up, you ma' eat me, but do, Maussa Wolf, whatebber you do, don't t'row me in de brier-bush! Ef you t'row me in de brier-bush I gwine dead!"[8]

Soon enough, the wolf realizes his mistake. After he throws the rabbit into the briar patch, the rabbit taunts the wolf: "Maussa Wolf, aint you know I *lib* in de brier-bush? Aint you know all my farmbly bawn an bred in de brier-bush? *Dat* what mek I tol' you for trow me yere." As the rabbit explains, the wolf has been fooled on two counts. First, the briar patch is inhabitable. It is where the rabbit lives. Second, it is the place that connects the rabbit to his family and his traditions. It is where the next generation is reared, and culture is reproduced. Famously,

FIG. 5.1. A. B. Frost, "[The Fox Watches the Rabbit Escape]." Pen and ink. From Joel Chandler Harris, *Uncle Remus: His Songs and His Sayings, with One Hundred and Twelve Illustrations by A. B. Frost* (New York: D. Appleton and Company, 1915), 19.

the rabbit is emphatic about his connection to the briar patch, as we see in stories collected by Frédéric Ortoli ("In these brambles I was born"), John Lomax ("This is my father's land"), and Charles Colcock Jones Jr. ("Dis de place my mama fotch me up"), but the rabbit's claim to nativity is most commonly expressed through the familiar refrain about being "bawn an bred," "bred an' born," or "born and raise" on this unenclosed land. One of the more unusual variations on this formula appears in a French story collected in Missouri by Joseph Médard Carrière, in which the rabbit persuades the wolf to throw him into the dew by telling him it will be too cold there. Most versions of the story are careful to separate the traditional society in the briar patch from the fantasy of open access captured in the trope of the dew, but in Carrière's version, they are oddly conflated.[9]

Almost everything we learn about the briar patch is deduced from what the wolf evidently does not know about it. When the wolf tricks the rabbit earlier in the story, he relies on what he knows about the rabbit, specifically what he knows about the rabbit's penchant for personification, and when the rabbit tricks the wolf in return, he relies on what he knows about the wolf, and what the rabbit knows about the wolf is that the wolf sees the briar patch as a place that could not possibly be a home. For the rabbit's trick to succeed, the wolf has to be inclined to believe that it would be a fate worse than death to be consigned there. The briar patch exists outside the world the wolf calls his own, beyond the territories parceled into properties and made productive and navigable by investment of labor and technology. Unlike the fields where the wolf grows his produce, which are sown and one day soon will be fenced and irrigated, and unlike the road where the wolf sets his trap, which is graded and one day soon will be paved and posted, the briar patch is wild. Figured in the negative terms attributed to the wolf, the briar patch is unimproved, unincorporated, unenclosed. It is land that belongs to nobody, where nobody survives for long, a remnant from the natural world that existed before the beginning of civilization. If the story starts by setting the rabbit's crime in relation to its cognates in political philosophy, it ends by returning to these precedents, staging its own version of the archetypal scene in which the captor has a choice to mitigate the punishment meted to the captive, banishing him to the wilderness rather than killing or enslaving him.

If the commons appears brutish and desolate to the wolf, it looks different to the rabbit. It gives the rabbit sustenance and protection, and it also gives him other less tangible things, like a community and a sense of direction, that he did not previously seem to have at his disposal. It gives him a perspective that appears to have been developed over generations in the conflict over the land, and it gives him not only ancestors but presumably allies with whom he makes common cause. Describing the orientation he derives from the land, the rabbit is careful in his choice of words, identifying the briar patch not only as his present refuge but as his birthplace and childhood home. The briar patch is where his perspective on the world was formed. Nothing further is said, however, about the composition of his perspective, whether it comes from blood or culture, nature or nurture, from where he was born or how he was bred. The story remains agnostic on these points. What matters to the story is that this grounding in the briar patch is strong enough to arrest the cycle of disorientation that begins in the previous episode. The rabbit's escape to the briar patch promises an answer to the questions posed in the encounter with the tar baby. The actual answer, however, is unanticipated. It comes after a parody of the politeness ("please, please") that the rabbit sought and did not receive from the tar baby, but otherwise it can seem disconnected or contrived in relation to the rest of the story. The rabbit derives his capacity to think politically not through his struggle with the wolf but through his connection to a place that was there before the struggle began.[10]

The story connects, through the briar patch, to the many inhospitable places in the world that have given refuge to fugitives like the rabbit—including the jungles, foothills, deserts, bottoms, marshlands, and deltas that sheltered maroon communities in places like Palmares in Brazil, the Great Dismal Swamp in North Carolina, and the fabled mountainous "cockpit" in Jamaica, an area of steep ridges that provided a natural line of defense against Spanish and British colonists.

Even after the wolf and his heirs claimed the coastal plains and valleys as property, these rugged places remained unincorporated. Fernand Braudel has described these places as "'black holes' outside *world time*." Like black holes, they exist in the modern world but they remain outside it, resisting assimilation to the interstate system of global accumulation. From the perspective of the people living in these places, the terrain provided security and subsistence. Accordingly, Gonzalo Aguirre Beltrán has called these unenclosed wastelands "regions of refuge." Similarly, Pierre Clastres has called them "shatter zones." Beltrán and

Clastres both emphasize that people choose to live in these places. They are not savages consigned to a state of nature due to their failure to develop agriculture and commerce. Rather, they are people who fled from slavery or colonial authorities, setting up in a remote location so as to defend themselves. Understood in these terms, the briar patch seems neither barbarous nor inescapably tragic. The aspects that make the briar patch so uninviting to the wolf—its inaccessibility, its obscurity, its resistance to improvement—look not like vestiges from a primordial state of nature but like characteristics of an ancestral home chosen by the rabbit's forebears for the protection it offered from predators.[11]

There are a few cases, including Christensen's version, in which the rabbit's escape is foreshadowed at the start when we are told that the rabbit lives in the briar patch. In most instances, however, the end comes as a surprise. As a plot device, the escape to the briar patch characteristically functions as a *deus ex machina* in that it resolves the rabbit's struggle in a way that is not only unanticipated but barred from representation in the previous stages. At the start, the story hinges on the fact that miscreants like the rabbit tend to evade punishment, whether by fleeing to the briar patch or by some other ruse. This is supposed to show the failure of custom, proving that custom on its own is not forceful enough to constrain bad actors. By the end, however, the briar patch symbolizes the strength of custom, affirming a way of life that prospers both before and outside the law. The story does not explain how this reversal is accomplished. The rabbit's perspective does not materialize step by step as tensions internal to the conflict are resolved, restated, and resolved again. Nor is there a transition when the consciousness of the rabbit is raised, as it appears the rabbit already knew everything he needed to know before the story began. Ending in effect before it started, the story insists on the priority of the rabbit's point of view.[12]

For these reasons, it appears that there is something forced, or very nearly uncanny, about the subjectivity fostered by the briar patch, as it arrives despite, rather than through, the story's machinations. If the rabbit's encounter with the tar baby is a dream that replays the encounter between the rabbit and the wolf, we might say that the escape to the briar patch is also a dream hatched from the encounter with the tar baby, a dream inside a dream, in which the rabbit's incoherence, and the mismatch between knowledge and identification, is not so much resolved as reoriented through the rabbit's aspiration to freedom. The image of the rabbit reflected in the briar patch is almost certainly more perfect, more sovereign, more self-sufficient, than the rabbit, or anyone else for that matter, will ever become. The questions raised in the preceding stages of the story are therefore not so much answered as unblocked by its ending. The briar patch gives the rabbit an orientation to action. It projects him into history, making it possible to see the struggle over the expropriation of land, labor, and resources from a standpoint that is otherwise criminalized, caricatured, or blacked out.

As an example, consider a version of the story that was published in *Negro Myths from the Georgia Coast* (1898), a folklore collection "taken down" by Charles Colcock Jones Jr. "from the lips of the old negroes" on the rice and cotton plantations in Liberty County, Georgia. Circumstantial evidence indicates that the most likely source for this version of the story is Jack Jones, a house servant who worked for Charles Jones's extended family. Like other versions of the story, "Buh Rabbit, Buh Wolf, and de Tar Baby" has been characterized as an "African tale" that "survived relatively unchanged on the Georgia Coast." Based on its context of origin and dissemination, critics have felt safe in assuming that "Buh Rabbit, Buh Wolf, and de Tar Baby" is a political allegory in which slaves identified with the rabbit against the wolf.[13]

At the start of "Buh Rabbit, Buh Wolf, and de Tar Baby," there is a drought, and water is scarce. The wolf digs a well to access the groundwater. The rabbit, however, is "too lazy an too scheemy fuh wuk fuh iself." Every day, when the wolf is away from the well, the rabbit slips off to fill his calabash, carrying the water back to his house. Confronted by a thief who refuses to respect the natural rights that follow from his labor, the wolf is left to fend for himself. The story is clear that property is impossible to protect in this situation. When the wolf confronts the rabbit, pointing out the tracks that the rabbit has made leading to the well, the rabbit is free to offer a flat denial and walk away, as there is no authority in the story to decide on the evidence or enforce community norms of property ownership. Questioned by the wolf, the rabbit says that he has "no casion fuh hunt water" as he "lib off de jew on de grass," a hollow excuse at best. The wolf does the best he can, standing guard and setting his trap, but ultimately he fails when the rabbit escapes to the briar patch. The rabbit is just "too scheemy." Under the circumstances, there is no way to stop him.[14]

Among the slaves and ex-slaves who were telling the tar baby story in Liberty County, the briar patch may have signified something abstract, like culture or community, but first and foremost it would have referred to a real place in the world. It would have called to mind the swamps, canebrakes, marshes, oak groves, bottom lands, and wiregrass savannas that provided refuge and resources for subsistence both during and after slavery. Homesteads in Liberty County were spread out, leaving room for the backcountry network of trails that could take you from Maybank to Carlawter plantation, or from some small farm to a tavern in Eden or Riceboro, without setting foot on a main road. This terrain included waterways navigable only with a canoe or flatboat, including the swampy tributaries of the Medway and North Newport rivers, which ran all the way to the coast. The hush harbors and other sanctuaries lodged in the recesses of this terrain are known only through anecdotal evidence, but their importance to slaves and their descendants is undeniable.[15]

The vast majority of land in Liberty County was unfenced, and it was custom there, as it was elsewhere in the southern states, that unfenced land, whether or not it was privately owned, was accessible to anybody for the purposes of hunting, fishing, foraging, or grazing. By some estimates, as much as nine-tenths of the territory in the southern states remained unfenced as late as 1850. In the antebellum decades, a tremendous amount of land was effectively in the public domain, and the customary right to access this land for subsistence purposes was generally shared with slaves. In most jurisdictions, it was against the law for slaves to head out by themselves at night hunting, with or without firearms, or to release their livestock for open-range grazing, but these practices were tolerated by planters who realized that this self-provisioning worked to their own advantage. It made sense to permit slaves to provide for themselves, as it reduced the expenditure that was required to sustain a bound workforce. In an economic downturn, slaves' capacity to feed themselves alleviated some of the fiscal pressure on their owners, and sometimes, it even became a make-or-break enterprise, keeping plantations viable that would have failed otherwise. This system also gave planters another way to discipline slaves, as they could threaten to take away these customary privileges if rules were broken.[16]

In Liberty County, it was commonplace for slaves to hunt, fish, forage, tend gardens, and graze livestock on the open range. Archeological as well as anecdotal evidence shows that self-provisioning accounted for a significant portion of the calories consumed by slaves in the Low Country. Undoubtedly, it was indispensable to their nutrition. The rice, corn, black-eyed peas, sweet potatoes, cane syrup, and occasional fatback they were given as rations were scarcely enough to sustain their labor routine. It was normal for slaves in Liberty County to keep chickens, hogs, and in some cases cattle, a practice that would not have been possible if they had not been able to feed these animals without expense by grazing them in nearby woods and barrens. Depending on the season, slaves also headed into the backcountry to gather blackberries, acorns, plums, muscadine grapes, walnuts, and hickory nuts. They also hunted and trapped geese, pheasants, deer, turkey, possums, turtles, alligators, and raccoons.

Slaves who lived on coastal plantations such as Maybank collected oysters, trapped crabs, and caught a variety of fish. Further inland, slaves caught freshwater bass, mullet, perch, drum, and catfish in the swamps and rice canals using hooks and night crawlers for bait. In their garden plots, slaves grew any number of fruits and vegetables, including local staples like okra, squash, and sugarcane. In addition, they were able to supplement their rations by pilfering some of the crop they grew for their masters or helping themselves to ham and bacon from the smokehouse, habits whose prevalence is unsurprising given the number of slave owners who preemptively reduced slaves' fixed diet to below subsistence on the grounds that slaves would steal food at any rate.[17]

With these practices, slaves were not simply fending for themselves. Resources harvested from the commons were often consumed by the slaves who appropriated them, but they were also bartered, sold, shared, and given away as gifts. Specialization led to surplus, and this surplus became the basis for a well-documented informal economy that included not only slaves but also white yeoman farmers and free persons of color. From the beginning, this informal economy included not only resources taken from nature but also prepared foods, clothing, crafts, and store-bought goods such as farming implements and furniture. The informal economy was especially strong in locations like Liberty County where labor was organized not into gangs but instead according to the task system. Gang labor required slaves to work continuously at a more or less constant pace for the entire day. Under the task system, by contrast, slaves were done when they finished their regular assignments, usually leaving them with a modicum of time of each day to devote to self-provisioning or petty production. This flexible division of labor allowed slaves to establish their own customary traditions of agriculture, manufacture, possession, and trade. These traditions included commerce in grain, fruits, vegetables, and legumes as well as in livestock, usually starting with poultry, from which profits could be parlayed and invested into larger animals like pigs, cattle, and horses. In Liberty County, petty commodities included raw and prepared foodstuffs (from wild fruits to honey, ground meal, and fish oil), crafts (bowls made from gourds, baskets from reeds), transportation and building materials (canoes from logs, cabin beams from driftwood), and store-bought goods (from tobacco to fishhooks to farming implements). Slaves also had property interest in cabins, storage sheds, and livestock enclosures, including beehives and hen houses, that they built for themselves.[18]

Extending from the commons, this informal economy was sustained over generations, during which slaves in Liberty County became accustomed to governing both personal and communal property in a variety of ways, most of them without legal authorization. Some historians have idealized this informal economy, stressing its communitarian aspects. Slaves shared with others in need, and they often governed property in common, but they were also able to dictate when property belonged to individuals, and they imposed customary penalties when these individual property norms were violated. Many transactions involved bartering with kin or neighbors, trading surplus goods for equivalent products for personal use, but slaves also exchanged products for money in the unsanctioned markets that existed throughout the county. In other cases, they traded their wares for some other tangible and perhaps less perishable commodity that could be traded again as needed.[19]

This economy was informal in the sense that it was based in custom and not condoned by law, and the petty property that belonged to slaves was therefore theoretically vulnerable to confiscation at any time. Left to their own devices, slaves evolved a set of self-imposed restraints to organize possession and exchange. "A whole rainbow of social relationships among people who were not related by blood or marriage," historian Dylan Penningroth explains, helped slaves to "overcome the hardships of getting and keeping property in the slave quarters." Because "each piece of property embodied the interests of several different people," the relations among owners had to be "flexible and negotiable" and responsive to noneconomic factors. In Liberty County, the medium for this economy was an "informal system of display" by which households and other collectives could claim ownership by storing their property in plain view in their yards. Under this system, as Penningroth describes, slaves' ability to transform "possession into property" depended on their substituting "informal public recognition for public law as the anchor to their title." Acknowledgment that an object belonged to a slave or a particular group of slaves resulted not from a single event, like the signing of a deed of sale, but instead from "a series of demonstrations over time" that accumulated to establish the "boundaries of ownership."[20]

After emancipation, former slaves continued to trade and make meaningful contributions to their subsistence through hunting, fishing, foraging, grazing, and gardening. They persisted in bartering, sharing, and selling their surplus, and they continued to apply the rules from the moral economy of slavery, which said that they had a customary right to some small portion of the harvest that they had worked to produce. With these resources at their disposal, some chose to avoid the labor market, and many more appreciated that there were new ways to turn these customary practices to their benefit, leveraging negotiations with their employers and bringing unprecedented flexibility to their work schedule. By continuing to supplement their income by gathering or growing their own food and producing commodities for sale, it was possible to take off days when needed, or even to opt for seasonal stints instead of a long-term contract. If things were bad, quitting was an alternative when you knew that you had a chance at weathering the loss of a job.[21]

Self-provisioning practices continued after slavery, but their circumstances changed. Planters knew that these customs, though they were beneficial under slavery, were now a threat to their interests. Labor-intensive staple crops like cotton, indigo, and rice required a predictable and inexpensive workforce, and planters worried that these established customs of mutual self-provisioning would undermine discipline on the plantations. They believed that they could not afford to let their former slaves adapt to the subsistence lifestyle that many non-slaveholding whites had chosen in the preceding decades—combining irregular jobs with gardening, grazing, and fishing—because it would mean the end of their plantations.[22]

Planters and their allies in government responded to this perceived crisis by outlawing or restricting access to unenclosed land for the purposes of hunting, fishing, foraging, and grazing. Fish and game codes were adopted for the first time in three Georgia counties in 1872, six more in 1875, eighteen in 1876, six in 1877, and six in 1878. In addition, the laws on criminal trespass were strengthened, sometimes listing foraging and gathering wood as activities that were specifically forbidden on land that did not belong to you. With a similar intention, laws were passed establishing wildly disproportionate penalties for petty larceny, prescribing outsized mandatory minimum sentences for stealing pigs or poultry. In these same counties, there was aggressive prosecution for "larceny after trust" brought against tenants in disputes over shared crops, and vagrancy laws were rewritten to include hunting and fishing "on the land of others" as adequate reason for an arrest. Hunting seasons were established, often timed from October to March to make sure that there would be an incentive to work during the months when crops were being planted, tended, and harvested. In 1873, Georgia passed a law prohibiting hunting on Sundays, ostensibly on religious grounds, although there were likely also other motives given that Sunday was the only day of the week that many agricultural workers had time to head into the woods or swamps. Still more codes were adopted both at the local and state level targeting particular activities, like hunting while you were camping; extracting wild honey; collecting oysters; or marketing fruits, vegetables, or other provisions after the sun had set.[23]

In 1881, Georgia passed a local-option law to facilitate the enclosure of its open range, something that became possible only after a significant proportion of black voters were disfranchised by poll taxes. Before the enclosure law was adopted, individuals with little or no property, including slaves, had been able to keep their own goats, pigs, and even cows by grazing them on unfenced land. The public right of access to the open range derived from custom, but it was also confirmed in law. During its first session in 1759, the Georgia General Assembly adopted a law on fencing that remained in force for more than a century. This law codified the established customary practice in the state, which prescribed that landowners were responsible for fencing their lands if they wanted to prevent individuals from trespassing or animals from grazing on their property. If you killed an animal that was eating your crops and the animal's owner could show that your fencing was inadequate, then you had to reimburse the owner. This changed for good after the success of the enclosure campaign. According to the new fence laws passed in 1880s, property owners did not have to enclose their land to prevent grazing. Instead, livestock owners had to fence their animals or else pay for the damage they caused. Animals, in other words, needed to be "fenced in" rather than "fenced out," a change that ended open-range grazing by forbidding access to private land whether or not it had been formally enclosed. As a result of these laws, former slaves and other household farmers found themselves cut off from traditional resources even as they were also burdened with new expenses: fences and pens had to be built, fines and licenses had to be paid to the government, and livestock feed had to be purchased at a store.[24]

With these legal reforms, Georgia abandoned the traditional commitment to the commons that residents had taken for granted before emancipation, bringing the state into line with the common-law tradition that had developed in northern states like Massachusetts, where the controlling cases on fences, such as *Rust v. Low* (1809), held that open-range grazing was tantamount to theft, as it assimilated one person's property (grass or acorns) into another person's property (pig or cow) without consent or contract. In Georgia, this was a departure from customary practice, but it was a departure that was justified in familiar terms derived from slavery. The intentions behind these measures are stated plainly in a petition sent by the Georgia State Grange to the State General Assembly in 1874. The Grange was a civic organization representing the interests of planters and the agricultural industries. The Grange demanded legal protection for their property: they had the exclusive right to the products of their lands. Like the wolf in the story of the tar baby, they complained that the fish, game, and crops on their land were vulnerable to "thieves," "plunderers," and "poachers."

If custom dictated that they had to surrender the "vast advantages" of their land to the "vagrant and vicious negro," then custom had to be overturned. The Grange urged action in circumstances where property was the product of labor (like "standing and gathered crops") and in cases where it was the product of nature (like the produce in "orchards" and "groves" and the "fish in private waters"). At the same time, the petition urged the enclosure of the state's "waste and unused lands," turning the commons to productive purposes rather than "surrendering" them to lazy rascals who lived on what they stole from others.[25]

There were strong precedents for this thinking in Liberty County and elsewhere in Georgia. Slave owners had long seen "the negro" in terms that anticipated the enclosure campaign. The Reverend Charles Colcock Jones, who built the plantations on which his son would later transcribe the story of the tar baby, provides one example. Based on his observations in Liberty County, Jones determines that "the negro" is "proverbially idle" and "improvident." Among free persons of color, Jones announces, the "golden season of labor" is "passed in lounging along the streets and basking in the sun, or in lazy, bungling, and fitful attempts at work." When the golden season is over and these lazy rascals find themselves without the basic necessities, they resort to "theft" without a second thought, turning to the crime that Jones calls the "characteristic vice" of the "negro race." In Liberty County, these ideas were expressed not only by slave owners and their apologists but by officials in the Union Army and the Freedmen's Bureau, who believed that ex-slaves knew nothing about property and would not work unless forced. This mindset was reduced to a formula in primers and textbooks like Helen E. Brown's *John Freeman and His Family* (1864) and Clinton B. Fisk's *Plain Counsels for Freedmen* (1865), which were written for the purpose of teaching ex-slaves about labor, thrift, and the nature of contracts on the assumption that these concepts would be foreign to people who had proven themselves predisposed to idleness. These reformers and educators were at odds on many points with former slaveholders like Charles Colcock Jones Sr., but they agreed with them on the basic point that emancipated slaves were like the rabbit—lazy by inclination and disposed to work only under compulsion—while also agreeing that anyone in the slave community who attempted to grow some corn or dig a well would find him or herself—like the wolf—without protection.[26]

There is evidence demonstrating that many people appreciated the connection between stories like the tar baby and the ideas about labor and property put to use in the enclosure campaign. It became common in Georgia newspapers, for example, to say that poachers were acting like "Brer Rabbit" when sneaking out at night. One local court case reported in the *Atlanta Constitution* under the headline "Brer Rabbit and the Collard Patch" adopts this conceit. The defendant, Hunter Bailey, accused of stealing collard greens from his neighbor's yard, is described throughout the report as "Brer Rabbit" and is represented as a rabbit in the accompanying cartoon. "The officer," the judge begins, "says you played Brer Rabbit last night." The judge asks, "Where do you work, Hunter?" Bailey replies, "At furs one place an den annudder." The judge asks, "And what are your wages?" Bailey replies, "Fuss one t'ing an' den annudder." The judge decides that this "labor is too uncertain," and sends the rabbit to the chain gang.[27]

As this newspaper sketch demonstrates, local residents understood that stories like the tar baby were connected to the battles over land, property, fencing, enclosure, poaching, and pilfering that were ongoing in Georgia in the late nineteenth century. At the same time as landowners were casting the enclosure campaign as a battle between lazy rabbits and the industrious wolves, ex-slaves and their descendants were turning to stories like the tar baby as a way to understand the attack on their traditional rights to hunt, fish, forage, and graze on unenclosed lands. Take the following verse, transcribed by Howard Odum somewhere on the Georgia coast in the opening decade of the twentieth century and printed for the first time in his collection *Negro Workaday Songs* (1926):

> De rabbit in de briar patch,
> De squirrel in de tree,
> Would love to go huntin',
> But I ain't free,
> But I ain't free,
> But I ain't free,
> Would love to go huntin',
> But I ain't free, ain't free.

Among the key aspects of this verse are its conflation of emancipation (or "freedom") with access to the land. The rabbit and the squirrel refer at once to the singer's quarry, the animals he would love to hunt, and also to the seemingly unalienated relationship to the natural world that the singer forfeits when he loses his freedom. The freedom that the singer desires is like the freedom the rabbit finds in the briar patch following his escape from the tar baby. The song is thereby even more specific about the connection between the briar patch and the unenclosed commons than the version of the tar baby story recorded in Liberty County.

In this verse, the briar patch is both tenor and vehicle: it stands figuratively for the singer's freedom but it also stands literally for the pastures, swamps, and forests where people like the singer were once free to hunt, even when, paradoxically, they were enslaved.[28]

Although Odum does not specify the circumstances under which this verse was collected, further indication of its meaning comes from its classification in his book as a convict song. One likely setting for the genesis of this verse would have been the prison labor camps instituted when Georgia began leasing convicts in 1868. Many of these camps were located in the pine barrens proximate to Liberty County that lined the second and third levels of the state's coastal plain. Prior to the 1870s, the area remained wild, standing as a buffer between the state's oceanside settlements and the growing towns and cities around its interior. With sandy soil and abundant wiregrass, the area had a reputation for being hard to improve, but it remained a great place to explore and camp, to gather wood and other resources, and most importantly, to hunt. This started to change following the passage of the new enclosure laws in the 1870s. At the same time as people like the singer were being arrested for hunting on land they had previously accessed by customary right, the state was transforming the pine barrens into an open-air prison where criminals were committed to hard labor. This transitional scene could well be the setting for the verse given by Odum. The singer, in other words, could be literally unfree, literally in chains, while literally looking out on the landscape where he used to hunt, reflecting on its transformation.[29]

This scenario appears even more plausible when we consider that the work required of prisoners in the camps in range of Liberty County included processing the raw gum from pine trees to manufacture materials for the naval stores industry, including turpentine, rosin, and—most importantly for the purposes of our interpretation—tar and pitch. In the 1870s, Georgia became a center for the naval stores industry following the exhaustion of the pine forests in the Carolinas. By 1890, it was the leading producer of naval stores in the United States, an achievement attributed to the work rate made possible by convict leasing. In the verse collected by Odum, there is no explicit reference to tar production, but the allusion to the rabbit in the briar patch is enough to establish an opposition between the singer's remembered orientation to the landscape (which he associates with hunting and personal autonomy) and his present orientation where his confinement ("I ain't free") is associated by implication with the abased blackness of the commodity he is producing for global export.[30]

In "Buh Rabbit, Buh Wolf, and de Tar Baby," the rabbit experiences the tar baby first and foremost as an existential threat, but the story is careful to make this threat comprehensible in relation to facts on the ground in Liberty County. Tar links the story not only to postbellum prison camps but also to antebellum plantations where tar was produced in winter months before spring planting. Tar was also a standard tool in the police repertoire of the plantations in Liberty County and elsewhere. Frederick Douglass famously recalls that tar was placed on fences around fruit and vegetable gardens to prevent slaves from following the rabbit's example and stealing their subsistence. On his plantation, Douglass explains that any slave caught with tar on his or her body was assumed to have been in the garden and was whipped accordingly. "The slaves," he concludes, "became as fearful of tar as of the lash. They seemed to realize the impossibility of touching tar without being defiled." Whether tar was understood as a product of prison labor, or remembered, in Douglass's sense, as police surveillance, or else known or intuited, in Blackstone's sense, as the stigma that results from the crime against nature, tar functions in the story as a cue that invites us to see everyday conflicts in the broadest possible terms.[31]

We will never be sure about the circumstances under which "Buh Rabbit, Buh Wolf, and de Tar Baby" was composed, nor will we know exactly how and when "I Ain't Free" entered the common stock of songs in Liberty County. There is, however, something that we can say for sure about this particular story and this particular song, which is that they would have been resources for people residing in Liberty County who were trying to steady themselves in unpredictable times. In both cases, we can see how the local struggle over pastures and pine barrens is recast in universal terms, as actions otherwise treated as simple larceny are staged in the story as contested rights whose meaning remains unresolved. Too often treated in vague terms, the story's theory of politics is based on the persistence of expectations that are banished in its backstory only to return during the encounter with the tar baby in a blurred and barely recognizable form. During the encounter, the rabbit struggles to find an orientation, and during the escape to the briar patch, this struggle is resolved as the rabbit becomes anchored again in customs that are otherwise represented only obliquely in the plot.

The story, in short, explains local conflicts by placing them in world history. This is the key to the story's political thinking and one of the contributing factors to its global popularity. From this perspective, the conflict that begins with the wolf's claim on the land, a conflict that the wolf sees only in hindsight as the prehistory to current events, never finished. Expropriation begins to look less like a foregone conclusion and more like an ongoing struggle—a struggle that is already happening before the start of the story, a struggle that is still happening when the cycle starts over at the story's end.

In contrast to the philosophical approaches that represent expropriation as a one-time event that divides everyone all at once into masters and slaves, settlers and natives, employers and landless workers, the tar baby sees expropriation as an ongoing process that does not end with the onset of capitalism. On the contrary, enclosure was a process that was still happening in Liberty County in the 1870s, when people were telling "Buh Rabbit, Buh Wolf, and de Tar Baby" and singing "I Ain't Free," and that is still happening everywhere in the world where things held in common are turned into property. We may not be able to say for sure how the story came to be in the places where it was told, but we know that it surfaces repeatedly in places where there is uncertainty about the proprietary claims made by settlers and slaveholders. Ending in a different place than it begins, the tar baby transcends the social problems that structure its plot by out-and-out refusing the terms in which these problems are initially posed, a refusal celebrated at last when the rabbit claims the briar patch as his home.[32]

EPILOGUE

As the most celebrated, the most thickly documented, and the most historiographically significant case in the global trickster tradition, the tar baby story provides something like a natural center for this book, an anchoring point around which associated ideas and examples can be set into a constellation that would not otherwise be available to analysis. The established ethnographic approach to the tar baby has led us to misconstrue the ways in which the story seeks to resolve the problems it sets before us. Restored to its full range, the tar baby presents nothing less than a comprehensive philosophy of world history.

My interpretation of the opening sequence emphasizes the formulaic representation of the trickster's crime against nature, which is sometimes depicted as illegitimate appropriation and other times as a defection from communal norms. In the next stage in the story, the thief is tricked into imagining that he has been insulted by an object that clearly has no capacity to address him. Even as the thief's mistake is dramatized in terms that invite our condescension, drawing associations from the colonial discourse on fetishism, the encounter with the tar baby asks to be taken seriously as the repetition of the conflict in the opening scene, restaged in this instance from the trickster's point of view. My discussion of the final episode focuses on versions that feature an escape to a briar patch or some other unenclosed terrain, such as a wilderness or desert. This conclusion builds on the fantasy staged in the encounter with the tar baby, insisting on the persistence of the commons as a resource for the trickster in his warfare with his enemies.

The tar baby story shares both substantive concerns and narrative conventions with formative passages in natural law where labor is mixed with nature or an incorrigible rascal commits an unforgivable crime. If philosophers and policymakers like Vitoria and Locke returns to these original scenes in an attempt to explain the developing global systems of slavery and colonialism, the tar baby returns this situation with a similar purpose in mind. When the tar baby is read this way, one of the things that becomes apparent is the story's capacious flexibility. The story seeks to portray expropriation simultaneously in all of its senses, with its characters standing at one and the same time for slaves and masters, natives and settlers, lazy workers and hardworking capitalists. If Locke provides a history of the world that assumes there is a basic distinction between freedom and slavery, metropole and colony, the tar baby does not respect these boundaries, preferring to speak all at once to peasants, slaves, convicts, vagrants, debt peons, unwaged household laborers, indentured servants, and dispossessed commoners as well as agricultural, industrial, and service workers bound by contract.[1]

At the end of the story, the freedom the rabbit finds in the briar patch does not represent individual emancipation. Rather, it represents a return to a self-organized community seeking to preserve its autonomy. It is impossible to understand the story without reckoning with the collective capacity for self-organization instantiated in commons institutions in locations like the South Carolina Sea Islands and the Visayan region of the Philippines. If the tar baby's opening scene is designed to assert the theoretical impossibility of these institutions, the story is shaped at every stage by its gradual acknowledgment of their continuing presence in the world. This acknowledgment manifests as a tension between the story (which denies the commons) and its contexts (in which the commons remains fundamental to everyday life) before it is internalized in the story as the formal incompatibility between its opening and closing scenes. If the story begins by pledging allegiance to principles of property and sovereignty, it ends by nullifying them.

The story of the tar baby addresses these conceptual problems in its three-part narrative structure, but it also addresses them through its representation of characters, objects, and environments—most notably its treatment of speaking animals. The tar baby is a fable that features animals as speaking characters, but it does not stop there. The story treats the speaking animal as a problem, representing its protagonist, in particular, not as a character whose agency and speaking capacity should be taken for granted but as an indeterminate entity. In the story, the rabbit is not merely an animal, nor is he merely a weaker animal who fights with other stronger animals. The rabbit's character is instead formed by something seemingly unremarkable yet distinctive to the world of the story—the fact that he is an animal who speaks.

As we have seen, the narrative problems in the tar baby are easiest to grasp when they are understood in relation to cognates in other intellectual traditions. The same is true for the story's representation of speaking animals. Speaking animals are a problem in the story, and they are also a longstanding problem in political philosophy. "Wherever the relevance of speech is at stake," Hannah Arendt proposes, "matters become political by definition, for speech is what makes man a political being." In *The Human Condition* (1958), Arendt addresses the prerequisites to political participation by returning to Aristotle's argument that speech is a uniquely human capacity. When she cites speech as a baseline for politics, Arendt is arguing for an expansion of the political domain, or more precisely for the politicization of the problem of political standing, or the "right to have rights." Her call for inclusion, however, is also notable for what it excludes. *The Human Condition* stands as the abbreviation, or maybe the apotheosis, of a tradition in philosophy that refuses recognition not only to nonhuman animals but also implicitly to some categories of humanity traditionally associated with the nonhuman on the grounds that their members lack the capacity for rational expression.[2]

Arendt follows a line of thought that predominated in many parts of the world before the rise of the empirical sciences, a tradition with a longstanding commitment to the idea that animals cannot speak. Speech, it was assumed in this tradition, was unique to humans. There were many theories about why this was the case—concerning the shape of the lips, tongue, and larynx—but the most common explanation was geared not to anatomy but to ontology. Following from Aristotle, speech was seen as a baseline that differentiated humans and animals. It was believed that animals had voices that conveyed pleasure or pain, but they lacked reason, and it was reason that distinguished the noises made by animals from human speech. Moreover, it was speech that enabled humans to distinguish right from wrong, and it was this capacity to make moral distinctions, in turn, that enabled humans to organize themselves politically. Speaking, in this tradition, meant having a capacity for politics. The corollary was also true. People not recognized by the state as citizens, whether women, or barbarians, or slaves, were like animals in that they were presumed to lack the inner reasoning capacity that was required to make their expression count as speech. According to this tradition, there was no such thing as a speaking bird, a speaking bullfrog, a speaking poodle, or a speaking rabbit. Animals imitated the inflections of human speech, and they displayed affection or apprehension in the pitch and timbre of their voices, but anyone who confused these speech-like sounds with articulate language was exhibiting more than a mere lapse in empirical judgment. This was a category mistake that called the speaker's own rationality into question. It was a failure of comprehension that told you everything you needed to know about the mentality of the savages who lived outside the walls of the city.[3]

By the nineteenth century, the proscription against naive faith in speaking animals was adopted in the new interpretive social science of anthropology as a universal standard by which the development of any culture or civilization could be measured in terms of its distance from this primordial fetishism. Every civilization in the world, it was presumed, passed through a primitive stage in which the mind was not yet able to distinguish fully between humans and the nonhuman world, a claim that scholars like E. B. Tylor sought to substantiate by documenting the perceived correspondences between primitive cultures that existed in earlier periods in history and the primitive cultures that were thought to exist on the edges of the colonial world system. Among populations that ascribed "to the lower animals a power of speech," Tylor explains, "beast-stories" were "one of the great staples" of communication, serving not only as entertainment but as a medium for constructing cosmology, managing conflict, and reproducing values. From what Tylor calls the "ordinary civilized point of view," these stories could be appreciated from an ironic distance as works of literature, as scientific specimens, or as apologues suitable for the amusement and edification of children, but in the primitive cultures that were their "first home," they remained socially functional as one of the primary sources of knowledge about the world.[4]

These assumptions about primitive mentality and animal communication were important to early collectors of the tar baby story. Among other things, this is a matter of genre. The story follows patterns present in the ancient fables attributed to Aesop, fables that, like the tar baby, were supposed to provide a bottom-up account of society by adopting an imaginary perspective attributed to symbolic animals and everyday objects. As is the case with the tar baby, collections like the *Aesop Romance* framed the fable as a mode of popular culture associated with the lower orders of society, a point that was emphasized in the extradiegetic narrative in which Aesop is identified as a slave who engages in an ongoing battle of wits with a philosopher who refuses to grant his freedom. Gradually, it became important to the interpretation of these fables that Aesop was not only a slave but an African slave whose predilection for fetishism was associated with his race.[5]

If this ethnographic classification links the tar baby to the genre history of the fable, it also licenses the condescension that collectors frequently expressed in their framing comments. "The negroes," Christensen observes, "even in common conversation, speak of animals as if they thought, talked, and behaved among themselves like rational beings." Although it is left unstated by Christensen, the double implication is supposed to be obvious. Animals cannot speak, and anyone who speaks about animals as if they can speak has committed a mistake so laughable as to call into question their own rationality. Belonging to a tradition in which turtles smoked cigars and spiders went to stores to buy gunpowder, the tar baby story took place in an enchanted setting conjured into existence by primitive storytellers whose signal mistake was the attribution of speech to rabbits, spiders, turtles, bears, possums, birds, foxes, and wolves.[6]

As we have seen, this interpretation took a significant turn in the twentieth century as anthropologists, folklorists, and historians developed a new theory of politics based on evidence they found in oral traditions featuring speaking animals as their trickster protagonists. In their view, these traditions were not the fanciful expression of people without politics. Rather, they were precisely a political tradition. Speaking animal stories were understood, in other words, to exemplify a distinctive style of politics practiced by people previously considered nonpolitical. No longer dismissed as a category error, anthropomorphism was seen as the symbolic idiom of subaltern politics.

If this approach has proven attentive to the political significance of the tar baby's circulation, it has failed to consider that the problem of subaltern consciousness is represented not only outside but also inside the story, before the fact as it were, through the story's self-conscious address to the philosophical problem of the speaking animal. The problem of the politics practiced by the people who have no politics, in other words, is figured in the speaking animal, a character who should not speak but does. Indispensable here is the tradition's recursive imagination, or its ability to take the story that is told about the people without politics and enfold it into a character so that other stories can be told about it. The tar baby, in other words, needs to be conceived as a story that is told about the story that is told about the people without politics. This is not something we can gauge when we see the story as an allegory featuring a weaker animal who fights with stronger animals. When interpretation focuses instead on the speaking animal, a figure that aggressively calls into doubt everything that the allegorical interpretation takes for granted, it becomes possible to ask again what it means to adopt the rabbit, and therefore the speaking animal, as a figure for subjectivity under duress.[7]

All stories about speaking animals suspend the distinction between animals and humans, but the tar baby goes further by staging an encounter between a speaking animal and an inanimate object whose speechlessness drives the animal to distraction. Something more than another story with speaking animals, the tar baby is a story *about* the speaking animal, a story organized around the problem the speaking animal poses for political philosophy broadly conceived. In this case, the rabbit encounters an object that embodies his predicament, an object that nominalizes the story told about why animals cannot speak. By turning this story into an object and staging a meeting between the object and a character whose existence is encapsulated by the object, the story provides a second-order examination of the problem of political subjectivity dramatized as a comedy of misrecognition. "Why don't you speak to me?" the rabbit asks the tar baby in Mexico. "Why," the rabbit repeats in South Carolina, "don't you speak to me?" "Are you," the rabbit demands in Mississippi, in utter disbelief, "not going to speak?"[8]

It matters that the gradually compounded irony in this situation is conveyed not only in the collector's commentary, which asks us to condescend to primitive storytellers for their failure to distinguish between humans and animals, but also inside the story, which encourages us to condescend to the rabbit based on his failure to tell the difference between an inanimate object and a creature with the capacity to respond to his greetings. Inside the story, the irony turns out to be more volatile than it first appears, as the story manages to destabilize its own drama by making it impossible to laugh at the rabbit's ignorance without implicating ourselves in the same mistake the rabbit is supposed to have made. There is something strange, in other words, about being asked to condescend to the rabbit because the rabbit thinks the tar baby can speak, when at the same time we are asked to believe the rabbit can speak. There is a difference between the rabbit's fetishism and our own willing suspension of disbelief, but the similarity is pronounced enough to unsettle our easy condescension to the rabbit. Indeed, from this vantage, the rabbit's confusion about the relations between subjects and objects seems not primitive but typically modern, or potentially even prophetic, as if it were anticipating the disorientation of the senses that occurs as the world is reorganized around the fox's claim.[9]

The tar baby approaches the embodiment of its characters with a self-consciousness that matches its skepticism about the other common terms that structure its plot. Several steps removed from the humanism that distinguishes its cognates in political philosophy, the tar baby endows itself and its characters with attributes—the capacity to speak, the capacity to recognize one's own image, the capacity to think recursively—that were once thought absent from the animal kingdom. During the encounter with the tar baby, the problem of the speaking animal's self-division is represented in light of the crime against nature the rabbit commits in the preceding scene. According to reasoning implied in this scene but stated in its cognates, criminals lower themselves to the condition of animals. For Locke, criminals are like "those savage wild beasts . . . with whom mankind can have neither society nor security." It is right, Locke adds, to destroy people who commit crimes against nature for the "same reason" that it is right to kill "a lion or a tiger," or any other "noxious creature," whose destructive instincts are immune to regulation. Whether Locke means that criminals are literally animals or whether he means that it is right to treat them as if they were animals based on their crimes, his argument is that criminals and animals have something in common, and what they have in common is their disqualification from civil society. This is a belief that Locke shared with other humanist philosophers, including Thomas Hobbes, Hugo Grotius, and Alberico Gentili. Criminals demonstrate through their actions that they are unable to express themselves in the rational manner required to contribute to a deliberation or establish an agreement, and it is for this reason, before all others, that they are to be "reckoned in the number of the beasts."[10]

Through this opening scene and its development in the encounter with the tar baby, the story finds a way to fuse the positions occupied by the slave, the native, and the peasant by figuring their common exile from humanity through the character of the speaking animal. If Locke pictures a crime that causes humans to lose the right to be considered as human, the tar baby uses this same crime for another purpose, which is to ask how the rabbit—an animal who is only ever represented as an animal—came to be who he is. Several versions of the story explicitly represent this transformation. In a Temne story, for example, we are told that the thief was once "round lek pusson" (round like a person) before he is flattened out and formed into the shape of a spider during the beating he receives while stuck to the tar baby. In another story referenced by John Arnott Mac-Culloch, the thief begins the story as a human, but he is chased over a cliff and is flattened on impact into a dugong, a marine mammal indigenous to Indo-Pacific waters. As in the scene imagined by Locke, these stories punish the criminal by turning him into a beast. This topos is relevant not only to the versions in which the thief's transformation is represented as an incident.

It speaks to the story as a whole, or to be exact, it speaks immediately, and in the most general terms, to its ontology. If we want to know how the rabbit became a rabbit, we need look no further than his crime.

It is also important to the meaning of the story that the struggle that begins with the rabbit's crime against nature does not end in transcendence: the rabbit does not sacrifice his animal embodiment in order to emerge as a full-fledged speaking character. Consciousness does not begin when the object turns subject or when the rabbit transcends his self-division by killing or winning recognition from the tar baby. Instead, it arrives with the rabbit's reconnection to an existing community embedded in the world. Politics appears not as individual agency but as a capacity for collective self-organization in connection with the given circumstances of natural existence. If the story begins with the wolf proving his capacity to regulate his desires, exercising the restraint needed for economic rationality and political obligation, these standards are suspended when we look backward from the story's conclusion, seeing things for the first time from the rabbit's consolidated viewpoint—a viewpoint previously blocked in the story due to its association with laziness, superstition, and crime.

As we reflect on the tar baby's anthropomorphism, it is certainly tempting to hope for something more in the story, perhaps a thoroughgoing antihumanism that would release us from the commitment to a political framework for interpretation. We need to reckon, for example, with Donna Haraway's complaint about the tendency to transform rabbits and wolves into "surrogates" for human themes. However we see the conflict in the story, we need to admit that its characters are more than vehicles for metaphor. We might even find virtue where others have found fault, embracing the tar baby's seeming enchantment as an antidote to the alienation—the division of subject and object—that comes with modernization. The story could even belong to a cosmomorphic world in which subject and object remain undivided, a world in which "being" is experienced, as Maurice Leenhardt proposes, in its "plenitude."[11]

For reasons I have tried to demonstrate throughout this book, I think it would be a mistake to characterize the tar baby as a cultural antidote or alternative to modernity. The story is not the product of a tradition isolated from the rest of the world. It has circulated from place to place, from continent to continent, not despite but literally through circuits formed by global trade networks. Not only was the story most often collected in places conditioned by the slave trade and settler colonialism, it is literally *about* these places, or more exactly about the experience of living in these places in the wake of expropriation. It matters, moreover, that the terms the story uses to frame this disorienting and often fragmented experience—person and property, crime and captivity, science and superstition—are universal and not aboriginal terms. The tar baby uses these terms not in order to transcend them but instead to assert its existence within them. Its double consciousness arrives gradually, possibly in the only way that it can, as the trickster's perspective merges with the story's own.[12]

FIG. 6.1. Edward Gorey, "[The Fox Sneaks Away]." Color pen and ink. From Ennis Rees, *Brer Rabbit and His Tricks, with Drawings by Edward Gorey* (New York: Young Scott Books, 1967). By permission of the Edward Gorey Estate.

TWELVE EXAMPLES

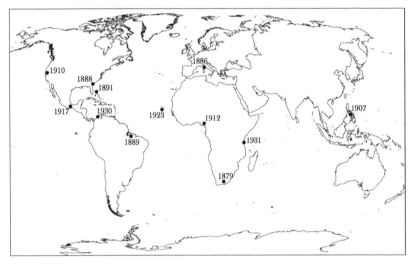

FIG. 7.1. Robert Lee, "Twelve Examples of the Tar Baby Story." Produced for this volume.

SOUTH AFRICA

1879

"The Story of the Dam" was published in July 1879 in *The Folk-Lore Journal*, a publication based in Cape Town, South Africa, whose purpose was to preserve superstitions, legends, and ballads discovered in the colonies. This version was common among the Khoikhoi, an ethnic group in southwestern Africa whom Dutch colonizers called "Hottentots." The story was submitted by Thomas Bain, a colonial road engineer and mineralogist, who remembered it from his youth. The story begins with a drought and shows the animals, led by the lion, working together to build a dam. The free rider, in this case, is the jackal, who is able to outwit several guards until he is caught by the proverbial tar baby, in this case, a tortoise with bijenwerk, a sticky black substance taken from beehives, smeared on his back.

The Story of the Dam

There was a great drought in the land; and Lion called together a number of animals so that they might devise a plan for retaining water when the rains fell.

The animals which attended at Lion's summons were Baboon, Leopard, Hyena, Jackal, Hare, and Mountain Tortoise.

It was agreed that they should scratch a large hole in some suitable place to hold water; and the next day they all began to work, with the exception of Jackal, who continually hovered about in that locality, and was overheard to mutter that he was not going to scratch his nails off in making water-holes.

When the dam was finished the rains fell, and it was soon filled with water, to the great delight of those who had worked so hard at it. The first one, however, to come and drink there, was Jackal, who not only drank, but filled his clay pot with water, and then proceeded to swim in the rest of the water, making it as muddy and dirty as he could.

This was brought to the knowledge of Lion, who was very angry and ordered Baboon to guard the water the next day, armed with a huge knobkirrie. Baboon was concealed in a bush close to the water; but Jackal soon became aware of his presence there, and guessed its cause. Knowing the fondness of baboons for honey, Jackal at once hit upon a plan, and marching to and fro, every now and then dipped his fingers into his clay pot, and licked them with an expression of intense relish, saying, in a low voice to himself, "I don't want any of their dirty water when I have a pot full of delicious honey." This was too much for poor

Baboon, whose mouth began to water. He soon began to beg Jackal to give him a little honey, as he had been watching for several hours, and was very hungry and tired.

After taking no notice of Baboon at first, Jackal looked round, and said, in a patronizing manner, that he pitied such an unfortunate creature, and would give him some honey on certain conditions, viz., that Baboon should give up his knobkirrie and allow himself to be bound by Jackal. He foolishly agreed, and was soon tied in such a manner that he could not move hand or foot.

Jackal now proceeded to drink of the water, to fill his pot, and to swim in the sight of Baboon, from time to time telling him what a foolish fellow he had been to be so easily duped, and that he (Jackal) had no honey or anything else to give him, excepting a good blow on the head every now and then with his own knobkirrie.

The animals soon appeared and found poor Baboon in this sorry plight, looking the picture of misery. Lion was so exasperated that he caused Baboon to be severely punished, and to be denounced as a fool.

Tortoise hereupon stepped forward, and offered his services for the capture of Jackal. It was at first thought that he was merely joking; but when he explained in what manner he proposed to catch him, his plan was considered so feasible that his offer was accepted. He proposed that a thick coating of "bijenwerk" (a kind of sticky black substance found on beehives) should be spread all over him, and that he should then go and stand at the entrance of the dam, on the water level, so that Jackal might tread upon him and stick fast. This was accordingly done and Tortoise posted there.

The next day, when Jackal came, he approached the water very cautiously, and wondered to find no one there. He then ventured to the entrance of the water, and remarked how kind they had been in placing there a large black stepping-stone for him. As soon, however, as he trod upon the supposed stone, he stuck fast, and saw that he had been tricked; for Tortoise now put his head out and began to move. Jackal's hind feet being still free he threatened to smash Tortoise with them if he did not let him go. Tortoise merely answered, "Do as you like." Jackal thereupon made a violent jump, and found, with horror, that his hind feet were now also fast. "Tortoise," said he, "I have still my mouth and teeth left, and will eat you alive if you do not let me go." "Do as you like," Tortoise again replied. Jackal, in his endeavors to free himself, at last made a desperate bite at Tortoise, and found himself fixed, both head and feet. Tortoise, feeling proud of his successful capture, now marched quietly up to the top of the bank with Jackal on his back, so that he could easily be seen by the animals as they came to the water.

They were indeed astonished to find how cleverly the crafty Jackal had been caught; and Tortoise was much praised, while the unhappy Baboon was again reminded of his misconduct when set to guard the water.

Jackal was at once condemned to death by Lion; and Hyena was to execute the sentence. Jackal pleaded hard for mercy, but finding this useless, he made a last request to Lion (always, as he said, so fair and just in his dealings) that he should not have to suffer a lingering death.

Lion inquired of him in what manner he wished to die; and he asked that his tail might be shaved and rubbed with a little fat, and that Hyena might then swing him round twice and dash his brains out upon a stone. This, being considered sufficiently fair by Lion, was ordered by him to be carried out in his presence.

When Jackal's tail had been shaved and greased, Hyena caught hold of him with great force, and before he had fairly lifted him from the ground, the cunning Jackal had slipped away from Hyena's grasp, and was running for his life, pursued by all the animals.

Lion was the foremost pursuer, and after a great chase Jackal got under an overhanging precipice, and, standing on his hind legs with his shoulders pressed against the rock, called loudly to Lion to help him, as the rock was falling, and would crush them both. Lion put his shoulders to the rock, and exerted himself to the utmost. After some little time Jackal proposed that he should creep slowly out, and fetch a large pole to prop up the rock, so that Lion could get out and save his life. Jackal did creep out, and left Lion there to starve and die.

CORSICA

1886

"Compère Bouc et Compère Lapin" is a composite of stories learned in Corsica by Jean-Baptiste Frédéric Ortoli, the preeminent scholar of Corsican literature and folklore in the nineteenth century. It was published in *Les Contes de la Veillée*, a collection of traditional stories adapted for young readers. It was subsequently translated into English by Joel Chandler Harris and published as "A French Tar-Baby." In the story, the goat proposes digging a well, and the rabbit responds that he gets all the water he needs from the cups of the flowers supplemented by the milk and cream he gets from the cows. The story is noteworthy for its explicit designation of the tar-doll as "little negro" and "little Congo." It concludes with the conventional escape to the briar patch, in this case called "the brambles." The English translation follows the French version.

Compère Bouc et Compère Lapin

Au temps des lutins et des fées, compère Bouc et compère Lapin habitaient dans la même plaine, non loin l'un de l'autre.

Fier de sa longue barbe et de ses cornes aiguës, compère Bouc se montrait fort dédaigneux pour compère Lapin; à peine le saluait-il quand il le rencontrait, et son plus grand plaisir était de lui jouer les tours les plus pendables.

—Compère Lapin, voici maître Renard! Et compère Lapin de fuir aussitôt.

—Compère Lapin, voici maître le Loup!

Et compère Lapin de trembler de tous ses membres.

—Compère Lapin, voici maître le Tigre!

Et compère Lapin de frémir et de croire venue sa dernière heure.

Fatigué de cette triste existence, messire Lapin réfléchit au moyen de changer en ami son terrible et puissant voisin.

Il trouva des raisons infaillibles et compère Bouc fut invité à dîner.

Le repas fut long et abondant; rien n'y manquait, les meilleurs plats furent servis. Compère Bouc s'en léchait la barbe de satisfaction; jamais il ne s'était trouvé à pareille fête.

—Eh bien! mon ami, s'écria au dessert, compère Lapin, es-tu content de ton souper?

—On ne peut davantage, mon cher hôte, toutefois mon gosier est bien sec et un peu d'eau ne ferait pas de mal.

—Ma foi, compère Bouc, je n'ai point de cave, aussi je ne bois jamais pendant les repas.

—Une idée, compère Lapin, moi non plus je n'ai pas d'eau; si tu veux venir par là, auprès du peuplier, nous allons creuser un puits.

Compère Lapin espéra se venger:

—Non, compère Bouc; à l'aube naissante je bois la rosée dans le calice des fleurs, et pendant la chaleur du jour, quand j'ai soif, je bois dans la piste des vaches.

—C'est bien; tout seul je le ferai et tout seul je profiterai de mon puits.

—Bon courage, compère Bouc!

—Merci, mon bon ami petit Lapin!

Compère Bouc s'en alla au pied de l'arbre et fouilla son puits; le voilà qui avance, qui se creuse, qui devient de plus en plus profond. Le puits est fait, l'eau jailli!, et compère Bouc se désaltère largement.

Compère Lapin qui l'avait suivi se mit alors à rire derrière un buisson tout en fleurs.

—Ah! mon pauvre ami, comme tu es innocent! ne put-il s'empêcher de dire.

Le lendemain, lorsque Bouc à la grande barbe et aux cornes pointues retourna chercher de l'eau à son puits, il aperçut la trace des pas de petit Lapin encore marquée dans la terre fraîche. Compère Bouc réfléchit profondément, se gratta la tête, tira sa barbe, se frappa le front, puis enfin s'écria:

—Mon bon ami, je vais t'attraper!

Et aussitôt il court prendre ses outils et fait une grosse poupée en bois de laurier; ensuite il la goudronne de-ci, delà, à droite, à gauche, en haut, en bas, jusqu'à ce qu'elle soit noire comme une petite négresse, une négresse de Guinée.

Cela fait, compère Bouc attendit tranquillement la fin de la journée; le soleil couché, il courut, se cachant derrière les arbres et les buissons, planter sa poupée au ras du puits.

La lune venait de se lever; au ciel brillaient des millions de petits flambeaux; compère Lapin crut l'instant arrivé. Il prend son baquet et va chercher de l'eau.

En route il a peur d'être surpris, il frémit au plus petit bruissement de feuilles, au plus léger souffle du vent. Il marche par sauts, se cachant ici derrière un monticule, se couvrant par là d'une touffe d'herbe.

Enfin, il arrive au puits. Compère Lapin aperçoit la petite négresse; il s'arrête effrayé, avance, recule, avance et s'arrête encore.

—Qu'est-ce là? se dit-il. Il écoute; les herbes ne parlaient pas, les feuilles et les branches restaient muettes. Il cligne des yeux, baisse la tête:

—Hé! l'amie, qui donc es-tu?

Petite Négresse ne bouge pas.

Compère Lapin avance un peu plus, puis crie encore. Petite Poupée ne répond pas.

Il respire, souffle plus à l'aise, puis s'approche du bord du puits.

Mais, quand il regarde dans l'eau, Petite Négresse regarde aussi.

Compère Lapin devient rouge de colère.

—Ecoute, petite, si tu regardes dans ce puits, je vais te flanquer sur le nez.

Il se baisse au ras du puits et voit la poupée qui lui sourit.

Il lève sa main droite et la lui envoie. Pan! Ah! sa main reste collée.

—Qu'est cela? lâche-moi, fille de démon, ou je vais te flanquer sur les yeux avec l'autre main. Il la lui flanque.

Bin!

Hé! la gauche se colle aussi.

Compère Lapin lève son pied droit.

—Petite Congo, fais attention et mûris bien mes paroles. Vois-tu ce pied-là? Ce pied, je te l'envoie dans l'estomac si tu ne me lâches à l'instant. Aussitôt dit que fait.

Boum!

Le pied se colle; compère Lapin lève l'autre.

—Tu vois, celui-ci? Si je te l'envoie, tu croiras que c'est la pierre de tonnerre qui te cogne.

Il la frappe.

Tarn!

Le pied se colle encore.

Compère Lapin tenait bien sa Guinée.

—Hé! la petite! j'ai déjà battu bien du monde avec mon front. Attention ou je brise ton affreuse tête en petits morceaux. Lâche-moi!

—Ha! ha! tu ne réponds pas?

Vlan!

—Négresse, es-tu morte? Ouais, que ma tête colle bien! Quand le soleil fut levé, compère Bouc se rendit au bord du puits pour prendre des nouvelles de son ami petit Lapin: le résultat avait dépassé ses espérances.

—Hé! hé! petit coquin, grand coquin, couquinasse. Hé! hé! compère Lapin, que fais-tu donc là? Je pensais que tu buvais la rosée dans le calice embaumé des fleurs ou dans la piste des vaches. Hé! hé! compère Lapin, je vais te punir pour me voler mon eau.

—Je suis ton ami, ne me tue pas.

—Voleur! voleur! crie compère Bouc. Et vite il court dans le bois, ramasse un gros tas de branches sèches, allume un grand feu, puis va chercher petit Lapin pour le brûler tout vivant.

Or, comme il passait près d'un tes de ronces avec compère Lapin sur son épaule, compère Bouc rencontra sa. fille Bélédie qui se promenait dans les champs.

—Où vas-tu, Bouc, mon papa, ainsi affublé d'un pareil fardeau? Viens manger l'herbe fraîche avec moi, et jette vilain compère Lapin dans ces ronces!

Petit voleur, tout penaud, dresse alors les oreilles et fait l'effrayé.

—Non, non, compère Bouc, ne me jette pas dans ces ronces; les piquants déchireraient ma peau, crèveraient mes yeux, me perceraient le cœur. Ah! je t'en prie, jette-moi plutôt dans le feu.

—Hé! hé! petit coquin, grand coquin, couquinasse, hé! hé! compère Lapin, tu n'aimes pas les ronces? Eh bien! alors, va rire là-dedans!

Et il l'y envoie sans pitié.

Compère Lapin roule en bas du tas d'épines, puis se met à rire:

—Kiak! kiak! kiak! compère Bouc, mon ami, que tu me sembles bête! kiak! kiak! kiak! Meilleur lit jamais je n'ai eu; kiak! kiak! C'est dans ces ronces que maman m'a fait naître!

Compère Bouc en fut désespéré mais compère Lapin eut la vie sauvée par sa présence d'esprit:

Longue barbe n'est pas toujours signe d'intelligence.

A French Tar-Baby

In the time when there were hobgoblins and fairies, Brother Goat and Brother Rabbit lived in the same neighborhood, not far from each other. Proud of his long beard and sharp horns, Brother Goat looked on Brother Rabbit with disdain. He would hardly speak to Brother Rabbit when he met him, and his greatest pleasure was to make his little neighbor the victim of his tricks and practical jokes.

For instance, he would say: "Brother Rabbit, here is Mr. Fox," and this would cause Brother Rabbit to run away as hard as he could. Again he would say: "Brother Rabbit, here is Mr. Wolf," and poor Brother Rabbit would shake and tremble with fear. Sometimes he would cry out: "Brother Rabbit, here is Mr. Tiger," and then Brother Rabbit would shudder and think that his last hour had come.

Tired of this miserable existence, Brother Rabbit tried to think of some means by which he could change his powerful and terrible neighbor into a friend. After a time he thought he had discovered a way to make Brother Goat his friend, and so he invited him to dinner.

Brother Goat was quick to accept the invitation. The dinner was a fine affair, and there was an abundance of good eating. A great many different dishes were served. Brother Goat licked his mouth and shook his long beard with satisfaction. He had never before been present at such a feast.

"Well, my friend," exclaimed Brother Rabbit, when the dessert was brought in, "how do you like your dinner?" "I could certainly wish for nothing better," replied Brother Goat, rubbing the tips of his horns against the back of his chair; "but my throat is very dry and a little water would hurt neither the dinner nor me."

"Gracious!" said Brother Rabbit, "I have neither wine-cellar nor water. I am not in the habit of drinking while I am eating."

"Neither have I any water, Brother Rabbit," said Brother Goat. "But I have an idea! If you will go with me over yonder by the big poplar, we will dig a well."

"No, Brother Goat," said Brother Rabbit, who hoped to revenge himself—"no, I do not care to dig a well. At daybreak I drink the dew from the cups of the flowers, and in the heat of the day I milk the cows and drink the cream."

"Well and good," said Brother Goat. "Alone I will dig the well, and alone I will drink out of it."

"Success to you, Brother Goat," said Brother Rabbit.

"Thank you kindly, Brother Rabbit."

Brother Goat then went to the foot of the big poplar and began to dig his well. He dug with his forefeet and with his horns, and the well got deeper and deeper. Soon the water began to bubble up and the well was finished, and then Brother Goat made haste to quench his thirst. He was in such a hurry that his beard got in the water, but he drank and drank until he had his fill.

Brother Rabbit, who had followed him at a little distance, hid himself behind a bush and laughed heartily. He said to himself: "What an innocent creature you are!"

The next day, when Brother Goat, with his big beard and sharp horns, returned to his well to get some water, he saw the tracks of Brother Rabbit in the soft earth. This put him to thinking. He sat down, pulled his beard, scratched his head, and tapped himself on the forehead.

"My friend," he exclaimed after a while, "I will catch you yet."

Then he ran and got his tools (for Brother Goat was something of a carpenter in those days) and made a large doll out of laurel wood. When the doll was finished, he spread tar on it here and there, on the right and on the left, and up and down. He smeared it all over with the sticky stuff, until it was as black as a Guinea negro.

This finished, Brother Goat waited quietly until evening. At sunset he placed the tarred doll near the well, and ran and hid himself behind the trees and bushes. The moon had just risen, and the heavens twinkled with millions of little star-torches.

Brother Rabbit, who was waiting in his house, believed that the time had come for him to get some water, so he took his bucket and went to Brother Goat's well. On the way he was very much afraid that something would catch him. He trembled when the wind shook the leaves of the trees. He would go a little distance and then stop and listen; he hid here behind a stone, and there behind a tuft of grass.

At last he arrived at the well, and there he saw the little negro. He stopped and looked at it with astonishment. Then he drew back a little way, advanced again, drew back, advanced a little, and stopped once more.

"What can that be?" he said to himself. He listened, with his long ears pointed forward, but the trees could not talk, and the bushes were dumb. He winked his eyes and lowered his head: "Hey, friend! Who are you?" he asked.

The tar-doll didn't move. Brother Rabbit went up a little closer, and asked again: "Who are you?"

The tar-doll said nothing. Brother Rabbit breathed more at ease. Then he went to the brink of the well, but when he looked in the water the tar-doll seemed to look in too. He could see her reflection in the water. This made Brother Rabbit so mad that he grew red in the face.

"See here!" he exclaimed, "If you look in this well I'll give you a rap on the nose!"

Brother Rabbit leaned over the brink of the well, and saw the tar- doll smiling at him in the water. He raised his right hand and hit her—bam! His hand stuck.

"What's this?" exclaimed Brother Rabbit. "Turn me loose, imp of Satan! If you do not, I will rap you on the eye with my other hand."

Then he hit her—bim! The left hand stuck also. Then Brother Rabbit raised his right foot, saying:

"Mark me well, little Congo! Do you see this foot? I will kick you in the stomach if you do not turn me loose this instant."

No sooner said than done. Brother Rabbit let fly his right foot—vip! The foot stuck, and he raised the other. "Do you see this foot?" he exclaimed. "If I hit you with it, you will think a thunderbolt has struck you." Then he kicked her with the left foot, and it also stuck like the other, and Brother Rabbit held fast his Guinea negro.

"Watch out, now!" he cried. "I've already butted a great many people with my head. If I butt you in your ugly face I'll knock it into a jelly. Turn me loose! Oho! You don't answer?" Bap!

"Guinea girl!" exclaimed Brother Rabbit, "Are you dead? Gracious goodness! How my head does stick!"

When the sun rose, Brother Goat went to his well to find out something about Brother Rabbit. The result was beyond his expectations.

"Hey, little rogue, big rogue!" exclaimed Brother Goat. "Hey, Brother Rabbit! What are you doing there? I thought you drank the dew from the cups of the flowers, or milk from the cows. Aha, Brother Rabbit! I will punish you for stealing my water."

"I am your friend," said Brother Rabbit; "don't kill me."

"Thief, thief!" cried Brother Goat, and then he ran quickly into the woods, gathered up a pile of dry limbs, and made a great fire. He took Brother Rabbit from the tar-doll, and prepared to burn him alive. As he was passing a thicket of brambles with Brother Rabbit on his shoulders, Brother Goat met his daughter Beledie, who was walking about in the fields.

"Where are you going, Papa, muffled up with such a burden? Come and eat the fresh grass with me, and throw wicked Brother Rabbit in the brambles."

Cunning Brother Rabbit raised his long ears and pretended to be very much frightened.

"Oh, no, Brother Goat!" he cried. "Don't throw me in the brambles. They will tear my flesh, put out my eyes, and pierce my heart. Oh, I pray you, rather throw me in the fire."

"Aha, little rogue, big rogue! Aha, Brother Rabbit!" exclaimed Brother Goat, exultingly, "You don't like the brambles? Well, then, go and laugh in them," and he threw Brother Rabbit in without a feeling of pity. Brother Rabbit fell in the brambles, leaped to his feet, and began to laugh.

"Ha-ha-ha! Brother Goat, what a simpleton you are!—ha-ha-ha! A better bed I never had! In these brambles I was born!"

Brother Goat was in despair, but he could not help himself. Brother Rabbit was safe.

A long beard is not always a sign of intelligence.

GEORGIA LOW COUNTRY

1888

"Buh Wulf, Buh Rabbit, an de Tar Baby" was transcribed by Charles Colcock Jones Jr. and published in his volume of Gullah folklore, *Negro Myths from the Georgia Coast*. The story was told on one of the Jones family plantations in Liberty County, Georgia. Evidence suggests the most likely source for this story is Jack Jones, a house servant known for his storytelling prowess. The occasion in this case is a drought, and the ownership is predicated on individual labor. The story also contains a classic instance of the rabbit's claim that he can get all the water he needs from the dew on the grass. The briar patch is described in this version as "de place me mammy fotch me up."

Buh Wulf, Buh Rabbit, an de Tar Baby

Buh Wolf and Buh Rabbit, dem bin lib nabur. De dry drout come. Ebry ting stew up. Water scace. Buh Wolf dig one spring fuh him fuh git water. Buh Rabbit, him too lazy an too scheemy fuh wuk fuh isself. Eh pen pon lib off tarruh people. Ebry day, wen Buh Wolf yent duh watch um, eh slip to Buh Wolf spring, an eh full him calabash long water an cah um to eh house fuh cook long and fuh drink. Buh Wolf see Buh Rabbit track, but eh couldnt ketch um duh tief de water.

One day eh meet Buh Rabbit in de big road, an eh ax um how eh mek out fur water. Buh Rabbit say him no casion fuh hunt water: him lib off de jew on de grass. Buh Wolf quire: "Enty you blan tek water outer me spring?" Buh Rabbit say: "Me yent." Buh Wolf say: "You yis, enty me see you track?" Buh Rabbit mek answer: "Yent me gone to you spring. Must be some edder rabbit. Me nebber bin nigh you spring. Me dunno way you spring day." Buh Wolf no question um no mo; but eh know say eh bin Buh Rabbit fuh true, an eh fix plan fuh ketch um.

De same ebenin eh mek Tar Baby, an eh gone an set um right in de middle er de trail wuh lead to de spring, an dist in front er de spring.

Soon a mornin Buh Rabbit rise an tun in fuh cook eh bittle. Eh pot biggin fuh bun. Buh Rabbit say: "Hey! me pot duh bun. Lemme slip to Buh Wolf spring an git some water fuh cool urn."

So eh tek eh calabash an hop off fuh de spring. Wen eh ketch de spring, eh see de Tar Baby duh tan dist een front er de spring. Eh stonish. Eh stop. Eh come close. Eh look at um. Eh wait fur um fuh mobe. De Tar Baby yent notice um. Eh yent wink eh yeye. Eh yent say nuttne. Eh yent mobe. Buh Rabbit, him say: "Hey titter, enty you guine tan one side an lemme git some water?" De Tar Baby no answer. Den Buh Rabbit say: "Leely Gal, mobe, me tell you, so me kin dip some water outer de spring long me calabash." De Tar Baby wunt mobe. Buh Rabbit say: "Enty you know me pot duh bun? Enty you know me hurry? Enty you yeddy me tell you fuh mobe? You see dis han? Ef you dont go long and lemme git some water, me guine slap you ober." De Tar Baby stan day.

Buh Rabbit haul off an slap um side de head. Eh han fastne. Buh Rabbit try fuh pull eh hand back, an eh say: "Wuh you hole me han fuh? Lemme go. Ef you dont loose me, me guine box de life outer you wid dis tarruh han." De Tar Baby yent crack eh teet. Buh Rabbit hit um, bim, wid eh tarruh han. Dat han fastne too same luk tudder. Buh Rabbit say: "Wuh you up teh? Tun me loose. Ef you dont leggo me right off, me guine knee you." De

Tar Baby hole um fas. Buh Rabbit skade an bex too. Eh faid Buh Wolf come ketch um. Wen eh fine eh cant loosne eh han, eh kick de Tar Baby wid eh knee. Eh knee fastne. Yuh de big trouble now. Buh Rabbit skade den wus den nebber. Eh try fuh skade de Tar Baby. Eh say: "Leely Gal, you better mine who you duh fool long. Me tell you, fuh de las time, tun me loose. Ef you dont loosne me han an me knee right off, me guine bus you wide open wid dis head." De Tar Baby hole um fas. Eh yent say one wud. Den Buh Rabbit butt de Tar Baby een eh face. Eh head fastne same fashion luk eh han an eh knee. Yuh de ting now. Po Buh Rabbit done fuh. Eh fastne all side. Eh cant pull loose. Eh gib up. Eh bague. Eh cry. Eh holler.

Buh Wolf yeddy um. Eh run day. Eh hail Buh Rabbit: "Hey, Budder! Wuh de trouble? Enty you tell me you no blan wisit me spring fuh git water? Who calabash dis? Wuh you duh do yuh anyhow?" Buh Rabbit so condemn eh vent hab one wud fuh talk. Buh Wolf, him say: "Num-mine, I done ketch you dis day. I guine lick you now." Buh Rabbit bague. Eh bague. Eh prommus nebber fuh trouble Buh Wolf spring no mo. Buh Wolf laugh at um. Den eh tek an loose Buh Rabbit from de Tar Baby, an eh tie um teh one spakleberry bush, an eh git switch an eh lick um tel eh tired. All de time Buh Rabbit bin a bague an a holler. Buh Wolf yent duh listne ter um, but eh keep on duh pit de lick ter um.

At las Buh Rabbit tell Buh Wolf: "Dont lick me no mo. Kill me one time. Mek fire an bun me up. Knock me brains out gin de tree." Buh Wolf mek answer: "Ef I bun you up. Ef I knock you brains out, you guine dead too quick. Me guine trow you in de brier patch, so de brier kin cratch you life out." Buh Rabbit say: "Do Buh Wolf, bun me: broke me neck, but dont trow me in de brier patch. Lemme dead one time. Dont tarrify me no mo." Buh Wolf yent bin know wuh Buh Rabbit up teh. Eh tink eh bin guine tare Buh Rabbit hide off. So, wuh eh do? Eh loose Buh Rabbit from de spakleberry bush, an eh tek um by de hine leg, and eh swing um roun, an eh trow um way in de tick brier patch fuh tare eh hide an cratch eh yeye out. De minnit Buh Rabbit drap in de brier patch, eh cock up eh tail, eh jump, an eh holler back to Buh Wolf: "Good bye, Budder! Dis de place me mammy fotch me up,—dis de place me mammy fotch me up:" an eh gone befo Buh Wolf kin ketch um. Buh Rabbit too scheemy.

BRAZIL

1889

This story was recorded by Frederico José de Santa-Anna Nery, a scholar based in Paris and the scion of a family whose great wealth derived from the colonial trade in latex extracted from rubber trees in the Amazon Basin. The story was recalled from the author's youth in Belém, and published in 1889 as the lead story in *Folk-Lore Brésilien*, the inaugural work of Brazilian folklore studies in Europe. This version is notable in that ownership of property—in this case, an orange grove—is assumed rather than predicated on labor or collective agreement. The tar baby is an image of a monkey made from wax, a mirror image of the trickster, also in this case a monkey. The English translation that follows the French version below is by Aurelio Espinosa.

Le Singe et le Mannequin de Cire

Il y avait une fois un Singe qui avait l'habitude d'aller manger des oranges d'un oranger toujours chargé de fruits. Le maître du jardin plaça sur une branche de l'oranger un mannequin de cire pour effrayer les oiseaux. Le Singe y vint le lendemain, comme d'habitude et aperçut le mannequin sur l'arbre. «Donne-moi une orange, dit-il à l'homme de cire, autrement je t'envoie un coup de pierre.» Le Mannequin ne répondit rien, naturellement, et le Singe lui jeta une pierre qui resta collée au Mannequin.

Le vent, qui soufflait très fort, fit alors tomber une orange. Le Singe la ramassa et la mangea. Puis il demanda encore une autre orange au Mannequin. Celui-ci, ne lui ayant pas répondu, il lui jeta une autre pierre, qui resta collée au Mannequin, comme la première. Voyant que l'homme ne bougeait pas, le Singe s'approche de l'arbre, y grimpe et flanque un croc-en-jambe à l'homme. Sa jambe reste collée au Mannequin. «Laisse-moi ma jambe, dit-il, autrement je te donne un coup de pied.» Voyant que l'autre ne bouge pas, il lui donne un coup-de-pied, et sa seconde jambe y reste collée. Alors, il lui donne une gifle; sa main reste collée; il lui applique une seconde gifle, et sa main gauche reste prise. Furieux, il se démène tant et si bien, que le Mannequin se décolle et dégringole. Le Singe dégringole avec, et roule sur les épines de l'oranger jusqu'à terre. Quand il tomba, il avait le corps tout meurtri, et s'en alla en gémissant.

A monkey steals oranges from an orange grove. The owner of the orange grove sets up a wax-monkey on one of the trees. The monkey arrives and says to the wax-monkey, "Give me an orange." Receiving neither the orange nor a reply he gets angry, picks up a stone and throws it at the wax-monkey. The stone sticks to the wax-monkey. Then an orange falls from the tree and the monkey eats it, thinking that his command had been obeyed after throwing the stone. He then asks for another orange. He does not get it so he throws another stone at the wax-monkey, and that stone sticks also. No more oranges fall so the monkey gets very angry, climbs up the tree and gives the wax-monkey a good kick. His foot sticks. Then the monkey attacks in the usual manner with his hands and both stick. He still fights to free himself and both monkey and wax-monkey fall together to the ground. He finally escapes all battered up.

BAHAMAS

1891

This story was collected by Charles L. Edwards, a biology professor, in the summer of 1888 on Green Turtle Cay, a tiny barrier island in the Bahamas. Edwards believed that he was likely to discover unadulterated folklore in this relatively isolated location, and he attempted to preserve this perceived authenticity by transcribing songs and stories in his phonetic approximation of local dialect. In this story, the rabbit shirks labor, refusing to dig a well or harvest the fields. The rabbit says that he has no worries, as he is able to rely on nature's bounty. Moreover, the rabbit's approach to the tar baby is explicitly sexualized. Following his capture and the mock plea, the rabbit escapes in this instance to the "fine grass."

B'Rabby an' B'Tar-Baby

So dis day B'Rabby, B'Booky, B'Tiger, B'Lizard, B'Helephant, B'Goat, B'Sheep, B'Rat, B'Cricket; all o' de creatures, all kind,— so now dey say, "B'Rabby, you goin' help dig vwell? "B'Rabby say, "No! "Dey say, "Vw'en you vwan' vwater, how you goin' manage?" 'E say, "Get it an' drink it." Dey say, "B'Rabby, you goin' help cut fiel'?" B'Rabby say, "No!" Dey say, "Vw'en you 'r' hungry, how you goin' manage?" "Get it an' eat it." So all on 'em gone to work. Dey vwen'; dey dig vwell first. Nex' dey cut fiel'.

Now dis day B'Rabby *come*. Dey leave B'Lizard home to min' de vwell. So now B'Rabby say, "B'Lizard, you vwant to see who can make de mostest noise in de trash?" B'Lizard say, "Yes!" B'Rabby say, "You go in dat big heap o' trash dere an' I go in dat over dere (B'Rabby did vwant to get his vwater now!). B'Lizard *gone* in de trash; 'e kick up. Vw'ile 'e vwas makin' noise in de trash, B'Rabby dip 'e bucket full o' vwater. 'E *gone!*

So now vw'en B'Helephant come, an' hall de hother animals come out de fiel', B'Helephant say, "B'Lizard, you goin' let B'Rabby come here to-day an' take dat vwater?" B'Lizard say, "I couldn't help it!" 'E say, "E tell me to go in de trash to see who could make the mostest noise." Now de nex' day dey leave B'Booky home to min' de vwell. Now B'Rabby come. 'E say, "B'Booky, you vwan' to see who can run de fastes'?" B'Booky say, "Yes." 'E say, "You go dat side, an' le' me go dis side." Good! B'Booky break off; 'e gone a runnin'. Soon as B'Booky git out o' sight B'Rabby dip 'e bucket; 'e *gone*.

So now vw'en B'Helephan' an' em come dey say, "B'Booky, you let B'Rabby come 'ere again to-day and take our vwater?" 'E say, " 'E tell me who could run de fastes', an' soon 's I git a little vays 'e take de vwater an' gone. So B'Helephan' say, "I know how to ketch him!"

Dey *gone*; hall on 'em in de pine yard. Dey make one big tar-baby. Dey stick 'im up to de vwell. B'Rabby *come*. 'E say, "Hun! dey leave my dear home to min' de vwell to-day." B'Rabby say, "Come, my dear, le' me kiss you!" Soon as 'e kiss 'er 'e lip stick fas'. B'Rabby say, "Min' you better le' go;" 'e say, "You see dis biggy, biggy han' here;" 'e say, " 'f I slap you wid dat I kill you." Now vw'en B'Rabby fire, so, 'e han' stick. B'Rabby say, "Min' you better le' go me;" 'e say, "You see dis biggy, biggy han' here; 'f I slap you wid dat I kill you." Soon as B'Rabby slap wid de hudder han', so, 'e stick. B'Rabby say, "You see dis biggy, biggy foot here: my pa say, 'f I kick anybody wid my biggy, biggy foot I kill 'em." Soon as 'e fire his foot, *so*, it stick. B'Rabby say, "Min' you better le' go me." *Good!* soon as 'e fire his foot, so, it stick. Now B'Rabby jus' vwas hangin'; hangin' on de Tar-baby.

B'Booky come runnin' out firs'. 'eE say, "Ha! vwe got 'im to-day! vwe got 'im to-day!" 'E gone back to de fiel'; 'e tell B'Helephan'; 'e say, "Ha! B'Elephan', vwe got 'im to-day!" Vw'en all on 'em gone out now dey ketch B'Rabby. Now dey did vwan' to kill B'Rabby; dey did n' know whey to t'row 'im. B'Rabby say, " 'f you t'row me in de sea" (you know 'f dey had t'row B'Rabby in de sea, dey'd a kill 'im),—B'Rabby say, "'f you t'row me in de sea you won' hurt me a bit." B'Rabby say, "'f you t'row me in de fine grass, you kill me an' all my family." Dey take B'Rabby. Dey t'row 'im in de fine grass. B'Rabby *jump* up; 'e put off a runnin'. So now B'Rabby say, "Hey! ketch me 'f you could." All on 'em gone now.

Now dis day dey vwas all sittin' down heatin'. Dey had one big house; de house vwas full o' hall kin' o' hanimals. B'Rabby *gone*; 'e git hup on top de house; 'e make one big hole in de roof o' de house. B'Rabby sing hout, "Now, John Fire, go hout!" B'Rabby let go a barrel o' mud; let it run right down inside de house. Vw'en 'e let go de barrel o' mud, *so*, every one on 'em take to de bush, right vwil'; gone right hover in de bush. B'Rabby make vwil', till dis day you see hall de hanimals vwil'.

PHILIPPINES

1907

Published in the *Journal of American Folklore*, "Masoy and the Ape" is a composite formed from several stories collected by W. H. Millington and Bertrand Maxfield in Iloilo and Mandurriao, two villages on Panay, an island in the Visayan region of the Philippines. According to their brief account, the tar baby story was told by Visayan parents to their children, and it was commonly conveyed by the public storytellers who worked the markets when people were out purchasing ingredients for the evening meal. The sequence begins by staging the crime against nature that is committed by the ape when he steals fruit from Masoy's garden. It also contains an elaborate example of the no-reply formula, and a notable ending, in which the ape is turned into a slave.

Masoy and the Ape

Masoy was a poor man who lived on a farm some miles from the town. His clothing was very poor, and his little garden furnished him scarcely enough to live on. Every week day he went to town to sell his fruits and vegetables and to buy rice. Upon his return he noticed each day that someone had entered the garden in his absence and stolen some of the fruit. He tried to protect the garden by making the fence very strong and locking the gate; but, in spite of all he could do, he continued to miss his fruit.

At length Masoy conceived the happy idea of taking some pitch and moulding it into the shape of a man. He put a bamboo hat on it and stood it up in one corner of the garden. Then he went away.

As soon as he was gone, the robber, who was none other than a huge ape, climbed the fence and got in. "Oh!" he said to himself, "I made a mistake! There is Masoy watching. He did not go away as I thought. He is here with a big bamboo hat, but he could not catch me if he tried. I am going to greet him, for fear he may consider me impolite."

"Good morning, Masoy," he said. "Why do you not answer me? What is the matter with you? Oh! you are joking, are you, by keeping so silent? But you will not do it again." On saying this, the ape slapped the man of pitch with his right hand, and of course it stuck, and he could not get it loose.

"For heaven's sake," cried the ape, "let me go. If you do not, I will slap you with my other hand." Then he struck him with the other hand, which, of course, stuck fast also.

"Well, Masoy," cried the ape, "you have entirely exhausted my patience! If you don't let go of me at once, I shall kick you." No sooner said than done, with a result which may easily be imagined.

"Masoy," cried the now enraged ape, "if you have any regard for your own welfare, let me go, for if you don't, I still have one leg left to kill you with." So saying, he kicked him with the remaining foot, getting so tangled up that he and the tar man fell to the ground, rolling over and over.

Then Masoy came, and, when he saw the ape, he said: "So you are the robber who has stolen my fruit! Now you will pay for it with your life."

But the ape cried, "Oh, spare my life, and I will be your slave forever!"

"Do you promise not to steal my fruit again?"

"I do, and I will serve you faithfully all my life." Masoy agreed to spare him.

From that time on the ape worked very hard for his master. He sold the fruit and bought the rice and was honest and industrious. One day, on his way to market, he happened to find a small piece of gold and another of silver. At that time this country was not ruled by any foreign power, but each tribe was governed by its own datto or chief. The chief was naturally the bravest and richest of the tribe.

The chief of Masoy's tribe had a very beautiful daughter. The ape schemed to have her marry his master. Now he hit upon a plan. He went to the chief's house and asked for a ganta, which is a measure holding about three quarts and used for measuring rice.

"My master," he said, "begs you to lend him a ganta to measure his gold with."

The chief was astonished at such an extraordinary request, and asked: "Who is your master?"

"Masoy, who owns many gantas of gold and silver, acres upon acres of land, and uncountable heads of cattle," was the reply.

The ape carried the ganta home, and there he stuck the piece of gold he had found on the inside of the bottom of the measure, and then returned it to the chief.

"Oh, ape!" said the datto, "your master has forgotten to take out one piece of gold. Take it and give it back to him."

"Nevermind, sir," answered the ape, "he has so much gold that that small piece is nothing to him. You may keep it."

Some weeks afterward, the ape went again to borrow the chief's ganta.

"What do you want it for now?" asked the chief.

"To measure my master's silver with," was the answer. So he carried it home, stuck inside the piece of silver he had found, and returned it. The chief found the piece of silver and offered to return it, but was answered as before, that it did not matter.

The chief believed all that the ape said, but was puzzled to know how such a rich man could be living in his territory without his having heard of him.

After a few days the ape, considering the way well prepared for his plans, called upon the datto and said: "My master requests you to give him your daughter in marriage. I am authorized to make all the arrangements with you for the wedding, if you consent to it."

"Very well," answered the chief, "but before we arrange matters I wish to see my future son-in-law. Ask him to come to see me, and I will receive him in a manner befitting his rank."

The ape returned home and said to Masoy, who knew nothing at all of the negotiations with the chief: "I have good news for you. The chief wants to see you, for he intends to give you his daughter in marriage."

"What are you chattering about?" answered Masoy. "Have you lost your senses? Don't you know that I am too poor to marry the chief's daughter? I have not even decent clothes to wear and no means of getting any."

"Do not worry about the clothes. I will get them for you somewhere," replied the ape. "And how shall I talk? You know that I am ignorant of city ways."

"Oh, Masoy, don't trouble about that! Just answer 'Yes' to the questions they ask you and you will be all right."

Finally Masoy consented to go, and went down to the river to wash off the dirt and grime. A rich merchant was bathing some distance up the river, and the ape slipped along the bank, stole the merchant's clothes, hat, and shoes, and running back swiftly to his master, bade him put them on. Masoy did so, and found himself, for the first time in his life, so well dressed that he no longer hesitated about going to the chief's house. When they arrived there they found that the chief was expecting them and had made a big feast and reception in honor of his future son-in-law. The chief began to talk about the wedding and said:

"Shall we have the wedding in your palace, Masoy?"

"Yes," answered Masoy.

"You have a large palace, I suppose, have n't you, sir?"

"Yes," was the reply.

"Don't you think it would be well for us to go there this afternoon?"

"Yes," was again the reply.

Meanwhile the ape had disappeared. He went along the road towards home and said to all the people he met: "The datto will be along this way pretty soon and when he asks you to whom all these farms and cattle belong, you must say that they are Masoy's, for otherwise he will kill you."

The ape knew that in a certain spot stood an enchanted palace invisible to men. He went to the place, and just where the front of the house appeared whenever it was visible, he began to dig a ditch. The witch who lived in the house appeared and asked: "What are you ditching there for, Mr. Ape?"

"Oh, madam," was his answer, "haven't you heard the news? The chief is coming this way soon, and is going to have all witches and the low animals like myself put to death. For this reason I am digging a pit to hide myself in."

"Oh, Mr. Ape!" said the witch, "let me hide myself first, for I am not able to dig for myself, and you are. Do me this favor, please."

"I should be very impolite, if I refused to do a favor for a lady," said the ape. "Come down, but hurry, or you will be too late."

The witch hurried as fast as she could and got down into the pit.

Then the ape threw stones down on her until she was dead. The house then became free from enchantment and always visible.

The ape then returned to the chief's house and reported that all was ready for the wedding. So the chief, Masoy, and the bride, escorted by a large number of people, set out for Masoy's palace. On the way they saw many rich farms and great herds of cattle. The chief asked the people who the owner of these farms and cattle was. The answer always was that they belonged to Masoy. Consequently the chief was greatly impressed by Masoy's great wealth.

The chief greatly admired the palace and considered himself fortunate to have such a son-in-law. That night the wedding took place, and Masoy lived many years in the palace with his wife, having the ape and a great number of slaves to serve him.

CALIFORNIA

1910

"Coyote and the Stump" was common among the Maidu, an indigenous people in Northern California. It was transcribed by Roland B. Dixon during ethnographic fieldwork in the lower Sierra region, and it was published by Edward Sapir in "Yana Texts," a volume in the University of California's series in *American Archaeology and Ethnology*, where it was acknowledged for the first time as a "version of the world-wide 'Tar Baby' myth." The story is distinctive in portraying the stickfast sequence, in this case as an encounter between a coyote and a stump, without any other narrative elements.

Coyote and the Stump

Coyote went to P'a'wi one day. It was early in the morning and it was very foggy. He met some one in the trail. Coyote stooped. "Whew! I'm tired. Where do you come from?" The man did not answer. Coyote sat down to rest, and said, "You came early, so did I." The man said nothing. Coyote said, "Talk! One must say something when he meets one." There was no reply. Said Coyote, "If you are angry, say so!" No answer. Coyote said, "If you want to fight, I can fight." Coyote got up. There was no answer. Coyote said, "I'll hit." He did so, and his right hand stuck. It was no man, it was a stump. Coyote said, "Let go my hand!" with no result. Coyote hit him with his left hand; it stuck. Coyote said, "Why do you hold my hands? Let go! That is no way to fight." No reply. Coyote kicked with his right foot; it stuck. He kicked with his left foot; it stuck. He butted; his head stuck. By and by a man came along and saw Coyote. He said, "Coyote is a fool. He has been fighting that stump."

NIGERIA

1912

Versions of "Why Nki Lives in the Tops of Palm Trees" were common among Ekoi people in southeastern Nigeria. It was published in a social and geographical survey, *In the Shadow of the Bush*, which was written by P. Amaury Talbot, a British bureaucrat in the Nigerian Political Service. Talbot claimed the stories included in his book were taken "from sources never before brought into contact with white influence." The conflict in the story concerns land cleared for common use as well as a communal cache of smoked meat that is raided repeatedly by the Nki, a kind of small dormouse, who eventually finds himself stuck fast to a rubber man before his mock plea leads to his escape into the palm trees.

Why Nki Lives in the Tops of Palm Trees

A new piece of land had been cleared by the people of a certain town. Next morning, when they went thither to work, they found the place befouled. Inquiry was made, but the offender was not to be found. The head chief therefore gave a gun to Ise and set him to watch.

When night fell, Ejaw crept out of the bush, and began to befoul the place as before. Ise took aim and shot him, then ran and told the people what he had done. At daybreak they all went forth and brought in the body. They cut up the flesh, and asked Ise to dry it in the smoke of the fire that they might feast upon it next day. Ise did as he was bidden, and, when he had laid the pieces in order upon the drying shelf, sat down to watch by the hearth.

Now Nki loved fresh meat, and thought of a way by which he alone might feast upon the kill. He took a great jar of palm wine, and went to visit Ise. The latter was very thirsty, so he drank a deep draught and then lay down and fell asleep. While he slept Nki stole all the meat, then, when dawn broke, before the theft could be discovered, this treacherous animal took a drum and stood in the open space before the Egbo house playing:

"Ofu awche, kpa kun edingi ane aba.
Day breaks, now we may know each other.
Mbana nyamm aba kare nyamm.
Drier of meat come give meat."

Ise awoke and found all the flesh gone, so he cried out:
"A thief has taken all the meat which was given me to guard. Take my flesh instead that the town may feast." On this the people said, "It is just," so they killed Ise and gave his body to Etuk, that it might be smoked before the fire.

Nki did as before, stole the meat, and at daybreak beat upon the summoning drum. So Etuk lost his life as Ise had done, and his flesh was entrusted to Nkongam.

On him Nki played the same trick, with the result that he also was slain, and his body given in charge to Ngumi. This latter also fell a victim to Nki in exactly the same manner as the other beasts, and this time Mbaw was chosen to smoke the meat.

Now the latter is a very cunning animal, and no sooner had he reached his house than he laid the flesh upon the drying shelf, and spread over it great lumps of rubber. Next he piled high the fire, so that the rubber grew soft, and sat down to wait for the thief.

After a while Nki appeared as before, but Mbaw only pretended to drink the palm wine, and poured it away little by little when his visitor was not looking. At length he too lay down as if overcome by sleep.

Nki called, "Mbaw, Mbaw, are you awake?" but the latter did not answer.

The thief thought that all was now safe, so he rose up softly, and laid his hand upon the meat. At once the rubber caught him and held him fast. Nki was angry and cried, "Let go of me, whoever you are, or I will punch your head." Still the rubber held fast. Then Nki drove his own head against the place where his hand was held, thinking to force back his enemy, but the rubber caught his hair and held that also. In vain he struggled and fought, threatening his unseen foe all the while. Rubber answered nothing, but only held the tighter.

At dawn Mbaw went out and beat upon the summoning drum, "Day breaks now, we may know each other; drier of meat come and give meat."

The people came together, and found the thief caught fast. They debated as to how he could best be punished for the deaths of all those beasts who had died through his fault.

While they talked together, each proposing some more cruel fate than the other, Nki began to wring his hands and to weep. With each new suggestion he heartily agreed, adding always, "Yes, yes, kill me in any of these ways, only do not fix spears in the ground, and throw me up so that I may fall upon their points."

The people were so angry that they shouted, "Since he dreads this death above all others, it is by this that he shall die." They got spears, and fixed them firmly in the earth, points upward. Then they freed Nki from the rubber which had held him till now, and placed him before the spears. Six of the strongest men advanced to seize him and fling him into the air, but to the surprise of everyone, he himself gave a great leap, and sprang up a palm tree which stood near.

At once the people got axes, and cut down the tree, but before it fell, Nki sprang to another.

Then they said "If we follow this man, we shall ruin all the palm trees. It is better to leave him alone."

That is why Nki always stays in the tops of palm trees. Up to that time he had lived on earth like all other animals, but since he caused the death of so many creatures, no one will be his friend, and he cannot come back to dwell among them any more.

OAXACA
1917

"El Machín y el Jardín con Muchas Frutas" was collected by Paul Radin from students at the Normal School of Oaxaca in Ixtlán de Juárez. It was published in cooperation with Aurelio Espinosa in *El Folklore de Oaxaca*, a collection sponsored by the Escuela Internacional de Arqueología y

Etnología Americanas. The story concerns a capuchin monkey that steals from a garden with many fruits and gets caught by a trap made from "cera negra" (black wax). The story ends when the fox is tricked into taking his place. An almud and an arroba are units for measuring weight. An English translation follows the Spanish version below.

El Machín y el Jardín con Muchas Frutas

Mi padre me contaba, que un señor tenía un jardín con muchas frutas y que un animal le causaba mucho daño en las noches. Tenía tres hijos y entonces el padre les dice a sus hijos:—¿Qué hacemos con el animal? Mucho daño nos ha causado. Entonces el mayor de edad le dice:—Yo lo agarro y te lo entrego, pero para esto, necesito que tú me des unas reatas de lazar, Cogió el padre y le dio las reatas. Aquel muchacho cogió y puso los lazos por los árboles y se acostó a dormir. En la mañana, cuando amaneció, pues más daño había en los árboles. Su padre regañó al muchacho.

En la noche, le dice el otro, menor de edad:—Papá, yo voy ahora. Cómprame un almud de cacahuete y una vihuela y las mismas reatas. Y se fué él a aquel jardín y puso los lazos y se puso a comer cacahuetes. Ya que le fastidiaron los cacahuetes, se puso a hacer ruido con su vihuela. Ya que tenía sueño, se acostó a dormir y cuando amaneció, lo mismo estaba y si se ofrece, peor. Luego se fué su padre a verlo. Cuando llegó, estaba quitando los lazos de los frutales, y le dijo:—¿Qué pasó? ¿No lo cogiste?—No, me fué mal.—Malvados muchachos. No más me han hecho comprar las cosas y no lo agarran. Entonces el más pequeño le dice:—Papá, mis hermanos nunca hacen una cosa buena. Yo iré, papá. Entonces el padre echa una carcajada muy fuerte, y le dice:—Tus hermanos que ya son grandes, no pudieron; contimás tú, chiquitín. Le dice:—No papá. ¡Mira! Cómprame dos arrobas de cera negra y yo te prometo traértelo mañana. Entonces el padre compró la cera negra y el muchacho la cogió y se fué. Llegó donde estaban los frutales y comenzó a hacer monos. Ya que acabó de hacer los monos, los fué a colocar en les árboles, y se acostó a dormir. Cuando llegó el machín, se fué encontrando el mono de cera y le dice:—¡Eh, buen amigo! ¿Qué, también tú vienes a comer frutas? ¡Mira! Déjame pasar y verás que buenas frutas hay por aquí. El mono, no había de contestar. Entonces le dice:—No seas malo. Déjame pasar o te pego. De ver que el mono no lo dejaba pasar el machín, le dice:—Me dejas pasar o te pego. Entonces levantó la mano el machín y le pegó en la cara al mono y se le quedó la mano estampada.—¡Oyes! No seas malo, amigo. Suéltame la mano. ¿No me la sueltas? Entonces le pegó con la otra mano y se le quedó estampada la otra.—Suéltame o te pego con el pie. Entonces le dio una patada y se le quedó pegado el pie.—Suéltame a la buena o te pego con el otro pie. Le dio otra patada y se le quedó estampado.—Me sueltas o te enrollo mi cola. De ver que no lo soltaba el mono, le enrolló la cola y se le quedó enrollada la cola.—Suéltame, buen amigo. No seas malo. Suéltame o te muerdo la cara. Entonces le mordió la cara y se quedó estampado el animal.

Cuando amaneció, se levantó el muchacho y cogió su lazo y se subió al palo. Cuando le vio que estaba estampado en el mono, luego lo amarró y lo despegó y lo bajó del palo y se lo llevó a su padre. Y el padre se puso muy contento. Lo metieron en una jaula de fierro y luego pusieron lumbre y metieron un hierro que se calentara.

Eso estaban haciendo, cuando pasó una zorra y le dice al machín:—¡Oh, buen amigo! ¿Qué haces ahí?—Amigo, aquí me tienen por mes. Me pagan cinco pesos al mes y me dan pura gallina. Pero ya me fastidia la gallina. ¿No te quieres estar por mi parte? ¡A ti te gustan tanto las gallinas! A mí, ya me hostigan. Entonces la zorra dijo que sí, que se estaba por su parte. Le dijo:—Abre la puerta y entra. Desátame para que yo te amarre. Luego amarró el machín a la zorra y cerró la puerta y se fué muy contento.

Cuando salieron con el fierro caliente y vieron que ya no era machín, sino que era ya zorra, entonces dijeron:—¿Qué clase de animal será porque se volvió zorro?, y luego lo sacaron de la jaula y le metieron el fierro caliente y comenzó a gritar y allí murió.

The Monkey and the Garden with Many Fruits

My father told me that there was a man who had a garden with a lot of fruit and that a capuchin monkey did it much damage at night. The man had three sons, and so he said to his sons, "What shall we do with the animal? It has caused us a lot of harm." Then the eldest says to him, "I'll catch him and hand him over to you, but in order to do this, I need you to give me some ropes for lassoing." The father got and gave him the ropes. That boy took them and put the ropes in the trees and lay down to sleep. In the morning, when the sun rose—well, there was more damage in the trees. The boy was scolded by his father.

In the evening, the other son, the younger one, says to him: "Papa, I'll go now. Buy me an almud of peanuts and a guitar and the same ropes." And he went to that garden and put up the same ropes and began to eat peanuts. Since he got tired of the peanuts, he began to make noise with his guitar. Since he got sleepy, he lay down to sleep, and when the sun rose, it was the same situation, and possibly worse. Then his father came to take a look. When he arrived, the son was taking the ropes off the fruit trees, and the father said to him, "What happened? You didn't catch him?" "No, it went badly for me." "Wicked boys. They haven't done anything other than make me buy things and then not capture the monkey."

Then the youngest says to him, "Papa, my brothers never do anything right. I'll go, Papa." Then the father laughs very hard, and he says to his son, "Your brothers are already big, and they couldn't do it: all the more so you, little guy."

The son says, "No, Papa. Look! Buy me two arrobas of black wax and I promise I will bring it to you tomorrow." And so the father bought the black wax, and the boy took it and left. He arrived where the fruit trees were and began to make monkeys. As soon as he was done making the monkeys, he went and hung them from the trees and he lay down to sleep.

When the capuchin monkey arrived, he happened upon another monkey and he says to him, "Eh, my good friend! What, have you also come to eat fruit? Look! Let me by and you will see what good fruit there is here." The monkey was not obliged to respond. And so the capuchin says to him, "Don't be evil. Let me by or I will hit you." Seeing that the monkey didn't let the capuchin pass by, he says to him, "Let me by or I will hit you." And so the animal raised his hand and hit the face of the monkey and his hand remained stuck. "Listen to me! Don't be evil, my friend. Let go of my hand. You're not going to let it go?" And so he hit it with his other hand, and the other hand remained stuck. "Let me go or I will hit you with my foot." And so he kicked the monkey and his foot remained stuck. "Let me go by the grace of God or I will hit you with my other foot." He kicked him again and his foot remained stuck. "Let me go or I will roll you up with my tail." Seeing that the monkey didn't let him go, he rolled him up with his tail and his tail remained stuck. "Let me go, good friend. Don't be evil. Let me go or I will bite your face." And so he bit its face and remained stuck.

When the sun rose, the boy got up and grabbed his rope and went up the tree. When he saw the animal was stuck to the monkey, then he tied him up and unstuck him and lowered him from the tree and carried him to his father. And his father was very happy. They placed the monkey in an iron cage and then they lit a stove and they placed an iron pot on to heat up.

This was happening when a fox passed by and said to the capuchin, "Oh, good friend! What are you doing there?" "Friend, here they have me for a month. They pay 5 pesos a month and they give me pure-bred hen. But I am already tired of hen. Don't you want to be here on my behalf? You like hens so much! For me, they are already a bother. "And so the fox said yes, that she would stay there on his behalf. He said to her, "Open the door and enter. Untie me so that I can tie you up." Then the monkey tied up the fox and closed the door and left very happy.

When the father and son returned with the hot pot and saw that there was no longer a monkey, but now it was a fox, then they said, "What type of animal is it since it became a fox?" And then they took it out of the cage and they put it in the hot iron pot and it began to shout and there it died.

Translation by Elena Schneider

CAPE VERDE ISLANDS

1923

With the simple title "Tar Baby," this story comes from Fogo, one of the islands in Cape Verde, a volcanic archipelago situated off the northwest coast of Africa and colonized by Portugal. Elsie Clews Parsons transcribed the story from her collaborator and translator Pedro Teixeira, who had recently emigrated from Fogo to Newport, Rhode Island. Parsons published the story in the first volume of her *Folk-Lore from the Cape Verde Islands*, an important series resulting from a research partnership between the American Folk-Lore Society and the Hispanic Society of America. The story is distinctive as it implies a domestic mode in which production and consumption are organized at the level of the household, resulting in a conflict when Uncle Wolf labors in the fields with his nephew but takes more

Twelve Examples

than his share from the family stock. The nephew uses a tar baby to capture his uncle, and in an original turn, the uncle tries to blame the theft on the tar baby, an appeal that is based on the mirroring that is frequently suggested in the scene of encounter.

Tar Baby

There was a wolf with a nephew. They worked on the land together. When the crops were ripe, Nephew found something stolen from the land each day. Nephew said, "I believe it's you stealing there, my Uncle Wolf." Uncle Wolf said to him, "No, it's not me, it's other people." Sir Wolf stole, stole, until almost everything was gone from the land. Nephew went to see a *saib*; he asked him, "How can I catch my Uncle Wolf?"—"Make a figure of tar, put it in the middle of the land." Next day Uncle Wolf came, he met the tar figure. He asked, "What are you doing here? It's you stealing on our land." The tar figure did not answer him. Wolf said, "You needn't speak. I'm going to knock you down, I'm going to keep you here until Nephew comes." He gave a punch with his right hand, his right hand stuck. He said, "If you want to fight with me, let my hand go!" The figure did not stir. "I have another hand," said Wolf, and he gave him one with his left hand. His left hand stuck. He kicked him with his right foot, his foot stuck. "Oh, you're fighting well! I've still a foot." He kicked him with his left foot, his left foot stuck. "You've got my foot, but I'm going to butt you with my belly." He gave it to him with his belly, his belly stuck. "Oh, you're doing well! but I'm going to bite you." He bit, his teeth stuck. At eight o'clock Nephew came by. Wolf said to him, "I was watching for this fellow who was stealing on our land, Nephew; I caught him, he caught me too."—"I'm glad you've got the man, my Uncle Wolf. Now I'm going to set fire to him to burn him up."—"Don't set fire to him!" begged Wolf; "if you burn him, you'll kill your Uncle Wolf too."—"I can't help it, my Uncle; I can't get you two apart, I've got to burn you both." Nephew set fire to the tar figure. That was the end of Uncle Wolf.

COLOMBIA
1930

This untitled story was in circulation on the Caribbean coast of Colombia. It was collected from an unnamed informant in the state of Magdalena by J. Alden Mason, an archaeologist and the curator of the University of Pennsylvania Museum of Archaeology and Anthropology. In this version, we see the rabbit eating a watermelon meant as a present for the king. The story refers to the tar baby as "el negro de cera" (the wax negro), a designation that makes explicit the racial symbolism essential to the story's general significance. The rabbit escapes not by making a mock plea but by persuading another animal to take his place. An English translation follows the original Spanish version.

Un señor tenía una rosa y le regaló una *patilla* al rey. Aquella patilla era muy grande y llegó el conejo y se la comió. Y ahí llegó y se metió adentro de la patilla y se la comió. Y la patilla se la regalará al rey. Cuando le llevaron la patilla al rey lo que tenía adentro era mierda del conejo. Cuando la abrieron creyeron que era cosa del hombre y iba a coger al hombre para fusilarlo. Dijo el que no, que eso era cosa del conejo. Le dijeron entonces que cogiera al conejo.

Ahí llegó el hombre y hizo un negro de cera y lo puso en la rosa con un juego de baraja. Conejo era muy jugador y cuando vió la luz se fué encima a jugar él también. Se puso a jugar con el

Twelve Examples

negro de cera. El décia al negro que le echara carta y el negro callado. Ahí llegó y le dió un puño y se quedó pegado al negro. Le dió con la otra mano y también se quedó pegado. Le dijo que le soltara porque era pateador. Y le dió una patada y también se quedó pegado de la pata. Le dió con la otra pata y también se quedó pegado. Le dijo que le daba con la cabeza. También se quedó pegado de la cabeza.

Allí lo cogieron y llegaron y lo amarraron. Lo amarraron de un palo grande y pusieron a calentar un fondo de agua. Y él se puso a llorar. En eso se apareció Tío Tigre y le dijo que por que lloraba. Y le dijo que lloraba porque se le iba a casar con la hija del rey. Entonces le dijo el tigre que lo amarrase a él. Y ahí llegó entonces y el tigre se amarró y soltó al conejo. Cuando llegó la gente con el agua caliente encontraron al tigre y al conejo suelto. Y ahí llegaron y le echaron el fondo de agua al tigre y le dejaron allí amarrado.

En eso iba un mico pasando y le dijo el tigre que le soltara. Él le dijo que después se lo comía. El tigre le dijo que no. El mico llegó y siempre lo sacó de las dos manos. Y ahí llegó y lo cogió para comérselo. Entonces dijo el mico que no lo comía así, que lo tirara arriba para que le sintiera más sabroso. El tigre lo tiró para arriba para pararlo en la boca y comérselo, y el mico se agarró de un ramo. Y entonces no comió el tigre nada. Y entonces salió atrás del mico para podérselo comer. Y el mico se le escondió.

A gentleman had a rose garden and gave a watermelon to the king. That watermelon was very large, and along came a rabbit who ate it. Along he came and climbed into the watermelon and ate it. And this was the watermelon the man was going to give to the king. When they carried the watermelon to the king all it had inside was rabbit shit. When they opened it, they thought it was human shit and they were going to grab the man and shoot him. He said no, that was rabbit shit. Then they told the gentleman to capture the rabbit.

Along came the man and made a black figure out of wax and put it in the rose garden with a deck of cards. Rabbit was a gambler and when he saw the light of day he went to play, too. He sat down to play cards with the negro made of wax. He told the black to give him a card and the black was quiet. And so he gave him a punch and remained stuck to the black. He punched him with the other hand, which also remained stuck. He told him to let him go because he was a kicker. And he gave him a kick and his foot also got stuck. He kicked him with the other foot, which also got stuck. He told him he would hit him with his head. He also got stuck by his head.

There they captured him and came and tied him up. They tied him to a big stick and put some water on to heat up. And he began to cry. Uncle Tiger appeared in the middle of this and he said to Rabbit, why was he crying. And Rabbit said he was crying because he was going to marry the daughter of the king. Then the tiger said to him that he should tie *him* up. And so along came Tiger and he tied himself up and freed Rabbit. When the people arrived with the hot water, they found Tiger and Rabbit running free. And along they came and they threw the water at the tiger and they left him there tied up.

In the middle of this there was a little monkey passing by and the tiger told him to untie him. The monkey said that then afterwards he would eat him. The tiger said no. And so the monkey freed the tiger with his two hands. And so it happened that the Tiger grabbed him in order to eat him. Then the monkey said not to eat him that way, that he should flip him over so that he would taste more flavorful. The tiger flipped him over in order to catch him in his mouth and eat him, and the monkey grabbed onto a branch. And so the tiger didn't eat anything. And then the Tiger left behind the monkey in order that the others would be able to eat him. And the monkey hid himself.

Translation by Elena Schneider

TANZANIA

1931

"Kalusimu Ka Lugano" was collected by Frederick Johnson from the Iramba, a people who, at the time this story was told, lived on the plateau north of the central railway in Tanganyika, an area in German East Africa now known as Tanzania. The story concerns a hare who steals groundnuts from a family and is caught by the tar baby, in this case the figure of a young woman smeared with bird lime who does not move when the hare tries to scare her into running away from the field. The hare manages to escape through a distinctive sequence of deceptions that result in the death of the family's child. Johnson's English translation follows the original Iramba version (Johnson's parenthetic explanatory translation notes have been omitted).

Kalusimu Ka Lugano

Msungu ali ukulima nzugu ku'mbuga sunga nazikonda mpunda nwilia. Msungu nuza nwagana nzugu ndige nuga "Wani ukulia nzugu zane?" Nigulo yoi intondo tumtum, nuga "Kantunge nantende." Sunga nuza mpunda nwikulilia "Talami talami ngombe zaporoka." Masalu nwishemula, msungu numanka, nugopa, numanka wenda kukaa, numuila wisheo, nuga "Muntu ukulia nzugu aza ntungile washemulanga lukundi, nogopa numanka, ipa kutendei mgosha wane?" Mgosha nuga "Tulya, tendekye masala nukumugwila." Welu nuzipia kota liza migulu zi muntu, mbelele zi muntu, nitue nishanga numtungulia kina mnanso nulipaka ntia tum, nutwala ku'mgunda waki nzugu nwika nulega. Mpindi nuza [*original unclear*] Mnangala nuga "Talami talami, ngombe zaporoka." Kota nalidu. Sunga nusu-gamila pipe, mpunda nuga "Mnanso, uwe, nikikukua." Nuamba nu mbelele nukamantila, nuga "Leka isasila, uwe nde-kela." Nalidu. Nuamba nu mkono mua nukamantila, nuga "Nukakusamba." Nusamba mgulu umwi nukamantila, samba nu mua nukamantila, nuga, "Nikukulume." Nukamantila ni mino tum nukatala. Mdau aporoka asungu atili napika namwa-gana mpunda mnangala nauga "Nantende tuyu nukilia nzugu zitu." Mkola nzugu nuga "Leti ikome numkue." Iya nauga "Leka kumkua kumgwile mpanga kutwale kukaa wendi telekwa numoto." Namugwila namtunga ndigi nauga "To mlisha mt-wale kukaa mwile mguru wako wamteleke na kwaza waluge ugali kumlie kina walilile nzugu zitu, *[original unclear]* "Num-sola numlongolya kukaa naigenda kua, mpumla nuga," *[original unclear]* Namlisha uwe umuilwe mbi ni amau ako?" "Nimwilwe uwe wenda telekwa nu mguru wane." Mnangala nuga "Sikawig-ulye kisa." "Aza augileli?" Nuga "Azaaugile iti." "Ee." "Twala mgulu wako wandugile ugali kwikisiga nu mwana." Mlisha nuga "Sika yoi, wilongopa." Mpunda nuga "Kweni kwendi kolya." Mlisha nulaa kuli, nuga "Yakonda gwa kweni sikazani-gulye kisa." Naenda kukaa, numwila yoi, mguli nuluga ugali numpela nulia naikisiga nu mwana, sunga naigona nakumbwa ntila imwi nagona ndoro. Naza iya nina nauga "Leti gwa inama ya Mnangala, walile na nguru nzugu zitu." Mguli nuga "I i mli-sha uyo siwaza ne, wambwila mlugile ugali isige nu mwana, ipa tuyo igonile ensi." Mpunda nwigulye nina nuga "Leti pini, numkue." Punda numanka palumwi nu mwana, yaikinga "Wat-wala nu mwana witu." Nwenda m'kilimbili nwigiIya mwana uyo nupuna kunzi wikumba ntila. Aza aone migulu m'kilimbili auga "Tuyu, mnawingila, leti miolo kusimbe, mwana witu tuyu ipa pana wamuika." Asimba sunga akumkina mwana wao, aona migali mu-'molo auga "Tiyi migali, wakia, kweni kumsole mwana witu." Akunukula ntila lamanka lampunda, ailila "I i i i kwamulaga mwana witu." Ashoka asimbula agana wakia. Atwala kukaa amuika mwana wao. Mpunda wendi, sikaamuona. Mwana wao wakia, ni nzugu zao nalilia, nalyakapa turu. Yoi kalusimu yane yasila.

A Wonderful Story

A woman cultivated some ground-nuts on a plain, until they flourished, and a hare ate them. The woman came and found the ground-nuts eaten and said "Who eats my ground-nuts?" In the evening it was the same, every day, and she said "To-day I will spy." Then the hare came crying "Run, run, the cattle are coming." And he threw up the sand and the woman ran away, she was afraid, and ran and went to the village and told her husband, and said "A person is eating the ground-nuts, I watched and he kicked up a dust and I was afraid and ran away. Now what shall we do, my husband?" The man said "Wait I shall make a plan to catch him." Next morning he prepared a nice pole, legs like a person, breasts like a person, and he dressed with beads like a young girl and he smeared it all with bird-lime and he took it to the garden of ground-nuts and placed it and came away. In the evening the hare came and said "Run, run, the cattle are coming." The pole was silent. Then he drew near and the hare said "Little girl you, I shall beat you." And he seized the breasts and stuck, and said "Leave off your foolishness, leave go of me." Silence. And he struck with his other hand and it stuck, and he said "I shall kick you." And he kicked with one leg and it stuck, and he kicked with the other and it stuck, and he said "I shall bite you." And he stuck with all his teeth and was tired. The next morning there came only women and they arrived and found the hare and said "The person who eats our ground-nuts, here he is." The owner of the ground-nuts said "Bring a stick and I will beat him." The others said "Don't beat him, let us catch him alive, let us send him to the village to be cooked with fire." So they caught him and fastened him with rope and said "Here boy, take him to the village and tell your sister to cook him, and when we come let her cook 'ugali' (food) to eat with him, because he has eaten our groundnuts." And he took him and took him to the village, and he went a distance and the hare said "You boy, what were you told by your mothers?" "I was told you go to be cooked by my sister." The hare said "You did not hear properly." "What did they say?" He said "They said this." "Well?" "Take him to your sister that she may cook for him '*ugali*' and he may play together with the child." The boy said "It was not that, you tell lies." The hare said "Go, go and ask." The boy looked back far (they were far off) and he said "Very well, never mind, let us go, I did not hear properly." And they went to the village and he told her that, and the sister cooked food and gave him and he ate, and played together with the child till they lay down and was covered with a hide (or cloth) and they slept. Then the mothers came and said "Very well, bring the meat of the hare, he has eaten with strength our ground-nuts." The sister said "I say, that boy, he did not come to me, he told me to cook food for him and let him play with the child, and now there he is, they sleep together." The hare heard the mother say "Bring a big stick and I will beat him." And the hare ran away together with the child and they chased him. "He takes our child." And he went to an ant-hill and put in the child and himself, he came out and covered himself with the cloth. They came and saw legs in the ant-hill and said "Here he is, he has gone inside, bring pointed sticks and let us dig, our child is there where he put him" (thinking that the child was covered with the cloth). And they dug till they pierced their child and they saw the blood on the pointed stick and said "Here is blood, he is dead, let us go and take our child." And they uncovered the cloth and that rascal of a hare ran away. And they cried "*I! i! i! i!* we have killed our child." And they returned and dug and found he was dead. They took him to the village and buried their child. The hare went, they did not see him. Their child was dead, and their ground-nuts were eaten, they missed both. Thus, my story is finished.

Translation by Frederick Johnson

ACKNOWLEDGMENTS

I would like to thank the following friends and colleagues for their questions, suggestions, and support during the writing process: Alex Benson, Stephen Best, Kelvin Black, Marianne Constable, Nadia Ellis, Brad Evans, Richmond Eustis, Catherine Gallagher, Robert Levine, Eric Lott, Kim Magowan, Giuliana Perrone, Beth Piatote, Lloyd Pratt, Kent Puckett, Megan Pugh, Leigh Raiford, Michael Ralph, Elena Schneider, Darieck Scott, Susan Schweik, Jonathan Simon, Leti Volpp, and Edlie Wong.

Portions of this book were presented as lectures at Bard College, Brown University, Linacre College at Oxford University, University of Maryland, New York University, and Rutgers University. I greatly appreciate the thoughtful feedback I received at these events.

At Princeton University Press, Anne Savarese has been an exemplary editor. Her close attention to the manuscript made the book much better than it would have been otherwise.

I would also like to thank Emory University Library Special Collections and the Bancroft Library at the University of California, Berkeley, for their research assistance, and the Edward Gorey Estate for generously giving permission to reproduce two beautiful drawings.

Grateful acknowledgment is made for permission to reprint the following previously published material: "Kalusimu Ka Lugano" and "A Wonderful Story" from "Kiniramba Folk Tales" by Frederick Johnson printed in *Bantu Studies*, Vol. 5:1 (1931), 327–56. Reprinted by permission of the publisher Taylor & Francis Ltd (www.tandfonline.com). Excerpts from "Notes on the Origin and History of the Tar-Baby Story" by Aurelio M. Espinosa and "Cuatro Cuentos Colombianos" by J. Alden Mason printed in the *Journal of American Folklore*, Vol. 43: 168 (1930), 162–63, 216. Permission courtesy of the American Folklore Society (www.afsnet.org).

NOTES

PROLOGUE

1. Joel Chandler Harris, *Uncle Remus: His Songs and His Sayings, the Folk-lore of the Old Plantation* (New York: D. Appleton and Company, 1881), 23–25, 29–31. Harris's version was first published in the *Atlanta Constitution*. [Joel Chandler Harris], "Uncle Remus's Folk Lore: Brer Rabbit, Brer Fox, and the Tar-Baby," *Atlanta Constitution,* 16 November 1879, 2; [Joel Chandler Harris], "Uncle Remus's Folk Lore: Showing How Brer Rabbit Was Too Sharp for Brer Fox," *Atlanta Constitution,* 30 November 1879, 2. Harris wrote the tar baby as he remembered hearing it in his youth on Turnwold Plantation in Eatonton, Georgia. He insisted that he wrote the tar baby and other stories as they were told to him without embellishment. Harris did, however, manufacture the character of Uncle Remus and the storytelling situation where Remus tells trickster stories to the little boy. Remus was an established stereotype from the plantation tradition, a dialect-speaking slave who remains loyal to his master's extended family following emancipation. Following the precedent in Harris's first publication, the standard classification in folklore studies breaks the story into two parts: "Tarbaby and the Rabbit" and "Briar-Patch Punishment for Rabbit." Antti Amatus Aarne and Stith Thompson, *The Types of the Folktale: A Classification and Bibliography, Second Revision* (Helsinki: Academia Scientiarum Fennica, 1961),

63–64, 389; Harris, *Uncle Remus*, 23–25, 29–31; *Song of the South* (Walt Disney Film-Studio Productions, 1946); Marion Palmer, *Walt Disney's "The Wonderful Tar Baby"* (New York: Grosset and Dunlap 1946). The comic strip, *Uncle Remus and His Tales of Brer Rabbit* (1945–72), was distributed by King Features and sponsored by Disney and products like Cheerios breakfast cereal. Brer Rabbit's Blackstrap Molasses is produced by B & G Foods. On Uncle Remus and the plantation tradition, see the following works: Thomas Nelson Page, "Immortal Uncle Remus," *Book Buyer* 12 (1895): 642–45; Sterling A. Brown, "Negro Character as Seen by White Authors," *Journal of Negro Education* 2 (1933): 179–203; Darwin T. Turner, "Daddy Joel Harris and His Old-Time Darkies," *Southern Literary Journal* 1 (1968): 20–41; Wayne Mixon, "The Ultimate Irrelevance of Race: Joel Chandler Harris and Uncle Remus in Their Time," *Journal of Southern History* 56 (1990): 457–80; Eric J. Sundquist, *To Wake the Nations: Race in the Making of American Literature* (Cambridge: Harvard University Press, 1993), 323–59; Walter M. Brasch, *Brer Rabbit, Uncle Remus, and the" Cornfield Journalist": The Tale of Joel Chandler Harris* (Macon, GA: Mercer University Press, 2000). On *Song of the South* and related ventures, see Jason Sperb, *Disney's Most Notorious Film: Race, Convergence, and the Hidden Histories of Song of the South* (Austin: University of Texas Press, 2012).

2. Mrs. William Preston Johnston, "Two Negro Tales," *Journal of American Folklore* 9 (1896): 195. Madeleine Holland, "Folklore of the Banyanja," *Folklore* 27 (1916): 116. Frank Edgar and Neil Skinner, *Hausa Tales and Traditions: An English Translation of Tatsuniyoyi Na Hausa* (New York: Africana Publishing Corporation, 1969), 41, 46. Joel Chandler Harris, *Nights with Uncle Remus: Myths and Legends of the Old Plantation* (Boston: James R. Osgood and Company, 1883), xii–xiv. Elsie Clews Parsons, "The Provenience of Certain

Negro Folk Tales: Tar Baby," *Folklore* 30 (1919): 227–34. Franz Boas, "Notes on Mexican Folk-Lore," *Journal of American Folklore* 25 (1912): 235–39. Franz Boas, *Race, Language and Culture* (New York: Macmillan Company, 1940), 519–22. Melville J. Herskovits, *The Myth of the Negro Past* (New York: Harper and Brothers, 1941), 254–60, 272–73.

3. M. J. Herskovits, "Tar Baby," in Maria Leach, ed., *Funk and Wagnalls Standard Dictionary of Folklore, Mythology, and Legend*, 2 vols. (New York, Funk and Wagnalls, 1950), 2:1104. E. Franklin Frazier, *The Negro Family in the United States* (Chicago: University of Chicago Press, 1939), 21. Stanley M. Elkins, *Slavery: A Problem in American Institutional and Intellectual Life* (Chicago: University of Chicago Press, 1959). "The folktale," Mary Berry and John Blassingame write, "was also a means of training young blacks to use their cunning to overcome the strength of the master, to hide their anger behind a mask of humility, to laugh in the face of adversity, to retain hope in spite of almost insuperable odds, to create their own heroes, and to violate plantation rules and still escape punishment." Mary Frances Berry and John W. Blassingame, *Long Memory: The Black Experience in America* (New York: Oxford University Press, 1982), 18.

4. Robert Chaudenson summarizes this longstanding methodological problem. "Many authors," Chaudenson explains, "including some of the most distinguished, are often somewhat rash in their conclusions, and, for lack of information (which may be sparse or difficult to obtain), formulate opinions implicitly based on highly incomplete comparative analyses." Robert Chaudenson with Salikoko S. Mufwene, *Creolization of Language and Culture*, trans. Sheri Pargman, Salikoko S. Mufwene, Sabrina Billings, and Michelle AuCoin (London: Routledge, 2001), 273.

5. The term "great transformation" was coined by Karl Polanyi to refer to the interconnected political and economic changes that led to the establishment of "market society." Karl Po-

lanyi, *The Great Transformation* (New York: Farrar and Rinehart, 1944).

6. Aarne and Thompson, *Types of the Folktale*, 63–64. Florence E. Baer, *Sources and Analogues of the Uncle Remus Tales* (Helsinki: Suomalainen Tiedeakatemia, 1980), 29–32. May Augusta Klipple, *African Folktales with Foreign Analogues* (New York: Garland Publishing, 1992), 96–106. Aurelio M. Espinosa, "A New Classification of the Fundamental Elements of the Tar-Baby Story on the Basis of Two Hundred and Sixty-Seven Versions," *Journal of American Folklore* 56 (1943): 31–37.

7. "Notes," *Nation* 7 (5 November 1868): 368–70. Gavin Jones, *Strange Talk: The Politics of Dialect Literature in Gilded Age America* (Berkeley: University of California Press, 1999), 14–36. Paul Hull Bowdre, "A Study of Eye Dialect" (dissertation, University of Florida, 1964). On the problematic concept of "primary orality," referring to cultures uncontaminated by print, see Walter J. Ong, *Orality and Literacy: The Technologizing of the Word* (London and New York: Methuen and Company, 1982). See also Susan Stewart, "Notes on Distressed Genres," *Journal of American Folklore* 104 (1991): 5–31. For the tar baby transformed into standard language, see Julius Lester, "Brer Rabbit and the Tar Baby," in *The Tales of Uncle Remus* (New York: Puffin Books, 1987), 10–13.

CHAPTER 1. IDEAS OF CULTURE

1. Writing in 1926 with an enthusiasm characteristic of the story's early collectors, Newbell Niles Puckett imagines a chain of connecting points across the Western Hemisphere. In the United States, Puckett observes, the "fox or the wolf" makes the tar baby. On the Bahama Islands, it is an "elephant." In Canada, it is a "Frenchman," and in Brazil, an "old woman." Newbell Niles Puckett, *Folk Beliefs of the*

Southern Negro (Chapel Hill: University of North Carolina Press, 1926), 66.

2. The most comprehensive survey of the story's collection appears in the series of essays published by Aurelio Espinosa between the 1920s and the 1940s. These essays should be interpreted with caution, as they are colored by an effort to diminish the importance of Africans and African Americans in the tar baby's diffusion. Aurelio M. Espinosa, "Notes on the Origin and History of the Tar-Baby Story," *Journal of American Folklore* 43 (1930): 129–209. Espinosa, "More Notes on the Origin and History of the Tar-Baby Story," *Folklore* 49 (1938): 168–81. Espinosa, "New Classification," 31–37.

3. Adolf Gerber estimates the tar baby was collected more than any other tale in North and South America in the late nineteenth century. Adolf Gerber, "Uncle Remus Traced to the Old World," *Journal of American Folklore* 6 (1893): 251. On the influence of Uncle Remus on the discipline of folklore in the late nineteenth century, see the following: William Wells Newell, "On the Field and Work of a Journal of American Folklore," *Journal of American Folklore* 1 (1888): 3–7; Fanny D. Bergen, "Uncle Remus and Folk-Lore," *Outlook* 48 (1893): 427–28; W. L. Weber, "Mississippi as a Field for the Student of Literature," *Publications of the Mississippi Historical Society* 1 (1898): 16–24; Julia Collier Harris, ed., *The Life and Letters of Joel Chandler Harris* (London: Constable, 1919), 162; Elsie C. Parsons, "Joel Chandler Harris and Negro Folklore," *Dial* 66 (1919): 491–93; Arthur Huff Fauset, "American Negro Folk Literature," in Alain Locke, ed., *The New Negro: An Interpretation* (New York: Albert and Charles Boni, 1925), 238–44; Stella Brewer Brookes, *Joel Chandler Harris—Folklorist* (Athens: University of Georgia Press, 1950); Kathleen Light, "Uncle Remus and the Folklorists," *Southern Literary Journal* 7 (1975): 88–104; Michael Flusche, "Joel Chandler Harris and the Folklore of Slavery,"

Journal of American Studies 9 (1975): 347–63. Harris's most serious and sustained attempt at comparative folklore study is Harris, *Nights with Uncle Remus*, xi–xxxvi. Among others, Harris cites the following examples of African-derived story-telling as points of comparison for Uncle Remus: Wilhelm Bleek, *Reynard the Fox in South Africa; or, Hottentot Fables and Tales* (London: Trübner and Company, 1864); Charles Frederick Hartt, *Amazonian Tortoise Myths* (Rio de Janeiro: William Scully, 1875), 1–15; George McCall Theal, *Kaffir Folk-lore: Or, A Selection from the Traditional Tales Current Among the People Living on the Eastern Border of the Cape Colony* (London: W. Swan Sonnenschein and Company, 1882).

4. David Dwight Wells, "Evolution in Folk Lore: An Old Story in a New Form," *Popular Science Monthly* 41 (May 1892): 45. Alice M. Bacon, "The Study of Folk-Lore," in John Wesley Edward Bowen, ed., *Africa and the American Negro* (Atlanta: Gammon Theological Seminary, 1896), 191, 194. Charlotte Sophia Burne, *The Handbook of Folklore* (London: Sidgwick and Jackson, 1914), 266. Alice Werner, *Myths and Legends of the Bantu* (London: G. G. Harrap and Company, 1933), 243. William Owens, "Folk-Lore of the Southern Negroes," *Lippincott's Magazine* 20 (1877), 748–55. Thomas F. Crane, "Plantation Folk-Lore," *Popular Science Monthly* 18 (1881): 824–33. Harris's influence in these decades is pronounced. If some collectors, following Harris, sought to prove that the Uncle Remus stories were told wherever there were people of African descent, others purported to have stumbled upon informants who looked like Remus and told the same stories, and still others crafted avowedly fictional conceits, more or less explicitly modeled on Harris's work, to frame their own collections. Charles Colcock Jones Jr., *Negro Myths from the Georgia Coast Told in the Vernacular* (Boston: Houghton, Mifflin and Company, 1888). Mary Pamela Milne-Home, *Mamma's Black Nurse Stories: West Indian Folk-*

lore (London: W. Blackwood and Sons, 1890). Abigail M. H. Christensen, *Afro-American Folk Lore: Told Round Cabin Fires on the Sea Islands of South-Carolina* (Boston: J. G. Cupples, 1892). Ruby Andrews Moore, "Superstitions from Georgia," *Journal of American Folklore* 7 (1894): 305–6. Arthur Fraser Sim, *Life and Letters of Arthur Fraser Sim* (Westminster: Universities Mission, 1896). Robert Hill, *Cuba and Porto Rico with the Other Islands of the West Indies* (New York: Century Company, 1898). Poultney Bigelow, *White Man's Africa* (New York and London: Harper and Brothers, 1898). Patricia C. Smith, *Annancy Stories* (New York: R. H. Russel, 1899). Anne V. Culbertson, *At the Big House, Where Nancy and Aunt'Phrony Held Forth on the Animal Tales* (Indianapolis, IN: Bobbs-Merrill Company, 1904); Walter Jekyll, *Jamaican Story and Song: Annancy Stories, Digging Sings, Ring Tunes, and Dancing Tunes* (London: D. Nutt, 1907). Andrews Wilkinson, *Plantation Stories of Old Louisiana* (Boston: Page Company 1914). Ambrose Gonzales, *With Aesop along the Black Border* (Columbia, SC: State Company, 1920). Martha Warren Beckwith and Helen Heffron Roberts, *Jamaica Anansi Stories* (New York: American Folklore Society, 1924).

5. Lloyd W. Daly, trans., "The Aesop Romance," in *Anthology of Ancient Greek Popular Literature*, ed. William F. Hansen (Bloomington: Indiana University Press), 111. Francis Barlow, Thomas Philipott, and Robert Codrington, *Aesop's Fables, with His Life, in English, French and Latin* (London: Printed by William Godbid for Francis Barlow, 1666), 1, 7. William Godwin, *Fables, Ancient and Modern* (Philadelphia: Benjamin Warner, 1818), 145–47. William Martin Leake, *Numismata Hellenica: A Catalogue of Greek Coins* (London: John Murray, 1856), 45. J. H. Driberg, "Aesop," *Spectator* 148 (1932): 858. Robert Temple, "Introduction," in *Aesop: The Complete Fables* (New York: Penguin Books, 1998), xx–xxi. Richard A. Lobban, Jr., "Was Aesop a Nubian Kummaji

(Folkteller)?" *Northeast African Studies*, 9 (2002): 11–31. Arna W. Bontemps, "Introduction," in Arna W. Bontemps and Langston Hughes, eds., *The Book of Negro Folklore* (New York: Dodd, Mead, 1958), vii.

6. James Weldon Johnson, *Native African Races and Culture* (Charlottesville, VA: Trustees of the John F. Slater Fund, 1927). Herskovits, *Myth of the Negro Past*, 254–60, 272–73. John A. Lomax, "Stories of an African Prince: Yoruba Tales," *Journal of American Folklore* (1913): 1–12. John Henry Weeks, *Congo Life and Folklore* (London: Religious Tract Society, 1911), 366–67. A. B. Ellis, "Evolution in Folklore: Some West African Prototypes of the 'Uncle Remus' Stories," *Popular Science Monthly* 48 (1895): 93–96. W.H.I. Bleek, "African Folk-lore," *The Cape Monthly Magazine* 1 (September 1870): 168–82. Abbie Holmes Christensen describes a situation similar to Lomax's story about Lattevi Ajaji, concerning a native informant named Prince Baskin, as does James Marion Sims in framing an informant named Cudjo. See Christensen, *Afro-American Folk Lore*, 1–5. James Marion Sims. *The Story of My Life* (New York: D. Appleton and Company, 1884), 70. For point-to-point analysis linking the Uncle Remus stories and African cognates, see the following: Owens, "Folk-Lore of the Southern Negroes," 748–55; "Brer Rabbit," *Saturday Review*, 51 (19 March 1881), 363–65; Harris, *Nights with Uncle Remus*, xii–xiv; Thomas Bain, "The Story of a Dam," *Folk-Lore Journal* 1 (1879): 69–73; Louis Pendleton, "Notes on Negro Folklore and Witchcraft in the South," *Journal of American Folklore* 3 (1890): 201–7; Wells, "Evolution in Folk Lore," 45–54; Frederick Starr, "Curiosities of African Folk-Lore." *Dial* 17 (1894): 261–63; Héli Chatelain, *Folk-Tales of Angola* (Boston and New York: Houghton, Mifflin and Company, 1894), 185, 295; Père Capus, *Zeitschrift für afrikanische, ozeanische und ostasiatische Sprachen* 3 (1898): 358; Henri A. Junod, *Les Chants et les Contes des Ba-Ronga de la Baie de Delagoa* (Lausanne: Georges

Bridel & Cie., 1897), 96–98; Emmeline H. Dewar, *Chinamwanga Stories* (Livingstonia, Malawi, 1900), 57; W. Lederbogen, "Duala Fables" in *Journal of the African Society* 13 (1904): 59–60; R. E. Dennet, *Notes on the Folk-Lore of the Fjort* (London: David Nutt, 1898), 90–93; W. H. Barker and Cecilia Sinclair, *West African Folk-Tales* (London: George G. Harrap and Company, 1917), 69–72; Robert Hamill Nassau, *Fetichism in West Africa: Forty Years' Observation of Native Customs and Superstitions* (New York: C. Scribner's Sons, 1904), 276; Florence Cronise and Henry W. Ward, *Cunnie Rabbit, Mr. Spider, and the Other Beef: West-African Folk-Tales* (New York: E. P. Dutton and Company, 1903), 101–9; Alice Werner, "The Tar-Baby Story," *Folklore* 10 (1899): 282–94; Adolph N. Krug, "Bulu Tales from Kamerun, West Africa," *Journal of American Folklore* 25 (1912): 106–24; W. S. Scarborough, "Negro Folk-Lore and Dialect," *Arena* 17 (1896–97): 186–92; Annie Weston Whitney, "Negro American Dialects," *Independent* 53 (1901): 1079–81, 2039–42; Mary Tremearne and Arthur John Newman Tremearne, *Fables and Fairy Tales for Little Folk, or Uncle Remus in Hausaland* (Cambridge: W. Heffer and Sons Ltd., 1910), 87–89; W. Norman Brown, "Hindu Stories in American Negro Folklore," *Asia* 21 (1920): 703–7, 730–32; Natalie Curtis Burlin, C. Kamba Simango, and Madikane Čele, *Songs and Tales from the Dark Continent* (New York: G. Schirmer, 1920), 45–47; Mrs. Vivian Costroma Osborne Marsh, "Types and Distribution of Negro Folk-Lore in America" (dissertation, University of California, 1922); W. Norman Brown, "The Tar-Baby Story at Home," *Scientific Monthly* 15 (1922): 228–34. Puckett, *Folk Beliefs of the Southern Negro*, 40; Arthur Huff Fauset, "Negro Folk Tales from the South (Alabama, Mississippi, Louisiana)," *Journal of American Folklore* 40 (1927): 213–303; W. Norman Brown, "The Stickfast Motif in the Tar-Baby Story," *Publications of the Philadelphia Anthropological Society* (Philadelphia,

Pa., 1937), 1–12; S. C. Hattingh, "Die Teerpopsprokie in Afrika," *Tydskrif Vir Volkskunde en Volkstaal* 1 (1944): 13–19; Wenzell Brown, "Anansi and Brer Rabbit," *American Mercury* 69 (1949): 438–43.

7. Harris, *Uncle Remus: His Songs and His Sayings*, 4–10. Harris, *Nights with Uncle Remus*, xi–xlii. Charles Frede Hartt, *Amazonian Tortoise Myths* (Rio de Janeiro: William Scully, 1875), 1–15. James Mooney, "Myths of the Cherokees," *Journal of American Folklore* 1 (1888): 97–108. For Harris's responses to Powell's letter, see the following. Joel Chandler Harris, "Negro Folk Lore," *Atlanta Constitution,* 9 April 1880. J. C. Harris, "Indian and Negro Myths," *Critic,* 9 September 1882, 239. [Joel Chandler Harris], "Sun-Myths and Negro Stories," *Atlanta Constitution* (29 December 1885). Harris eventually expressed his disdain for the professional folklorists in a parody, "The Late Mr. Watkins of Georgia: His Relation to Oriental Folk-Lore," in *Tales of the Home Folks in Peace and War* (Boston: Houghton Mifflin and Company, 1898), 97–113. For the development of this debate, see the following: A. F. Chamberlain, "African and American: The Contact of Negro and Indian," *Science* 17 (1891): 85–90; Frank Gouldsmith Speck, "The Negroes and the Creek Nation," *Southern Workman* 27 (1908): 106–10; J. H. Johnson, "Documentary Evidence of the Relations of Negroes and Indians," *Journal of Negro History* 14 (1929): 21–43. On Uncle Remus's centrality to this debate, it is useful to consult the annual reports on current research in the new folklore journals. In 1889, *Folklore* describes the evidence for the diffusion thesis only to concede that the case "cannot be deemed to be wholly solved" until "thorough and scholarly" attention is paid to the "problem" of the "origin" of the Uncle Remus tales. E. Sidney Hartland, "Report on Folk-Tale Research in 1889," *Folklore* 1 (1890): 113. Three years later the journal would again frame the "burning question of folk-tale diffusion" around Uncle Remus. Noting that "the place of origin

of any folk-tale" is often "regarded as insoluble," the journal argues that such "disbelief" is "premature" given the promising research that was already being done into Uncle Remus's tar baby story. See the following: E. Sidney Hartland, "Report on Folk-Tale Research," *Folklore* 4 (1892): 82, 85, 90. Crane, "Plantation Folk-Lore," 824–33. W. A. Clouston, "'Uncle Remus' and Some European Popular Tales," *Notes and Queries* 7 (1890): 301–2. Joseph Jacobs, *Indian Fairy Tales* (London: David Nutt, 1892), 251–53. F. M. Warren, "'Uncle Remus' and 'The Roman de Renard,'" *Modern Language Notes* 5 (May 1890): 257–70. Lee J. Vance, "Folk-Lore Study in America," *Popular Science Monthly* 43 (1893): 586–88, 596, 598. It was not uncommon for commentators to scoff at the idea that stories like the tar baby could have been "an independent conception among the aborigines of Africa," as they believed there was no such thing as African culture. See Gerber, "Uncle Remus Traced to the Old World," 264. For critical discussion of the debate after the original publication of the Uncle Remus stories, see the following: Joseph Griska, "Uncle Remus Correspondence: The Development and Reception of Joel Chandler Harris's Writing, 1880–1885," *American Literary Realism* (1981): 26–37; Brasch, *Brer Rabbit, Uncle Remus, and the 'Cornfield Journalist,'* 70–74; Brad Evans, *Before Cultures: The Ethnographic Imagination in American Literature, 1865–1920* (Chicago: University of Chicago Press, 2005), 51–81. This debate was rekindled in the 1960s and 1970s, following Richard Dorson's claim that the "first declaration to make is that this body of tales does not come from Africa." Richard M. Dorson, *American Negro Folktales* (Greenwich, CT: Fawcett Publications, 1967), 15; William D. Pierson, "An African Background for American Negro Folktales?" *Journal of American Folklore* 84 (1971): 204–14; William Bascom, "Folklore and the Africanist," *Journal of American Folklore* 86 (1973): 253–59; Richard M. Dorson, "African and Afro-American Folklore: A Reply to Bascom and Other Misguided Critics," *Journal of American Folklore* 88 (1975): 151–64; Alan Dundes, "African and Afro-American Tales," *Research in African Literatures* 7 (1976): 181–99; On diffusion as the motor for cultural syncretism, see Sidney W. Mintz, "Creating Culture in the Americas," *Columbia University Forum* 13 (1970): 4–11.

8. William Wells Newell, "Individual and Collective Characteristics in Folk-Lore," *Journal of American Folklore* 19 (1906), 4–5. Newell explains that folklore scholarship had been committed to the assumptions of romantic nationalism, associated with Jacob and Wilhelm Grimm, which proposed that nations and races were bound by an organic unity expressed in culture. Increasingly, the wayward diffusion of stories like the tar baby caused scholars to question whether culture was more capricious than they had previously thought. See also Franz Boas, "The Occurrence of Similar Inventions in Areas Widely Apart," *Science* (1887): 485–86.

9. Parsons, "Provenience of Certain Negro Folk Tales: Tar Baby," 227–34. Elsie Clews Parsons, "Tar Baby," *Journal of American Folklore* 35 (1922): 330. Boas, *Race, Language and Culture*, 520–22. Mooney, "Myths of the Cherokees," 97–108. Franz Boas, "Dissemination of Tales among the Natives of North America," *Journal of American Folklore* 4 (1891): 13–20. Chamberlain, "African and American," 85–90. James Mooney, *Myths of the Cherokee* (Washington, DC: Government Printing Office, 1902), 232–36. Frank Gouldsmith Speck, "The Negroes and the Creek Nation," 106–10. Franz Boas, "Mythology and Folk-Tales of the North American Indians," *Journal of American Folklore* 27 (1914): 374–410. John M. McBryde, "Brer Rabbit in the Folk-tales of the Negro and Other Races," *Sewanee Review* 19 (1911): 185–206. Paul Radin, *Literary Aspects of North American Mythology* (Ottawa: Government Printing Bureau, 1915), 8, 29–30, 47–50. J. H. Johnson, "Documentary Evidence of the Rela-

tions of Negroes and Indians," *Journal of Negro History* 14 (1929): 21–43. For a summary of the evolution of this debate in later decades, see Alan Dundes, "African Tales among the North American Indians," *Southern Folklore Quarterly* 29 (1965): 207–19. On the tar baby's potential origins in Western Europe including its relation to the Roman de Renard, see the following: Lee J. Vance, "Plantation Folk-Lore," *Open Court* 2 (1888): 1029–32, 1074–76, 1092–95; Thomas F. Crane, "The Diffusion of Popular Tales," *Journal of American Folklore* 1 (1888): 8–15; F. M. Warren, " 'Uncle Remus' and 'The Roman de Renard,' " 129–35; A. Gerber, F. M. Warren, S. Garner, O. B. Super, J. B. Henneman, and W. A. Clouston, " 'Uncle Remus' and Some European Popular Tales," *Notes and Queries* 7 (1890): 301–2; F. M. Warren, S. Garner, O. B. Super, J. B. Henneman, S. Garner, and A. Gerber, "The Tales of Uncle Remus Traced to the Old World," *Publications of the Modern Language Association of America* (1892): xxxix–xliii; Lee J. Vance, "Folk-Lore Study in America," 586–88, 596, 598; Annie Weston Whitney, "De los' ell an' Yard," *Journal of American Folklore* 10 (1897): 293–98; C. W. Previte Orton, "Uncle Remus in Tuscany," *Notes and Queries* 10 (1904): 183–84; Parsons, "Provenience of Certain Negro Folk-Tales," 408–14; Elsie Clews Parsons, *Folk-lore from the Cape Verde Islands* (Cambridge, MA: American Folk-lore Society, 1923), 30–33, 90–94; Aurelio M. Espinosa, "European Versions of the Tar-Baby Story," *Folklore* 40 (1929): 217–27; Aurelio M. Espinosa, "A Third European Version of the Tar-Baby Story." *Journal of American Folklore* 43 (1930): 329–31; J. W. Ashton, "A Fourth European Tar Baby Story," *Journal of American Folklore* 45 (1932): 267–68; Archer Taylor, "The Tarbaby Once More," *Journal of the American Oriental Society* 64 (1944), 4–7. On precedents in Spain and Portugal and generally on the story's hispanophone diffusion, see the following: Charles Carroll Marden, "Some Mexican Versions of the 'Brer Rabbit Stories,' " *Mod-*

ern Language Notes 11 (1896): 22–23; Boas, "Notes on Mexican Folk-Lore," 235–39; Aurelio M. Espinosa, "Comparative Notes on New-Mexican and Mexican Spanish Folk-Tales," *Journal of American Folklore* 27 (1914): 211–31; Aurelio M. Espinosa, "A Folk-Lore Expedition to Spain," *Journal of American Folklore* 34 (1921): 129; J. Alden Mason, "Porto-Rican Folk-Lore. Folk-Tales (Continued)," *Journal of American Folklore* 35 (1922): 35; Aurelio M. Espinosa, "New Mexican Versions of the Tar-Baby Story," *New Mexico Quarterly* 1 (1931): 85–104; Aurelio M. Espinosa. "Another New Mexico Version of the Tar-Baby Story," *New Mexico Quarterly* 3 (1933): 31–36; Aurelio M. Espinosa, "More Spanish Folk-Tales," *Hispania* 22 (1939): 103–14; Aurelio M. Espinosa, "Three More Peninsular Spanish Folktales That Contain the Tar-Baby Story," *Folklore* 50 (1939): 366–77; Aurelio M. Espinosa, "Peninsular Spanish Versions of the Tar-Baby Story," *Journal of American Folklore* 56 (1944): 210–11; Laurence Cecil Boydstun, "Classification and Analysis of the Spanish-American Versions of the Tar-Baby Story" (dissertation, Stanford University, 1947); Aurelio M. Espinosa, "Spanish and Spanish-American Folk Tales," *Journal of American Folklore* 64 (1951): 151–62; Enrique Margery, "The Tar-Baby Motif," *Latin American Literatures Journal* 6 (1990): 1–13. On the story's francophone diffusion and the possibility that it arrived in North America through Louisiana before making its way to Georgia, North Carolina, and Virginia, see the following: Alcée Fortier, "Bits of Louisiana Folk-Lore," *Transactions and Proceedings of the Modern Language Association of America* 3 (1887): 101–15; Alcée Fortier, *Louisiana Folk-Tales: In French Dialect and English Translation* (Boston and New York: Houghton, Mifflin and Company, 1895), 35, 95–96, 98–109; George Reinecke, "The African 'Tar-Baby' Tale: Its Survival in Creole Louisiana," *Urban Resources* 4 (1967): 18; Barry Jean Ancelet, *Cajun and Creole Folktales: The French Oral Tradition of South Louisiana*

(New York, Garland, 1993), 5–8. Even Herskovits was prepared to admit the difficulty. "The Uncle Remus, or Anansi,
stories found in the United States, or Jamaica, which parallel
animal tales all over the African continent, also resemble so
closely as to remove the similarities from the dictates of
chance the fables of Aesop, the Reynard cycle of Europe, the
Panchatantra of India, and the Jātakas tales of China, to
name but a few of the best-known series." Herskovits, *Myth
of the Negro Past*, 273.

10. For influential reformulations of these questions in the late
twentieth century, see the following: Roger Bastide, *African
Civilizations in the New World* (New York: Harper and Row,
1971); Sidney W. Mintz, *Caribbean Transformations* (Chi-
cago: Aldine Publishing Company, 1974); Edward Kamau
Brathwaite, *Folk Culture of the Slaves in Jamaica* (London:
New Beacon Books, 1981); Robert Farris Thompson, *Flash
of the Spirit: African and Afro-American Art and Philosophy*
(New York: Vintage Books, 1984); Sterling Stuckey, *Slave
Culture: Nationalist Theory and the Foundations of Black
America* (New York: Oxford University Press, 1987); Sidney
W. Mintz and Richard Price, *The Birth of African-American
Culture: An Anthropological Perspective* (Boston: Beacon,
1992); Gwendolyn Midlo Hall, *Africans in Colonial Louisi-
ana the Development of Afro-Creole Culture in the Eighteenth
Century* (Baton Rouge: Louisiana State University Press,
1992); Paul Gilroy, *The Black Atlantic: Modernity and
Double-Consciousness* (Cambridge, MA: Harvard University
Press, 1993); Michael Gomez, *Exchanging Our Country
Marks: The Transformation of African Identities in the Colonial
and Antebellum South* (Chapel Hill: University of North
Carolina Press, 1998).

11. Joseph Jacobs, *Indian Fairy Tales*, 9, 251–53; Joseph Jacobs,
The Earliest English Version of The Fables of Bidpai (London:
David Nutt, 1888), xliv–xlvi; Joseph Jacobs, *The Fables of
Aesop as First Printed by William Caxton* (London: David

Nutt, 1889), 113, 136–37. This argument is summarized by Adolph Gerber. "Brer Rabbit," Gerber writes, "has taken the place of Buddha himself in the story of the Tar-Baby." Adolph Gerber, "Great Russian Animal Tales," *Publications of the Modern Language Association of America* 6 (1891): 85. See also "Mr. Joel C. Harris and Buddha," *New York Times*, 10 April 1897. Before Espinosa, the most systematic elaboration of Jacobs's theory appears in Oskar Dähnhardt, *Natursagen: Eine Sammlung naturdeutender Sagen Märchen Fabeln und Legenden*, 4 vols. (Leipzig and Berlin: B. G. Teubner, 1907–12), 4:26–45. Elaborating on this theory, Ruth Cline claims that the tar baby was originally a water sprite. Ruth I. Cline, "The Tar-Baby Story," *American Literature* 2 (1930): 72–78. See also Ananda K. Coomaraswamy, "A Note on the Stickfast Motif," *Journal of American Folklore* 57 (1944): 128–31. For the theory about Portuguese sailors, see Boas, *Race, Language and Culture*, 520–22. On the tar baby's circulation in Japan, Indonesia, and the Phillipines, see the following: William Elliot Griffis, "The Original of Uncle Remus Tar Baby in Japan," *The Folk-lorist* 1 (1892): 146–49; William Elliot Griffis, *The Japanese Nation in Evolution: Steps in the Progress of a Great People* (London: George G. Harrap, 1907); 115–16. Otto Mänchen-Helfen, "Zu den Zwerghirschgeschichten," *Anthropos* 30 (1935): 554–57; W. H. Millington and Berton L. Maxfield, "Visayan Folk-Tales III," *Journal of American Folklore* (1907): 311–18; Dean S. Fansler, *Filipino Popular Tales* (New York: G.E. Stechert & Co., 1921), 326–37, 342.

12. Espinosa, "Notes on the Origin," 129–209; Espinosa, "More Notes," 168–81; Espinosa, "New Classification," 31–37. Melville Herskovits regards Espinosa's theory as "scarely tenable" given that it was based on "one or two" versions when the general "weighting" of "distribution" was "toward Africa." "New World Negroes," Herskovits adds, "have everywhere preserved this story, many versions of it having been

recorded in Brazil, the Guianas, and the West Indies, in addition to its famous nominative form from the United States." Herskovits, "Tar Baby," 1104. On the Finnish historical-geographical method geared to detection of "cognate parallels," see Alan Dundes, "The Anthropologist and the Comparative Method in Folklore," *Journal of Folklore Research* 23 (1986): 125–46.

13. Summarizing his polemic, Espinosa writes: "In spite of the fact that the tar-baby story has been found in India and practically all the countries settled by Europeans, the erroneous theory still prevails that it is of African origin." Espinosa, "Notes on the Origin," 217. On anti-African bias in comparative tale-type analysis, see Alan Dundes, "The Motif-Index and the Tale Type Index: A Critique," *Journal of Folklore Research* 34 (1997): 195–202. On the ideophone and honorific titles as African retentions, see Baer, *Sources and Analogues of the Uncle Remus Tales*, 41–42, 167. Given the disagreement between Espinosa and Herskovits about the diffusion of the tar baby, it is striking that Herskovits also imagines that the flow of culture can be objectively charted precisely in the ways that Espinosa tries to achieve with the tar baby. Melville J. Herskovits, "The Negro in the New World: The Statement of a Problem," *American Anthropologist* 32 (1930): 149. From the start, collectors concerned with the tar baby's circulation tried to manage these problems by deferring their final analysis to an unspecified point in the future. Other times they simply engaged in colorful speculation. "The event of a canoe-load of visitors from another island," Charlotte Sophia Burne writes, "a stay of a single night, a sociable evening spent together, and a story may be left behind to be told and retold from generation to generation, and perhaps to afford evidence of former communication between peoples since separated by warfare, by migration, by wholesale shipwreck, or some other catastrophe." Burne, *The Handbook of Folklore*, 266.

14. Franz Boas, *Race, Language and Culture*, 520. Thomas F. Crane, "The Diffusion of Popular Tales," 14.
15. Aurelio M. Espinosa, "New-Mexican Spanish Folk-Lore," *Journal of American Folklore* 23 (1910): 395. Arguments about the "probable origins" of the tar baby and related stories, Paul Radin complains, are merely "opinion based on impression." Paul Radin, "The Nature and Problems of Mexican Indian Mythology," *Journal of American Folklore* 57 (1944): 28. "With the material in our hands at present," Franz Boas confesses, "it is impossible to decide just what happened." Boas, *Race, Language and Culture*, 521. "As to the origin of these stories," C. C. Marden proposes in 1896, "nothing definite can be said. They may be indigenous, they may be borrowed from the negroes of Texas and other Southern States, they may represent folk-lore of the West Indies, or they may be popular versions of the European collections which were introduced by the Spaniards." Marden, "Some Mexican Versions of the 'Brer Rabbit' Stories," 46. On the importance of the rhetoric of deferral to the paradigm of folklore study in its early years, see William Wells Newell, "Additional Collection Essential to Correct Theory in Folklore and Mythology," *Journal of American Folklore* 3 (1890): 23–32. The feud between Espinosa and Norman Brown over the origin of the tar baby story is recorded in their correspondence with Ruth Benedict. See Folders 1.5–2.7, Ruth Fulton Benedict Papers, Archives and Special Collections Library, Vassar College Libraries. "Now it is one of the fundamental methodological principles of anthropology," Benedict explains to Brown about his polemic against Espinosa, "that *direction* of diffusion cannot be shown except when there is some special circumstance that gives us relative dates" (Ruth Benedict to Norman Brown, 14 November 1932, Folder 2.6, Ruth Benedict Fulton Papers, Archives and Special Collections Library, Vassar College Libraries). See also Claude Brèmond, "Traitement des Motifs dans un Index des Ruses," in

Geneviève Calame-Griaule, Veronika Görög-Karady, and Michèle Chiche, eds., *Le Conte, Pourquoi? Comment?* (Paris, Éd. du CNRS, 1984), 35–52. On the early formulation of the age-area hypothesis, see especially Clark Wissler, *The American Indian* (New York: McMurtrie, 1917).

16. For James Scott, "little traditions" like the tar baby were organized to solicit identification with the trickster to legitimate the "evasive and cunning" tactics employed by oppressed populations throughout the world. James C. Scott, *Weapons of the Weak: Everyday Forms of Peasant Resistance* (New Haven, CT: Yale University Press, 1985), 300. This approach to the tar baby has been predominant since the 1970s, but it has also been evident across the history of its interpretation. Following an approach taken by Abbie Holmes Christensen, William Owens, and Joel Chandler Harris, for example, an anonymous critic would suggest in 1881 that the "selection of the rabbit as hero" was anything but accidental, as the rabbit was "surrounded on every side by enemies" and "liable to attack from every quarter and from almost every creature," a situation that "resembled" the condition of his storytellers. "Brer Rabbit," *Saturday Review,* 51 (1881), 363–65. The "choice of the hero," John McBryde agrees, was based on the shared experiences of oppressed people, as is shown in "the folk-tales of Africa, of the Indians of North America, and even of distant Asia," which when taken together demonstrate that "the rabbit is the hero" of common people throughout the world. McBryde, "Brer Rabbit in the Folk-tales of the Negro and Other Races," 188. See also Paul Radin, *The Trickster* (New York: Philosophical Library, 1956).

17. Scott, *Weapons of the Weak*, 241–303. A brilliant application of Scott's concept of the hidden transcript appears in Robin D. G. Kelley, " 'We Are Not What We Seem': Rethinking Black Working-Class Opposition in the Jim Crow South," *Journal of American History* (1993): 75–112.

18. Benjamin Botkin describes this intuitive identification as "in line with the universal tendency on the part of oppressed people to identify themselves with the weaker and triumphant animal in the pitting of brains against brute force and superior strength." B. A. Botkin, "Brer Rabbit," *Funk and Wagnalls Standard Dictionary of Folklore, Mythology, and Legend*, 2 vols. (New York: Funk and Wagnalls, 1950), 1:163. See also Benjamin A. Botkin, "The Slave as His Own Interpreter," *Library of Congress Quarterly Journal of Current Acquisitions* 2 (1944): 37–63; Sterling Brown, "Negro Folk Expression: Spirituals, Seculars, Ballads and Work Songs," *Phylon* 14 (1953): 45–61; Roger D. Abrahams, *Deep Down in the Jungle: Negro Narrative Folklore from the Streets of Philadelphia* (Hatboro, PA: Folklore Associates, 1964), 65–86; Bill R. Hampton, "On Identification and Negro Tricksters," *Southern Folklore Quarterly* 31 (1967): 55–65; Lewis Hyde, *Trickster Makes This World: Mischief, Myth, and Art* (New York: Macmillan Publishing, 1999). For an influential tropological account that follows the trickster from oral tradition into African American literature, see Henry Louis Gates, Jr., *The Signifying Monkey: A Theory of African-American Literary Criticism* (New York: Oxford University Press, 1988)

19. The new social history derives much of its methodology and many of its preoccupations from the precedent set in E. P. Thompson, *The Making of the English Working Class* (London: Victor Gollansz Limited, 1963). The tar baby has remained a point of reference especially for the new social history of North American slavery. Charles Nichols, *Many Thousand Gone: The Ex-Slaves' Account of Their Bondage and Freedom* (Leiden, Netherlands: Brill, 1963); Julius Lester, *To Be a Slave* (New York: Dial Press, 1968); Eileen Southern, *The Music of Black Americans: A History* (New York: W. W. Norton, 1971); John W. Blassingame, *The Slave Community: Plantation Life in the Antebellum South* (New York: Oxford

University Press, 1972); George P. Rawick, *From Sundown to Sunup: The Making of the Black Community* (Westport, CT: Greenwood Press, 1972); Peter H. Wood, *Black Majority: Negroes in Colonial South Carolina from 1670 through the Stono Rebellion* (New York: Alfred A. Knopf, 1974); Gladys-Marie Fry, *Night Riders in Black Folk History* (Knoxville: University of Tennessee Press, 1975); Herbert G. Gutman, *The Black Family in Slavery and Freedom, 1750–1925* (New York: Pantheon Books, 1976); Willie Lee Rose, *A Documentary History of Slavery in North America* (Oxford University Press, 1976); Leslie H. Owens, *This Species of Property: Slave Life and Culture in the Old South* (New York: Oxford University Press, 1977); Lawrence W. Levine, *Black Culture and Black Consciousness: Afro-American Thought from Slavery to Freedom* (New York: Oxford University Press, 1977); Albert J. Raboteau, *Slave Religion: The "Invisible Institution" in the Antebellum South* (New York: Oxford University Press, 1978); Deborah Gray White, *Ar'n't I a Woman: Female Slaves in the Plantation South* (New York: W. W. Norton, 1985); Charles Joyner, *Down by the Riverside: A South Carolina Slave Community* (Urbana: University of Illinois Press, 1985); Jacqueline Jones, *Labor of Love, Labor of Sorrow: Black Women, Work, and the Family from Slavery to the Present* (New York: Basic Books, 1985); John W. Roberts, *From Trickster to Badman: The Black Folk Hero in Slavery and Freedom* (Philadelphia: University of Pennsylvania Press, 1990); Roger D. Abrahams, *Singing the Master: The Emergence of African American Culture in the Plantation South* (New York: Pantheon Books, 1992); Tera W. Hunter, *To 'Joy My Freedom: Southern Black Women's Lives and Labors after the Civil War* (Cambridge, MA: Harvard University Press, 1997); Stephanie M. H. Camp, *Closer to Freedom: Enslaved Women and Everyday Resistance in the Plantation South* (Chapel Hill: University of North Carolina Press, 2004); Stephanie A. Smallwood, *Saltwater Slavery: A Middle Passage from Africa to*

American Diaspora (Cambridge, MA: Harvard University Press, 2007).

20. Raymond A. Bauer and Alice H. Bauer, "Day to Day Resistance to Slavery," *Journal of Negro History* 27 (1942): 388–419. Kenneth M. Stampp, *The Peculiar Institution: Slavery in the Antebellum South* (New York: Knopf, 1956), 86–140. George Fredrickson and Christopher Lasch, "Resistance to Slavery," *Civil War History* 13 (1967): 315–329. Blassingame, *Slave Community* (1972 ed.), 105–48. Rawick, *Sundown to Sunup*, 95–119. Levine, *Black Culture and Black Consciousness*, 121–28. White, *Ar'n't I a Woman*, 91–141. Robin D. G. Kelley, *Race Rebels: Culture, Politics, and the Black Working Class* (New York: The Free Press, 1994), 17–102. Hunter, *To 'Joy My Freedom*, 44–73. On social crime and other "pre-political" acts, see Eric Hobsbawm, *Primitive Rebels: Studies in Archaic Forms of Social Movement* (Manchester: Manchester University Press, 1959). On everyday resistance as an accommodation to existing conditions, see Eugene Genovese, *Roll, Jordan, Roll: The World the Slaves Made* (New York, Pantheon, 1974), 597–609. See also James Oakes, "The Political Significance of Slave Resistance," *History Workshop Journal* 22 (1986), 89–107. For a critique of the concept of the pre-political, see Ranajit Guha, *Elementary Aspects of Peasant Insurgency in Colonial India* (New Delhi: Oxford University Press, 1983), 1–17, 77–108. For theoretical synthesis of the debate over social crime and everyday resistance, see Stuart Hall, Chas Critcher, Tony Jefferson, John Clarke, and Brian Roberts, *Policing the Crisis: Mugging, the State and Law and Order* (London: Macmillan Publishing, 1978), 181–217.

21. As an alternative to the "great men" featured in more conventional histories, Certeau imagines an "anonymous hero" who "is the murmur of societies." He adds: "Popular cultures, proverbs, tales, folk wisdom, have long seemed to be the place in which such a hero might be sought and reidenti-

fied." Michel de Certeau, "On the Oppositional Practices of Everyday Life," *Social Text* 3 (1980): 3. For elaboration on this concept of "practice," see Saidiya V. Hartman, *Scenes of Subjection: Terror, Slavery, and Self-Making in Nineteenth-Century America* (New York: Oxford University Press, 1997), 49–78.

22. Zora Neale Hurston, *Mules and Men* (Philadelphia: J. B. Lippincott, 1935), 1. Boas, *Race, Language, and Culture*, 191–95. Clifford Geertz, *The Interpretation of Cultures* (New York: Basic Books, 1973), 448, 5. See also James Clifford, *The Predicament of Culture: Twentieth-Century Ethnography, Literature, and Art* (Cambridge, MA: Harvard University Press, 1988). On the culture concept in the new social history, see Daniel T. Rodgers, *Age of Fracture* (Cambridge, MA: Harvard University Press, 2011), 77–110. On associated intellectual movements, see Michael Denning, *Culture in the Age of Three Worlds* (London: Verso, 2004), 75–168.

23. Roger D. Abrahams, *Positively Black* (Englewood Cliffs, NJ: Prentice Hall, 1970), 52, 53, 90. Houston Baker, *Black Literature in America* (New York: McGraw Hill, 1971), 22–23. Genovese, *Roll, Jordan, Roll*, 1, 486–87, 535. Wood, *Black Majority*, 209–11, 217. Philip S. Foner, *History of Black Americans: From Africa to the Emergence of the Cotton Kingdom* (Westport, CT: Greenwood Press, 1975), 82. Owens, *This Species of Property*, 121–22. Levine, *Black Culture and Black Consciousness*, 125–30. Raboteau, *Slave Religion*, 285. John W. Blassingame, *The Slave Community: Plantation Life in the Antebellum South*, rev. ed. (New York: Oxford University Press, 1979), 21, 26, 31–32, 57, 122, 128. Robert Hemenway, "Introduction," in Joel Chandler Harris, *Uncle Remus: His Songs and His Sayings*, ed. Robert Hemenway (New York: Penguin Books, 1982), 26–27. Joyner, *Down by the Riverside*, 177, 194. Stuckey, *Slave Culture*, 17–22, 35, 38, 40, 57, 169, 256. Roberts, *From Trickster to Badman*, 17–64. Leon F. Litwack, *Trouble in Mind: Black Southerners*

in the Age of Jim Crow (New York: Alfred A. Knopf, 1998), 26, 43, 187.

24. Harold Cruse long ago complained that the historiography of slave resistance had reduced the politics of the enslaved to interest-group agitation, representing the individuals involved as rational actors seeking to maximize their own welfare. Interpretation of the tar baby has exhibited a similar tendency, representing the rabbit as always intrinsically self-centered and his victory therefore as a clever response to short-term necessity. The irony in this interpretation, as I attempt to show in this book, is that it conflates the concept of economic rationality derived from the zero-sum game staged at the story's outset with the freedom the rabbit finds at the end. Rational choice is important to the story, but it is relevant primarily as a foil that helps to define the freedom found in the briar patch. Harold Cruse, *Crisis of the Negro Intellectual: A Historical Analysis of the Failure of Negro Leadership* (New York: William Morrow, 1967), 206–24. Cruse is writing in response to Herbert Aptheker, *American Negro Slave Revolts* (New York: Columbia University Press, 1943). Following Aptheker's line of interpretation, Michael Flusche attributes a style of rational-choice agency to the trickster tradition: "The common trait of these characters was their relentless pursuit of their own self-interest as they outrageously flaunted social conventions and their companions' expectations." Michael Flusche, "Joel Chandler Harris and the Folklore of Slavery," *Journal of American Studies* 9 (1975): 352.

25. The "individual and the event," John and Jean Comaroff write, "have everywhere to be treated as problematic." They continue: "Just how are they constituted, culturally and historically? What determines, or renders indeterminate, the actions of human beings in the world? What decides whether, in the first place, the bounded individual is even a salient unit of subjectivity?" John and Jean Comaroff, "Ethnography

and the Historical Imagination," in John and Jean Comaroff, *Ethnography and the Historical Imagination* (Boulder, CO: Westview Press, 1992), 26–27. On the "'naturally articulate' subject of oppression" as fantasy as well as "implicit demand, made by intellectuals," see Gayatri Chakravorty Spivak, "Can the Subaltern Speak?" in *Marxism and the Interpretation of Culture*, ed. Cary Nelson and Lawrence Grossberg (Urbana: University of Illinois Press, 1988), 271–313. On various problems attending the concept of agency, see especially the following: Walter Johnson, "On Agency," *Journal of Social History* 37 (2003): 113–24; Hartman, *Scenes of Subjection*, 115–63; William H. Sewell, "A Theory of Structure: Duality, Agency and Transformation," *American Journal of Sociology* 98 (1992): 1–29; Joan W. Scott, "The Evidence of Experience," *Critical Inquiry* 17 (1991): 773–97.

26. My attempt in this book to understand the tar baby as coextensive with these competing philosophical traditions owes much to the critical example set by Stephan Palmié. "The contrasts resulting from typological reconstructions," Palmié writes, "impart artificial closure to 'traditions' that should initially be approached as fuzzy sets of ideas and practices whose boundedness in social space needs to be established rather than presumed." He continues, describing "the need to shift our focus away from conventional emphases on integration, homogeneity, boundedness, and seemingly passive 'endemic' reproduction of social and cultural forms and toward perspectives capable of analytically accommodating constellations of heterogeneous but contiguous, perhaps overlapping, forms of knowledge and practice: 'syndromatic' clusterings of cultural materials whose distribution in local social space at specific temporal junctures need coincide neither with their historical origins, nor with structurally identifiable collectivities, nor even with the boundaries maintained by self-identified social groups." Stephan Palmié, *Wizards and Scientists: Explorations in Afro-*

Cuban Modernity and Tradition (Durham: Duke University Press, 2002), 115, 139.

CHAPTER 2. STATES OF NATURE

1. Robin D. G. Kelley and Earl Lewis, *To Make Our World Anew: A History of African Americans* (New York: Oxford University Press, 2000), 181–82. An excellent overview of the African American vernacular tradition is available in the following anthologies and annotated bibliography. Bruce Jackson, ed., *The Negro and His Folklore in Nineteenth-Century Periodicals* (Austin: University of Texas Press, 1967). Alan Dundes, ed., *Mother Wit from the Laughing Barrel: Readings in the Interpretation of Afro-American Folklore* (Englewood Cliffs, NJ: Prentice-Hall, 1973). Eileen Southern and Josephine Wright, *African-American Traditions in Song, Sermon, Tale, and Dance, 1600s–1920* (New York: Greenwood Press, 1990).

2. This interpretation was elaborated in histories like Kenneth Stampp's *The Peculiar Institution* (1956), which made resistance into one of the central themes in the study of slavery. "The tales of Br'er Rabbit, in all their variations," Stampp asserts (p. 367), "made virtues of such qualities as wit, strategy, and deceit—the weapons of the weak in their battles with the strong." On the politics of the trickster tradition in the context of slavery and its aftermath, see the following. Hurston, *Mules and Men*. Sterling Allen Brown, Arthur Paul Davis, and Ulysses Lee, eds., *The Negro Caravan* (New York: Dryden Press, 1941). Benjamin A. Botkin, ed., *Lay My Burden Down: A Folk History of Slavery* (Chicago: University of Chicago Press, 1945). Arna Bontemps and Langston Hughes, eds., *The Book of Negro Folklore* (New York: Dodd, Mead, 1958). The standard themes in Kelley and Lewis's interpretation are anticipated in the following works. Abrahams, *Posi-*

tively Black, 52, 53, 90. Houston Baker, *Black Literature in America* (New York: McGraw-Hill, 1971), 22–23. Genovese, *Roll, Jordan, Roll*, 1, 486–87, 535. Wood, *Black Majority*, 209–11, 217. Foner, *History of Black Americans*, 82. Owens, *This Species of Property*, 121–22. Levine, *Black Culture and Black Consciousness*, 125–30. Raboteau, *Slave Religion*, 285. Blassingame, *The Slave Community* (1979 ed.), 21, 26, 31–32, 57, 122, 128. Joyner, *Down by the Riverside*, 177, 194. Stuckey, *Slave Culture*, 17–22, 35, 38, 40, 57, 169, 256. Roberts, *From Trickster to Badman*, 17–64. Litwack, *Trouble in Mind*, 26, 43, 187.

3. Harris, *Uncle Remus: His Songs and His Sayings* (1881), 9. Christensen, *Afro-American Folk Lore*, xi–xii.

4. Langston Hughes and Arna Wendell Bontemps, *The Book of Negro Folklore* (New York: Dodd, Mead, 1958), vii–xv. John Mason Brewer, *American Negro Folklore* (Chicago: Quadrangle Books, 1968), 3–4. Houston A. Baker, *Long Black Song: Essays in Black American Literature and Culture* (Charlottesville: University Press of Virginia, 1972), 22. Baker's use of the masculine ("black man") is a tendency that occasionally surfaces in commentary on the tar baby, building on the representation of the rabbit's bravado and appetite. Blassingame, *Slave Community* (1972 ed.), 57. Levine, *Black Culture and Black Consciousness*, 112–15. It was also common for historians to invoke the rabbit as a metaphor. "Blacks," Robert Cruden writes, "had to learn to take advantage of every conscious or unconscious opportunity afforded by white power. . . . They were 'Br'er Rabbit' to the white 'Br'er Fox.'" Robert Cruden, *The Negro in Reconstruction* (Englewood Cliffs, NJ: Prentice-Hall, 1969), 105. Describing the wily strategies adopted by African American power brokers such as Booker T. Washington, John Hope Franklin and August Meier describe the necessity of working in the "cracks" of society, moving like "Brer Rabbit through the brier patch," and thereby outwitting "powerful whites." John Hope Frank-

lin and August Meier, eds., *Black Leaders of the Twentieth Century* (Urbana: University of Illinois Press, 1982), 9

5. Kelley and Lewis, *To Make Our World Anew*, 181–82. Elsie Clews Parsons notes that the tar baby "almost always" begins with theft. "The most notable exception" to this pattern, Parsons explains, appears ironically in the "most familiar of all the versions of the tale," namely the one attributed to Uncle Remus. Elsie Clews Parsons, "The Provenience of Certain Negro Folk Tales: Tar Baby," *Folklore* 30 (1919): 227. Alan Dundes speculates that this "omission" may have resulted from the disproportionate attention devoted to the version that appeared in "Joel Chandler Harris's Uncle Remus books." Dundes, "African and Afro-American Tales," 182–83. See also John F. Callahan, *In the African-American Grain* (Urbana: University of Illinois Press, 1988), 34–35. For another exception, in this case a story that features the stickfast sequence as a standalone unit without context or resolution, see the story "Coyote and the Stump" in Edward Sapir, "Yana Texts," *University of California Publications in American Archaeology and Ethnology* 9 (1919): 227–28. It is worth noting that Harris restores the characteristic opening scene in a later version set in verse, which begins: "In Levemteen Hunder'd-an'-Full-er-Fleas, / When dey raise sech a crap er gooba peas, / De creeturs wuz all des ez chummy ez you please. . . . An' dey wa'n't no doubt, an' no perhaps, / Dat dey holp one anudder out wid der craps." This cooperation is soon interrupted, however, by the rabbit's selfish actions. Joel Chandler Harris, *The Tar-Baby, and Other Rhymes of Uncle Remus* (New York: D. Appleton & Company, 1904), 3.

6. Abrahams, *Positively Black*, 52, 53, 90. Genovese, *Roll, Jordan, Roll*, 1, 486–87, 535. Wood, *Black Majority*, 209–11, 217. Foner, *History of Black Americans*, 82. Owens, *This Species of Property*, 121–22. Levine, *Black Culture and Black Consciousness*, 125–30. Raboteau, *Slave Religion*, 285. Joyner, *Down by the Riverside*, 177, 194. Stuckey, *Slave Culture*,

17–22, 35, 38, 40, 57, 169, 256. Roberts, *From Trickster to Badman*, 17–64. Litwack, *Trouble in Mind*, 26, 43, 187. A review published in the *Saturday Review* in 1881 anticipates this strain of criticism, describing the tar baby story as an example of "allegorized resistance." Noting fox's superior strength and sharp teeth and the rabbit's "ridiculously inadequate weapons of self-defense," the reviewer poses this interpretation as a rhetorical question: "What more natural allegory," she asks, "than the quarrel of the wolf with the fox?" "Brer Rabbit," *Saturday Review* 51 (19 March 1881), 363–65.

7. Parsons, "Tar Baby," 227. Elsie Clews Parsons, *Folk-lore from the Cape Verde Islands* (Cambridge: American Folk-lore Society, 1923), 30–33, 90–94. Charles Baissac, *Le Folk-lore de L'Isle-Maurice* (Paris: Maisonneuve et C. Leclere, 1888), 2–14. Provisional statistics on thief-catching and other motifs are provided in Espinosa, "Notes on the Origin," 183–204.

8. Mooney explains that the tar baby has variants not only "among the Cherokee" but also in "New Mexico, Washington, and southern Alaska—wherever, in fact, the piñon or the pine supplies enough gum to be molded into a ball for Indian uses." For Mooney, the primacy of this geneaology is proven by the fact that stories similar to the tar baby are told by "widely separated tribes among whom there can be no suspicion of Negro influences." Mooney, *Myths of the Cherokee*, 233–34. For recent examples and including some extensions of Mooney's argument, see the following: Anne Dyk, ed., "Tarbaby," in *Mixteco Texts* (Norman, OK: Summer Institute of Linguistics of the University of Oklahoma, 1959), 3344; Pedro Aguilar, "The Rabbit and the Coyote," in *Mitla Zapotec Texts: Folklore Texts in Mexican Indian Languages*, ed. Carol Stubblefield and Morris Stubblefield (Dallas: Summer Institute of Linguistics, 1994), 10; Bruce Beatham and Candice Beatham, eds., *Leso xí'in ñ u má t u ún / El Conejo y la*

Cera Negra (Tlalpan, D.F., Mexico: Instituto Lingüístico de Verano, 2011).

9. The property in dispute changes from story to story. Property is one of the tar baby's most unstable variables although its function in the plot remains relatively constant. The object most commonly contested is water, as in the Cherokee example cited by Mooney. Other resources under dispute in the story include chicken, venison, plantains, corn, apples, oranges, yams, peanuts, butter, chilarro, watermelons, wheat, beans, chiles, potatoes, and black-eyed peas. There are also stories where the dispute concerns not an object but rather access to land, whether a spring, pasture, or berry patch. Daniel J. Crowley, *I Could Talk Old-Story Good: Creativity in Bahamian Folklore* (Berkeley: University of California Press, 1966), 91–92; Elsie Clews Parsons, "Spirituals and Other Folklore from the Bahamas," *Journal of American Folklore* 41 (1928): 515–16; Robert H. Nassau, *Where Animals Talk: West African Folk Lore Tales* (London: Duckworth & Co., 1914), 18–26; Arthur Huff Fauset, *Folklore from Nova Scotia* (New York, G. E. Stechert and Co., 1931), 45–46; Melville J. Herskovits and Frances S. Herskovits, *Suriname Folk-Lore* (New York: Columbia University Press, 1936), 167–68; Paul Radin, *El Folklore de Oaxaca* (Havana: Imprenta de Aurelio Miranda, 1917), 153–54; F. J. de Santa-Anna Nery, *Folk-lore Brésilien* (Paris: Perrin et Cie., 1889), 213; Arthur John Newman Tremearne, *Hausa Superstitions and Customs* (London: John Bale, Sons & Danielsson, 1913), 212–14; R. E. Dennett, *Notes on the Folklore of the Fjort* (London: David Nutt, 1898), 90–93; Boas, "Notes on Mexican Folk-Lore," 235–39. "Tales from Venezuela." *Ethnology* 12 (1888): 307–8; Elsie Clews Parsons, "Folk-Lore from Aiken, S.C." *Journal of American Folklore* 34 (1921): 4–5, 15; Jean Bassett Johnson, "Three Mexican Tar Baby Stories," *Journal of American Folklore* 53 (1940): 215–17; Charles Edward Brown, *Wigwam Tales: Indian Short*

Stories for the Fireside and Camp Fire (Madison, WI: C.E. Brown, 1930), 20; Thaddeus Norris, "Negro Superstitions," *Lippincott's Magazine* 6 (1870): 90–95; Fauset, "Negro Folk Tales from the South," 228–29.

10. On the trickster as "lazy one," see Sanni Metelerkamp, *Outa Karel's Stories: South African Folk-Lore Tales* (London: Macmillan and Co., Limited, 1914), 94. The following stories begin with a commons dilemma in which one animal, the trickster, defects from a communal resource arrangement established by customary agreement. "Negro Fables," *Riverside Magazine for Young People* 2 (1868): 505–7. Anna Porter, "Negro Stories," *The Independent* 30 (1878): 27–28. Bain, "The Story of a Dam," 69–73. Charles L. Edwards, "Some Tales from Bahama Folk-Lore," *Journal of American Folklore* 4 (1891): 50–51. Dennett, *Notes on the Folklore of the Fjort*, 90–93. Dudley Kidd, *Savage Childhood: A Study of Kafir Children* (London: Adam and Charles Black, 1906), 240–43. Robert Sutherland Rattray, "The Rabbit and the Elephant," in *Some Folk-Lore Stories and Songs in Chinyanja* (London: Richard Cray & Sons, Limited, 1907), 139–42. James A. Honeÿ, *South-African Folk-Tales* (New York: The Baker & Taylor Company, 1910), 73–83. John R. Swanton, "Animal Stories from the Indians of the Muskhogean Stock," *Journal of American Folklore* 26 (1913): 214–15. Metelerkamp, *Outa Karel's Stories*, 88–100, 101–7. Burlin, Simango, and Čele, *Songs and Tales from the Dark Continent*, 45–47. John H. Johnson, "Folk-Lore from Antigua, British West Indies," *Journal of American Folklore* 34 (1921): 53. Parsons, "Aiken, S. C.," 4–5, 15. Elsie Clews Parsons, *Folk-Lore of the Sea Islands, South Carolina* (New York: G.E. Stechert & Co., 1923), 27. M. W. Walters, *Cameos from the Kraal* (Alice, South Africa: Lovedale Press, 1926), 28–30.

11. Alfred Burdon Ellis, *The E'we-Speaking Peoples of the Slave Coast of West Africa* (n. p.: Chapman and Hall, Limited, 1890), 275–77.

12. Mooney, *Myths of the Cherokee*, 233–34. Alfred Burdon Ellis, *The Ewe-Speaking Peoples of the Slave Coast of West Africa* (London: Chapman and Hall, Ltd., 1890), 275–77. The claim that the animals "deliberated a long time" appears in Ellis, *Ewe-Speaking*, 275. For the animals "assembled in council," see A. F. Mockler-Ferryman, *Imperial Africa: The Rise, Progress and Future of the British Possessions in Africa* (London: The Imperial Press, Limited, 1898), 1:464. Drought is the plot motivation in the following versions of the story. Burlin, Simango, and Čele, *Songs and Tales from the Dark Continent*, 45–47. John Harrington Cox, "Negro Tales from West Virginia." *Journal of American Folklore* 47 (1934): 341–57. Johnson, "Folk-Lore from Antigua," 53. Fauset, "Negro Folk Tales from the South," 228–30. Robert Sutherland Rattray, "The Rabbit and the Elephant," in *Some Folk-Lore Stories and Songs in Chinyanja* (London: Richard Cray & Sons, Limited, 1907), 139–42. Calvin Claudel and J.-M. Carrière. "Three Tales from the French Folklore of Louisiana," *Journal of American Folklore* 56 (1943): 39–41. Fortier, *Louisiana Folk-Tales*, 2:98–115. Alfred Burdon Ellis, *The Ewe-Speaking Peoples of the Slave Coast of West Africa* (London: Chapman and Hall, Ltd., 1890), 275–77. Honeÿ, *South-African Folk-Tales*, 73–83. For a story that begins with the communal labor of clearing arable land, see Percy Amaury Talbot, *In the Shadow of the Bush* (New York: George H. Doran Company; London: Heinemann, 1912), 397–400. For the Kaffir version of the "Story of the Hare" in which one animal eats grease belonging to the other animals, see Gerber, "Uncle Remus Traced to the Old World," 248. On the building of the kraal, see Sophonia Machabe Mofokeng, "The Development of Leading Figures in Animal Tales in Africa" (dissertation, University of Witwatersrand, 1954), 166–67. For examples where the theft is from a shared cache, see Dennett, *Folklore of the Fjort*, 90–93; and Joseph-Médard

Carrière, *Tales from the French Folk-Lore of Missouri* (Evanston, IL: Northwestern University, 1937), 29–36.

13. James Mooney, *Myths of the Cherokee*, 272. Mancur Olson, *The Logic of Collective Action: Public Goods and the Theory of Group* (Cambridge, MA: Harvard University Press, 1965). John G. Cross and Melvin J. Guyer, *Social Traps* (Ann Arbor: University of Michigan Press, 1980). R. Duncan Luce and Howard Raiffa, *Games and Decisions* (New York: Wiley, 1957). Anatol Rapoport and Albert M. Chammah, *Prisoner's Dilemma* (Ann Arbor: University of Michigan Press, 1965). Robert M. Axelrod, *The Evolution of Cooperation* (New York: Basic Books, 1984). Peter Kollock, "Social Dilemmas: The Anatomy of Cooperation," *Annual Review of Sociology* 24 (1998): 183–214.

14. Garrett Hardin, "The Tragedy of the Commons," *Science* 162 (1968): 1243–48.

15. Bernard Wolfe, "Uncle Remus and the Malevolent Rabbit," *Commentary* 8 (1949): 34. Hardin, "Tragedy of the Commons," 1244. Wolfe's interpretation of the world of the animals as a state of natural warfare is echoed in later commentary, which describe the setting for the stories as "an arena of life-and-death struggle." Charles W. Joyner, *Remember Me: Slave Life in Coastal Georgia* (Atlanta: Georgia Humanities Council, 1989), 49.

16. The state of nature has sometimes been conceived as a thought experiment without empirical reference. John Rawls, for instance, characterizes it as a "purely hypothetical situation" rather than an "actual historical state of affairs." John Rawls, *A Theory of Justice* (New York: Oxford University Press, 1972), 12. Others have rejected this interpretation, arguing that the state of nature was a concept that was understood to have material application in the law of war and in the sphere of international relations. See Richard Tuck, *The Rights of War and Peace: Political Thought and the Inter-*

national Order from Grotius to Kant (New York: Oxford University Press, 1999).

17. Arthur Huff Fauset, "Tales and Riddles Collected in Philadelphia," *Journal of American Folklore* 41 (1928): 532. Fauset, *Folklore from Nova Scotia*, 45–46. Among others, see the following for versions of the tar baby that feature a dispute over private property in which the natural right to property is determined by individual labor. [Abigail M. H. Christensen], "A Negro Legend: De Wolf, De Rabbit and De Tar Baby," *Springfield Daily Republican*, 2 June 1874. Owens, "Folk-Lore of the Southern Negroes," 750–51. Jean-Baptiste Frédéric Ortoli, *Evening Tales*, trans. Joel Chandler Harris (New York: Charles Scribner's Sons, 1893), 1–12. Héli Chatelain, ed., *Folk-Tales of Angola* (Boston: G. E. Stechert & Co., 1894), 183–89, 295. Tremearne, *Hausa Superstitions and Customs*, 212–14. Parsons, *Sea Islands*, 28. Beckwith and Roberts, *Jamaica Anansi Stories*, 23–26, 64–66. Frederick Johnson, "Kiniramba Folk Tales," *Bantu Studies* 5 (1931): 328–30. Fauset, *Folklore from Nova Scotia*, 45–46. D. C. Simmons, "Specimens of Efik Folklore," *Folklore* 66 (1955): 418–19.

18. Lomax, "Yoruba Tales," 5. Héli Chatelain, *Folk-Tales of Angola* (Boston and New York: Houghton, Mifflin and Company, 1894), 183–89. Aurelio M. Espinosa, "Los Cuentos Populares Cubanos de H. Portell Vilà in Volumen en Homenaje a La Dra. Da Concepcion Casado Lobato," *Revista de Dialectologia y Tradiciones Populares* 43 (1988): 240–41. Boas, "Notes on Mexican Folk-Lore," 235–39.

19. Christensen, *Afro-American Folk Lore*, 62–68. [Christensen], "A Negro Legend: De Wolf, De Rabbit and De Tar Baby." On Christensen's life and career as folklore collector, see Monica Maria Tetzlaff, *Cultivating a New South: Abbie Holmes Christensen and the Politics of Race and Gender, 1852–1938* (Columbia: University of South Carolina Press, 2002). On Christensen, see also Cameron C. Nickels, "An Early

Version of the 'Tar Baby' Story," *Journal of American Folklore* 94 (1981): 364–69.

20. Millington and Maxfield, "Visayan Folk-Tales," 311–18. On the possibility of direct transmission of the tar baby from India to the Philippines, see Fansler, *Filipino Popular Tales*, 337. The moralism involved in this opening gambit is perfectly condensed in a version of the story published by Anna Porter in 1878, in which we are told that "Rabbit an' Bear an' Fox had done settle fur to make a bargain an' to make a garden, an' all work an' sell vegetables. So Bear he work, and Fox he work; but Rabbit he won' work. But when night come he slip in tro' de fence and steal de cabbages. An Bear an' Fox say: 'Mus' be Rabbit steal dem cabbages; kase he don' work, so he mus' steal." Porter, "Negro Stories," 27–28.

21. [Christensen], "A Negro Legend." Millington and Maxfield, "Visayan Folk-Tales," 311–14. Jeremy Waldron, *The Right to Private Property* (Oxford: Clarendon Press, 1988), 253–84.

22. On the themes of waste and improvement, see the following. Edwards, "Some Tales from Bahama Folk-Lore," 50–51. Porter, "Negro Stories," 27–28. Ortoli, *Evening Tales*, 1–12. David Benji Mudge-Paris, "Tales and Riddles from Freetown, Sierra Leone," *Journal of American Folklore* 43 (1930): 320. George P. Rawick, ed., *The American Slave: A Composite Autobiography: Supplement, Series 2* (Westport, CT: Greenwood Press, 1979), 2209.

23. John Locke, *Two Treatises of Government*, ed. Peter Laslett (Cambridge: Cambridge University Press, 1988), 285–302. See the following tar baby stories for cases in which property rights are claimed without labor being represented, where for instance ownership is asserted (as in the statement "Once de farmer had a spring of very good water," contained in a story that Parsons reports from Guilford County) or built into characterization (where one personage is glossed by Thaddeus Norris as "the owner of the patch"): Thaddeus Norris, "Negro Superstitions," *Lippincott's Magazine* 6 (1870), 90–

95; Elsie Clews Parsons, "Tales from Guilford County, North Carolina," *Journal of American Folklore* 30 (1917): 171–72; Mary Hose, "Bushy and Jack," *Harper's New Monthly Magazine* 34 (May 1867): 662–63; A. M. Bacon and Elsie Clews Parsons, "Folk-Lore from Elizabeth City County, Virginia," *Journal of American Folklore* 35 (1922): 259–60.

24. Owens, "Folk-Lore of the Southern Negroes," 750–51. Claudel and Carrière, "French Folklore of Louisiana," 39–41.

25. Both common and private property themes appear in the versions of the story concerned with the domestic mode of production—a situation in which property and subsistence are organized predominantly through kinship collectives in which the contribution of labor at one stage of life (often in one's youth) is repaid at another (often in old age). See for instance the version collected by Parsons on the Cape Verde Islands, where a wolf steals from his nephew, or the version from the African Gold Coast where a husband feigns death in order to eat his family's food. Elsie Clews Parsons, *Folk-Lore from the Cape Verde Islands*, vol. 1 (New York: G.E. Stechert & Co., 1923), 90–96. Harold Courlander and Albert Kofi Prempeh, *The Hat-Shaking Dance and Other Tales from the Gold Coast* (New York: Harcourt, Brace, 1957), 109–10. On the domestic mode of production, see Marshall Sahlins, *Stone Age Economics* (Chicago: Aldine-Atherton, 1972). For an alternate view, see Claude Meillasoux, *Maidens, Meal, and Money: Capitalism and the Domestic Community* (Cambridge: Cambridge University Press, 1981).

26. Claudel and Carrière, "French Folklore of Louisiana," 39–41. Swanton, "Animal Stories," 214–15. Mooney, *Myths of the Cherokee*, 271–73. E. W. De Huff, *Taytay's Tales: Folklore of the Pueblo Indians* (New York: Harcourt, Brace, and Company, 1922), 61–64. Ortoli, *Evening Tales*, 1–12. See also the following examples where the rabbit claims that he meets his subsistence needs by scavenging in nature: "Negro Fables," 505–7; Ortoli, *Evening Tales*, 1–12; Fauset, "Negro Folk

Tales from the South," 228–30; Parsons, *Sea Islands*, 25, 27, 28; Alcée Fortier, "Bits of Louisiana Folk-Lore," 104; Edwards, "Tales from Bahama Folk-Lore," 50–51; Federal Writers' Project, "Tar-Baby," in *South Carolina Folk Tales: Stories of Animals and Supernatural Beings* (Columbia, SC: Federal Works Agency, 1941), 29–31.

27. Owens, "Folk-Lore of the Southern Negroes," 750–51.

28. Swanton, "Animal Stories," 194. Concerning the distinction between common and open access, see Matthew Taylor, *The Possibility of Cooperation* (Cambridge: Cambridge University Press, 1987), 1–12. On their conflation in natural rights philosophy and political economy, see Allan Greer, "Commons and Enclosure in the Colonization of North America," *American Historical Review* 117 (2012): 365–86.

29. The plot-motivating characterological contrast between lazy and industrious actors is a commonplace in cultures throughout the world, from Aesop's fable of "The Ant and the Cricket" to stories like "Bunnyyarl the Flies and Wurrunnunnah the Bees," collected by Katie Langloh Parker in Australia. The latter begins by establishing the innate difference between the Wurrunnunnah (who were "hardworking") and the Bunnyarl (who "gave no heed to the future, but used to waste their time playing around any rubbish"), a difference that eventually transforms the Wurrunnunnah into bees and the Bunnyarl, an outcome that is supposed to prove, or in MacCulloch's interpretation of the story, that "character" becomes "indelible." Laura Gibbs, ed., *Aesop's Fables* (N.p.: Oxford World's Classics, 2008), 65–66. Katie Langloh Parker, *Australian Legendary Tales: Folklore of the Noongahburrahs as Told to the Piccaninnies* (London: D. Nutt, 1897), 106–7. John Arnott MacCulloch, *The Childhood of Fiction: A Study of Folk Tales and Primitive Thought* (New York: E.P. Dutton and Company, 1905), 182. There are also close cognates not only in Uncle Remus but elsewhere in the global trickster tradition featuring Brother Rabbit. Harris, for example, of-

fers several cognates in his second book of Uncle Remus stories. Harris, *Nights with Uncle Remus*, 11–14 ("Brother Rabbit and the Little Girl"), 25–32 ("Brother Rabbit Secures a Mansion"), 327–33 ("How Wattle Weasel Was Caught"). The version of "Playing Dead Twice in the Road," recorded by Elsie Clews Parsons in North Carolina, follows the same pattern in generating conflict from the moral contrast between character types. "Ol' rabbit an' fox went afishin'," the story begins, "Ol' rabbit he was lazy an' he wouldn't fish none, an' ol' fox kep' atellin' him he'd better fish. An' he started home an' ol' rabbit tol' him to give him some fish." Elsie Clews Parsons, "The Provenience of Certain Negro Folk-Tales," *Folklore* 28 (1917): 408–11. For the Kaffir version of the "Story of the Hare" in which one animal eats grease belonging to the other animals, see Gerber, "Uncle Remus Traced to the Old World," 248. On the building of the kraal, see Mofokeng, "The Development of Leading Figures in Animal Tales in Africa," 166–67. For "The Story of the Well," another close cognate of the versions of the tar baby that are motivated by the problem of free riding, see Alice Werner, *Myths and Legends of the Bantu*, 243–46. May Augusta Klipple, "African Folk Tales, with Foreign Analogues" (dissertation, Indiana University, 1938), 421–22. Mofokeng, "The Development of Leading Figures in Animal Tales in Africa," 11, 57, 120, 158, 160, 162, 163, 249. Erastus Ojo Arewa, "A Classification of the Folktales of the Northern East African Cattle Area by Types" (dissertation, University of California, 1967), 102–7. Jones, *Negro Myths from the Georgia Coast*, 49–53. Parsons, *Sea Islands*, 30–32, 145–46.

30. Adam Smith's theory of "prior" accumulation is conventionally credited with making this morality tale foundational to capitalism's understanding of its own beginnings. Adam Smith, *An Inquiry into the Nature and Causes of the Wealth of Nations*, ed. Edwin Canaan (New York: Modern Library,

1937), 259–60. Marx famously argues that Smith accounts for capitalism's "origin" by telling an "anecdote about the past," an anecdote that explains the unequal distribution of resources in the present by proposing that there were once, and implicitly still are, "two sorts of people" in the world, one sort like the fox who are "diligent" and "intelligent" and "frugal," and another sort like the rabbit who waste their time and resources in "riotous living." This moral contrast is supposed to explain how some people accumulated wealth and others "had nothing to sell except their own skins." Karl Marx, *Capital: A Critique of Political Economy*, trans. Ben Fowkes (New York: Penguin Books, 1976), 1:873. It is acknowledged that Marx reduces Smith's argument for polemical purposes, not least in the sense that Smith represents industry and indolence, thrift and self-indulgence, not in two archetypal individuals but instead as competing tendencies within each individual no matter their station. Following Smith, there are other thinkers, from Benjamin Franklin to Harriet Martineau, Andrew Carnegie to Booker T. Washington, who are more inclined to personify their precepts in characters that are reducible to aphorism. Adam Smith, *An Inquiry into the Nature and Causes of the Wealth of Nations*, ed. Edwin Cannan, 2 vols. (Chicago: University of Chicago Press, 1977), 1:5–20. Benjamin Franklin, *The Sayings of Poor Richard*, ed. Thomas Herbert Russell (Chicago: Edward T. Kelly Company, 1950). Harriet Martineau, *Illustrations of Political Economy* (London: C. Fox, 1834). Horatio Alger, *Ragged Dick, or, Street life in New York* (Boston: A. K. Loring, 1868). Booker T. Washington, *Up from Slavery* (Garden City, NY: Doubleday and Company, 1901). Max Weber, *The Protestant Ethic and the Spirit of Capitalism*, trans. Talcott Parsons (New York: Charles Scribner's Sons, 1958). For a counterstatement that would become important to subsequent interpretation of the tar baby and kindred stories, see E. P. Thompson, "Time, Work-Discipline, and Industrial Capitalism," *Past and Present* 38 (1967): 56–97. Like the new social historians who came after him, Thompson sees "laziness" not as moral defect but as the persistence of a preindustrial sense of time. On recent approaches to the mythology of primitive accumulation, see also Jason Read, *The Micro-Politics of Capital: Marx and the Prehistory of the Present* (Albany: State University of New York Press, 2003), 19–60.

31. Locke, *Two Treatises of Government*, 285–302. On the broad influence of Locke's ideas about colonization, see the following. James Tully, *An Approach to Political Philosophy: Locke in Contexts* (Cambridge: Cambridge University Press, 1993). David Armitage, *The Ideological Origins of the British Empire* (Cambridge: Cambridge University Press, 2000). Denise Ferreira da Silva, *Toward a Global Idea of Race* (Minneapolis: University of Minnesota Press, 2007). Ned Blackhawk, *Violence over the Land: Indians and Empires in the Early American West* (Cambridge, MA: Harvard University Press, 2006).

32. Locke, *Two Treatises of Government*, 285–302; see especially 288. The labor-mixing argument and the problem of "justice in initial acquisition" are addressed in Robert Nozick, *Anarchy, State, and Utopia* (New York: Basic Books, 1974), 174–82. For an interpretation of Locke's labor-mixing argument as an apology for capitalist exploitation, see C. B. Macpherson, *The Political Theory of Possessive Individualism: Hobbes to Locke* (Oxford: Oxford University Press, 1962). An influential critique of the Macpherson thesis is James Tully, *A Discourse on Property: John Locke and His Adversaries* (Cambridge: Cambridge University Press, 1980).

33. Hugo Grotius, *The Rights of War and Peace*, ed. Jean Barbeyrac and Richard Tuck, 3 vols. (Indianapolis, IN: Liberty Fund, 2005), 2:423. For Grotius's account of property in the state of nature, see the chapters "Things which Belong in Common" and "Of the Original Acquisition of Things" in *Rights of War and Peace*, 420–82. Samuel Pufendorf, *De Jure Natuae et Gentium Libri*, trans. C. H. Oldfather and W. A.

Oldfather, 8 vols. (Oxford: Clarendon Press), 2: 537–39, 550–54. William Blackstone, *Commentaries on the Laws of England*, 4 vols. (Oxford: Clarendon Press), 2:2–16. On the four-stage theory of world history, see Ronald L. Meek, *Social Science and the Ignoble Savage* (Cambridge: Cambridge University Press, 1976). The arguments made by Grotius, Pufendorf, Locke, and Blackstone about the emergence of property in the state of nature are distinguishable from Thomas Hobbes's claim that the state of nature was indistinguishable from the state of warfare and was therefore too chaotic to sustain claims to personal property. According to Hobbes, property becomes possible only with the state. Thomas Hobbes, *Leviathan*, ed. Richard Tuck (Cambridge: Cambridge University Press, 1996). See also Andrew Fitzmaurice, *Sovereignty, Property, and Empire, 1500–2000* (Cambridge: Cambridge University Press, 2014).

34. Henry Sumner Maine, *Ancient Law: Its Connection with the Early History of Society, and Its Relation to Modern Ideas* (London: John Murray, 1870), 259. Locke, *Two Treatises of Government*, 285–302. See also Andrew Fitzmaurice, "The Genealogy of Terra Nullius," *Australian Historical Studies* 38 (2007), 1–15. On the coincident global diffusion of legal ideas, see Lauren Benton, *Law and Colonial Cultures: Legal Regimes in World History, 1400–1900* (New York: Cambridge University Press, 2002).

35. Jones, *Negro Myths from the Georgia Coast*, 7–11. Nery, *Folklore Brésilien*, 213. Hose, "Bushy and Jack," 662–63. Parsons, "Tar Baby," 227. Espinosa, "New Classification," 31–37. Harris, *Tar-Baby and Other Rhymes*, 3–18. Labor is also an ambiguous element in natural law. If thinkers like Grotius insisted that objects were owned not when they were merely seen but when they were "[held]" and land was owned not when it was discovered but when it was "bounded and guarded," the difference between finding and holding, or discovering and enclosing, was often elided in the so-called

"doctrine of discovery." Hugo Grotius, *The Free Sea*, trans. Richard Hakluyt, ed. David Armitage (Indianaopolis: Liberty Fund, 2004), 14. For an example concerning American Indian land tenure, see *Johnson v. M'Intosh*, 21 U. S. 543, 5 L. Ed. 681 (1823).

36. On the absolute conceptual limits to Locke's labor-mixing metaphor, see Nozick, *Anarchy, State, and Utopia*, 175. The range and importance of *res nullius* in the English, French, Spanish, and Portuguese empires remains an open question. Anthony Pagden, *Lords of All the World: Ideologies of Empire in Spain, Britain, and France, c.1500–c.1800* (New Haven, CT: Yale University Press, 1995). J. H. Elliott, *Empires of the Atlantic World: Britain and Spain in America, 1492–1830* (New Haven, CT: Yale University Press, 2006), 3–56. Christopher Tomlins, *Freedom Bound: Law, Labor, and Civic Identity in Colonizing English America, 1580–1865* (Cambridge: Cambridge University Press, 2010), 21–190. A concise overview of recent thinking on these points is Lauren Benton and Benjamin Straumann, "Acquiring Empire by Law: From Roman Doctrine to Early Modern European Practice," *Law and History Review*, 28 (February 2010): 1–38.

37. Francisco de Vitoria, "On Civil Power," "On the American Indians," and "On the Law of War," in *Francisco de Vitoria: Political Writings*, ed. Anthony Pagden and Jeremy Lawrance (Cambridge: Cambridge University Press, 1996), 1–44, 231–92, 293–328. Hugo Grotius, *De Jure Belli ac Pacis Libri Tres*, quoted in Tuck, *Rights of War and Peace*, 103. See also Tuck, *Rights of War and Peace*, 58–61, 68–75.

38. Vitoria, "On Civil Power," 37. Vitoria, "On the American Indians," 231–92. Tuck, *Rights of War and Peace*, 103. Grotius, *Rights of War and Peace*, 1024. Blackstone, *Commentaries*, 4:765–68. Emer de Vattel, *The Law of Nations*, ed. Béla Kapossy and Richard Whitmore (Indianapolis, IN: Liberty Fund, 2008), 543–44. Francis Bacon, "Advertisement

Touching a Holy War," in *The Works of Francis Bacon*, ed. James Spedding, Leslie Ellis, and Douglas Denon Heath, 15 vols. (Boston: Houghton Mifflin, 1900), 7:1–36.

39. Locke, *Two Treatises*, 278–82, 283–85. Tuck, *Rights of War and Peace*, 103, 109–39. For a variation on Locke's formulation, see Blackstone, *Commentaries*, 4:70–71. Orlando Patterson, *Slavery and Social Death: A Comparative Study* (Cambridge, MA: Harvard University Press, 1982), 106–15. See also Claude Meillasoux, *The Anthropology of Slavery: The Womb of Iron and Gold*, trans. Alide Dasnois (Chicago: University of Chicago Press, 1991), 67–96. The intellectual background and precedents for Locke's adapation of classical thinking about slavery and captivity are sketched in Mary Nyquist, *Arbitrary Rule: Slavery, Tyranny, and the Power of Life and Death* (Chicago: University of Chicago Press, 2013). See also Ellen Meiksins Wood, *Liberty and Property: A Social History of Western Political Thought from the Renaissance to the Enlightenment* (London: Verso Books, 2012), 85–108, 211–88.

40. Blackstone, *Commentaries*, 4:380. See also Joan Dayan, "Legal Slaves and Civil Bodies," *Nepantla* 2 (2001): 3–39.

41. Millington and Maxfield, "Visayan Folk-Tales," 311–14. Fansler, *Filipino Popular Tales*, 327. Melville J. Herskovits and Frances S. Herskovits, "Tales in Pidgin English from Nigeria," *Journal of American Folklore* 44 (1931): 462.

42. Rawick, *American Slave*, 2209. Millington and Maxfield, "Visayan Folk-Tales," 311–14. For a case where the rabbit is imprisoned for his crimes, see Fortier, "Bits of Louisiana Folk-Lore," 101–15. For elaboration on the trope of captivity, see Thaddeus Norris, "Negro Superstitions," *Lippincott's Magazine* 6 (1870), 90–95.

43. Blackstone, *Commentaries*, 4:380. According to Marx, the discipline of political economy "does not recognize the unemployed worker." Characters like the rabbit "do not exist

for political economy but only for other eyes, those of the doctor, the judge, the gravedigger, and bum-bailiff." Karl Marx, *Economic and Philosophical Manuscripts of 1844*, trans. Martin Milligan (Moscow: Progress Publishers, 1974), 76. For a contrasting account, in which Marx argues for rather than analyzes the lack of perspective associated with the lumpenproletariat, see Karl Marx, "The Eighteenth Brumaire of Louis Bonaparte," in *Surveys from Exile: Political Writings* (New York: Penguin Books, 1973), 143–249. On the "radical absence of memory" entailed in the myth of prior accumulation and the consequent erasure of the point of view associated with the lazy rascal, see Louis Althusser and Étienne Balibar, *Reading Capital*, trans. Ben Brewster (London: New Left Books, 1970), 283, 215. See also Michael Denning, "Wageless Life," *New Left Review* 66 (2010): 79–97.

44. Karl Marx, *Capital,* 1:873–904. The trickster is described specifically as "vagabond" in Metelerkamp, *Outa Karel's Stories*, 95. There is at least one interpretation that takes seriously the story's opening gambit while maintaining the assumption of identification. Poultney Bigelow reconciles these two seemingly incompatible ideas by pointing to the inherent immorality of the African race. "We can recall very few tales of pure negro origin having the slightest moral point to them," Bigelow writes. "In general, these negro tales glorify the weak animal who triumphs by deception over a stronger one. . . . This triumph is accompanied usually by cruel circumstances, and it does not seem to spoil the story that the rabbit should be wholly wanton in his provocations, and his victim a good-natured, innocent member of the community. The African reader or listener rejoices in the triumph of duplicity . . . quite irrespective of the merits involved." Poultney Bigelow, *White Man's Africa* (New York: Harper and Bros., 1898), 175–76.

CHAPTER 3. STICKING FAST

1. On the erasure of this subaltern perspective in European philosophy and political science, see Gayatri Chakravorty Spivak, *A Critique of Postcolonial Reason: Toward a History of the Vanishing Present* (Cambridge, MA: Harvard University Press, 1999). Spivak describes how this "perspective is foreclosed in some of the backbone thinking of the modern Atlantic tradition," beginning with Immanuel Kant's *Critique of Judgment*, in which access to the sublime is denied to the "Inhabitant of Tierra del Fuego" (110, 26, 30). According to Spivak, this figure, the "native informant," remains indispensable to the major works of critical philosophy in the nineteenth and twentieth centuries even as its standpoint is summarily "foreclosed" within them (ix–x, 4). For a contrasting perspective on "unthinkable" history, see Michel-Rolph Trouillot, *Silencing the Past: Power and the Production of History* (Boston: Beacon Press, 1995).

2. Parsons, "Tar Baby," 227. Espinosa, "New Classification," 31–37.

3. Espinosa, "More Notes," 170–77. Ananda K. Coomaraswamy, "A Note on the Stickfast Motif," *Journal of American Folklore* 57 (1944): 128–31. Herskovits agrees that "in essence" the story is reducible to the thief being caught by a "figure made out of tar or some other sticky substance." Herskovits, *Myth of the Negro Past*, 272. For a critique of this reduction, see especially Brown, "The Stickfast Motif," 1–12. See the following versions for stories that specify the variety of natural and supernatural substances used to build the trap. Substances include tar, pitch, rubber, glue, tree gum, bird lime, and wax—both palm wax and black wax collected from the floor of beehives. The sticky substance is shaped to look like a girl, a man, a monkey, and sometimes an image of the trickster's adversary. "Tales from Venezuela," 307–8. Junod,

Les Chants et les Contes, 96–98. Dennett, *Folklore of the Fjort,* 90–93. Florence M. Cronise and Henry W. Ward. *Cunnie Rabbit, Mr. Spider and the Other Beef* (New York: E. P. Dutton and Company, 1903), 101–9. Tremearne, *Hausa Superstitions and Customs,* 212–14. Boas, "Notes on Mexican Folk Lore," 235–39. Paul Radin, *El Folklore de Oaxaca,* 153–54. Beckwith and Roberts, *Jamaica Anansi Stories,* 23–26, 64–66. Cox, "Negro Tales from West Virginia," 341–57. Johnson, "Three Mexican Tar Baby Stories," 215–17. Simmons, "Specimens of Efik Folklore," 418–19. Courlander and Prempeh, *The Hat-Shaking Dance,* 109–10. Samuel G. Armistead, "Two Brer Rabbit Stories from the Eastern Shore of Maryland," *Journal of American Folklore* 84 (1971): 443–44. Frank G. Speck, *The Creek Indians of the Taskigi Town,* vol. 2 of *Memoirs of the American Anthropological Association* (New York: Kraus Reprint Co., 1974), 149.

4. Thomas Gamble, *Naval Stores: History, Production, Distribution and Consumption* (Savannah, GA: Review Publishing and Printing Company, 1921), 9–42. Percival Perry, "The Naval-Stores Industry in the Old South, 1790–1860," *Journal of Southern History* 34 (1968): 509–26. Robert B. Outland, *Tapping the Pines: The Naval Stores Industry in the American South* (Baton Rouge: Louisiana State University Press, 2004), 8–36.

5. Outland, *Tapping the Pines,* 8–36. John Brickell and John Lawson, *The Natural History of North-Carolina* (Raleigh, NC: Trustees of the Public Libraries, 1911), 266–67.

6. Outland, *Tapping the Pines,* 8–36. Thomas Harriot, *A Briefe and True Report of the New Found Land of Virginia* (New York: Dover Publications, 1972), 88. Gamble, *Naval Stores,* 19–20. On tar as currency, see Paul Einzig, *Primitive Money in Its Ethnological, Historical and Economic Aspects* (London: Eyre and Spottiswoode, 1948), 278–85. Jeffrey R. Dobson and Roy Doyon, "Expansion of the Pine Oleoresin Industry

in Georgia: 1842 to ca. 1900," *West Georgia Studies in the Social Sciences* 18 (1979): 43–75. Michael Williams, *Americans and Their Forests: A Historical Geography* (Cambridge: Cambridge University Press, 1992), 85, 158.

7. Hose, "Bushy and Jack," 662–63. Espinosa, "More Notes," 171.

8. For Wofford's version, see Mooney, *Myths of the Cherokee*, 271–72. Melville J. Herskovits and Frances S. Herskovits, *Rebel Destiny: Among the Bush Negroes of Dutch Guiana* (New York: Whittlesey House, 1934), 13–15.

9. On the story collected by Père Capus, see Alice Werner, "The Tar-Baby Story," 282–86. Junod, *Les Chants et Les Contes*, 96–98.

10. Harris, *Uncle Remus: His Songs and His Sayings* (1881), 23.

11. Robert H. Nassau, "Fetishism, a Government," *Bulletin of the American Geographical Society* 33 (1901): 305–17. Mary Alicia Owen, *Ole Rabbit's Plantation Stories as Told among the Negroes of the Southwest Collected from Original Sources* (Philadelphia: G. W. Jacobs and Company 1898), 183. Weeks, *Congo Life and Folklore*, 366–68. A.J.N. Tremearne, *The Tailed Head-Hunters of Nigeria: An Account of an Official's Seven Years' Experience in the Northern Nigerian Pagan Belt* (Philadelphia: J.B. Lippincott, 1912), 206. Louis Pendleton, "Notes on Negro Folk-Lore and Witchcraft in the South,", 201–2. Herskovits, *Myth of the Negro Past*, 254. Willis D. Weatherford and Charles S. Johnson, *Race Relations: Adjustment of Whites and Negroes in the United States* (Boston: D.C. Heath and Company, 1934), 460–62. MacCulloch, *The Childhood of Fiction*, 200. Mary H. Kingsley, "Fetish View of the Human Soul," *Folklore* 8 (1897): 141.

12. Nassau, *Where Animals Talk*, 22–23. Mary Alicia Owen, *Old Rabbit, the Voodoo, and Other Sorcerers* (London: T. Fisher Unwin, 1893), v–ix, 183. Gerber, "Uncle Remus Traced to the Old World," 251. Another mixed variation in this for-

mula appears in versions of the story where the trap is not disguised as a sentient creature and yet the rabbit still performs his apostrophe. In Guilford County, North Carolina, for instance, the trap is an undisguised tar bucket that is still personified by the rabbit. "Who's this?" the rabbit asks. When the bucket says nothing, the rabbit launches into his threats: "If you don' speak, I'll hit you." Reflecting on a similar story involving lime smeared on a plain fence, Adolf Gerber argues that this extra improbability is a likely reason that these versions are less well known, as "it is quite unnatural" for the trickster "to talk to the fence as the prisoners of the other versions speak to the tortoise or the baby." Elsie Clews Parsons, "Tales from Guilford County, North Carolina," *Journal of American Folklore* 30 (1917): 171–72. For discussions of the fetish as conceived by collectors of the tar baby story, see Alfred Burdon Ellis, *The Land of the Fetish* (London: Chapman and Hall, 1883). Robert Hamill Nassau, "The Philosophy of Fetishism," *Journal of the Royal African Society* 3 (1904): 257–70. Alfred Cort Haddon, *Magic and Fetishism* (London: A. Constable and Co., Ltd., 1906), 66–90.

13. Weeks, *Congo Life and Folklore*, 366–67, 388–90. Edward B. Tylor, *Primitive Culture: Researches into the Development of Mythology, Philosophy, Religion, Art, and Custom* (London: J. Murray, 1871), 16. MacCulloch, *The Childhood of Fiction*, 201.

14. Willem Bosman, *A New and Accurate Description of the Coast of Guinea, Divided into the Gold, the Slave, and the Ivory Coasts* (Midwinter: Printed for J. Knapton et al., 1705). Charles de Brosses, *Du Culture des Dieux Fétiches, ou Parallèle de L'Ancienne Religione de l'Égypte avec la Religion Actuelle de Nigritie* (Paris: Fayard, 1989). William Pietz, "The Problem of the Fetish, I," *Res* 9 (1985), 5–17. William Pietz, "The Problem of the Fetish, II: The Origin of the Fetish," *Res* 13 (1987), 23–45. William Pietz, "The Problem of the Fetish,

IIIa: Bosman's Guinea and the Enlightenment Theory of Fetishism," *Res* 16 (1988), 105–24. On fetishism as an idea that emerges in tandem with the settler's purposive rationality to justify settlement, see Patrick Wolfe, *Traces of History: Elementary Structures of Race* (London: Verso Books, 2016), 141–71.

15. "The peculiarity of the African character," according to Hegel, is that it lacks "the principle which naturally accompanies all our ideas—the category of Universality." Africans worship "the first thing that comes their way. This, taken quite indiscriminately, they exalt to the dignity of a 'Genius'; it may be an animal, a tree, a stone, or a wooden figure. . . . [I]n the Fetich, a kind of objective independence as contrasted with the arbitrary fancy of the individual seems to manifest itself; but as the objectivity is nothing other than the fancy of the individual projecting itself into space, the human individuality remains master of the image it has adopted. If any mischance occurs which the Fetich has not averted, if the rain is suspended, if there is a failure in the crops, they bind and beat or destroy the Fetich and so get rid of it, making another immediately, and thus holding it in their power. Such a Fetich has no independence as an object of religious worship; still less has it aesthetic independence as a work of art; it is merely a creation that expresses the arbitrary choice of its maker, and which always remains in his hands. Hence there is no relation of dependence in this religion." See G.W.F. Hegel, *The Philosophy of History*, trans. J. Sibree (New York: Dover, 1956), 93–94. On the uses of fetishism in Hegel's *Philosophy of History*, see especially Pietz, "The Problem of the Fetish, I," 7–8. On the African "tendency to personify everything," see Frederick Starr, *Some First Steps in Human Progress* (New York: Flood and Vincent, 1895), 209.

16. On the tar baby as a "queer black thing," see Mooney, *Myths of the Cherokee*, 272. For the tar baby looking "as black as a

Guinea negro" and addressed as "little Congo" and "little negro," see Ortoli, *Evening Tales*, 6. For "little black boy," see Parsons, *Cape Verde Islands*, 96. For "black police," see Mudge-Paris, "Tales and Riddles," 320. For "You black man," see "Tales from Venezuela," 307–8. For "Good day to you, old blackie," see Johnson, "Three Mexican Tar Baby Stories," 215–17.

17. Frederick S. Church's line drawing of the rabbit facing off with the tar baby appears in Joel Chandler Harris, *Uncle Remus, His Songs and His Sayings* (New York: D. Appleton and Company, 1881), 23. On the negroid class in forensic anthropology, see Ashley Montagu, *An Introduction to Physical Anthropology* (Springfield, IL: Charles C. Thomas Publisher, 1951), 302–12.

18. For a standard account of how identification works in the tar baby story, see Levine, *Black Culture and Black Consciousness*, 112–15.

19. The crucial point about the rabbit's fetishism, again, is the fact that it stands in the story as a marker for individual and collective inadequacy, a synecdoche not only for mental but for social condition. Writing in 1940, Meyer Fortes and Edward Evans Pritchard summarize this point: "Africans have no objective knowledge of the forces determining their social organization and actuating their social behavior . . . Myths, dogmas, ritual beliefs and activities make his social system intellectually tangible and coherent to an African and enable him to think and feel about it. Furthermore, these sacred symbols, which reflect the social system, endow it with mystical values which evoke acceptance of the social order that goes far beyond the obedience exacted by the secular sanction of force. The social system is, as it were, removed to a mystical plane." M. Fortes and E. E. Evans-Pritchard, eds., *African Political Systems* (New York: Oxford University Press, 1940), 17–18. In 1901, Robert Nassau makes the same

point more succinctly. "Fetishism," he says, is "government." Nassau, "Fetishism, a Government," 305.

20. Harris, *Uncle Remus: His Songs and His Sayings*, 23–25, 29–31. Jones, *Negro Myths from the Georgia Coast*, 7–11. Ortoli, *Evening Tales*, 1–12. On astonishment as a sensory overload that leaves the body "immobile as a statue," see René Descartes, *The Philosophical Writings of Descartes*, trans. John Cottingham, Robert Stoothoff, and Dugald Murdoch, 2 vols. (Cambridge: Cambridge University Press, 1985), 1:354.

21. Harris, *Uncle Remus: His Songs and His Sayings*, 23–25, 29–31.

22. Ralph Ellison, "Hidden Name and Complex Fate" in *The Writer's Experience* (Washington, DC: Library of Congress, 1964), 1–15. Jean-Paul Sartre, *Being and Nothingness: An Essay on Phenomenological Ontology*, trans. Hazel E. Barnes (London: Methuen, 1958). Frantz Fanon, *Black Skin, White Masks*, trans. Richard Philcox (New York: Grove Press, Rev. Ed., 1986), 113. See also Albert Memmi, *The Coloniser and the Colonised*, trans. Howard Greenfield (Boston: Beacon Press, 1965). On blackness as a visual impression of absence experienced when no reflected light reaches the eye, see Michel Pastoureau, *Black: the History of a Color* (Princeton, NJ: Princeton University Press, 2009).

23. Examples of "tar baby" as figure of speech include the following: "Populism: Mississippi Politics," *Atlanta Constitution*, 17 February 1895; "The Tar-Baby Outdone," *Life,* 14 July 1898, 32; "The Tar-Baby," *Baltimore Afro-American*, 12 August 1899; "Mr. Randolph Barton and the Tar-Baby," *Baltimore Afro-American*, 28 October 1899); "Bryan and 'Subsidies': He Ignores Both Party Pledges and National Practice," *San Francisco Chronicle*, 14 April 1914; "Br'er Donkey and the Tar Baby," *Wall Street Journal*, 31 March 1924; Zygmund Dobbs, *Red Intrigue and Race Turmoil* (New

York: Alliance Incorporated, 1958), 34; Don A. Proudfoot, "'The Tar Baby': Maritime Personal-Injury Indemnity Actions," *Stanford Law Review* 20 (1968): 423–47; C. L. Sulzberger, "Saigon and Hanoi are Going to Be Left Face-to-Face," *New York Times*, 19 January 1973; Tom Wicker, "Still Fast to the Tar Baby," *New York Times*, 15 September 1974; Ross K. Baker, "Stuck with Nixon: The GOP and the Tar Baby," *The Nation* 219 (2 November 1974), 423–25; "UNESCO's Tar Baby," *Wall Street Journal*, 29 November 1976; Anthony A. Lake, *The "Tar Baby" Option: American Policy towards Southern Rhodesia* (New York: Columbia University Press, 1976); Jim Castelli, "The Separation 'Tar-Baby' Is Fading," *Chicago Tribune*, 15 July 1983; Arthur Schlesinger Jr., "Mr. Reagan's Tar Baby," *Wall Street Journal*, 1 March 1985; "Trouble with the Tibetan Tar Baby," *Chicago Tribune*, 13 March 1989; Donald F. Kettl, "The Savings-and-Loan Bailout: The Mismatch between the Headlines and the Issues," *Political Science and Politics* 24 (1991): 441–47; W. H. Von Dreele, "Medicare as Tar Baby," *National Review*, 29 May 1995, 14; Charmaine Seitz, "The Tar Baby of Foreign Aid: How Palestinians Are Trying to Keep Their Hands Clean," *Middle East Report* 234 (2005): 28–33; "Massachusetts Governor Apologizes for 'Tar Baby' Remark," *New York Times*, 1 August 2006; John V. Walsh, "The Tar Baby and China," *Dissident Voice* 1 (2014), 1. See also D. G. Martin, "The Term 'Tar Baby'—A Political Tar Baby," *Chatham Journal*, 17 September 2006.
24. Lucinda MacKethan, "Racism Not Part of the Tar Baby Tale," *Atlanta Journal-Constitution*, 7 May 2006. John McWhorter, "'Tar Baby' Isn't Actually a Racial Slur," *New Republic*, 3 August 2011. See also Anita Henderson, "What's in a Slur?" *American Speech* 78 (2003): 52–74.
25. Early examples where "tar baby" is used as a racial epithet include the following: "A Quarrel," *Saturday Evening Post*, 16 November 1839; A North Carolina Lawyer, "A Trip to

County Court," *Spirit of the Times*, October 5, 1844; "The Tar Baby—The Jay Bird," *Atlanta Weekly Constitution*, 27 June 1882; Joel Chandler Harris, *Little Mr. Thimblefinger and His Queer Country: What the Children Saw and Heard There* (New York: McKinlay, Stone, and MacKenzie, 1894), 38–39; William Safire, "The Tar Baby Strikes Again," *New York Times*, 13 November 1986; William Safire, "Tar Baby," *New York Times*, 13 May 1990. Other early cases in which the term is used as an epithet include the following: "Some Real Darkey Boys," *The Sunny South*, 9 December 1882; "A Tar Baby: The Romantic Adventure of a Small Negro," *Atlanta Constitution*, 16 November 1887; "Some Police," *Atlanta Constitution*, 24 July 1898; Gordon Noel Hurtel, "Police Matinee Pen Shots," Atlanta Constitution, 21 May 1901; "Henry Plays the Tar Baby," *Atlanta Georgian and News*, 6 May 1907; " 'Tar Baby' No Myth: Brooklyn Woman's Cherub Temporarily Transformed, but Mystery Solved," *Washington Post*, 23 June 1913. Complaints about the term's use as a racial epithet include the following: Nettie George Speedy, "Two 'Abyssinians' Get Death Penalty," *Chicago Defender*, 22 January 1921; "An Open Letter," *Cleveland Gazette*, 19 September 1925; " 'Georgia Governor Called Me a Tarbaby,' Says Milton P. Webster," *Arkansas State Press*, 9 July 1943; "Says Xmas Story Is Offensive," *New Journal and Guide*, 14 December 1946.

26. Stanley M. Elkins, *Slavery: A Problem in American Institutional and Intellectual Life*. Elkins is anticipated in this position by historians and sociologists such as U. B. Phillips, Robert Park, and E. Franklin Frazier. Ulrich Bonnell Phillips, *American Negro Slavery: A Survey of the Supply, Employment and Control of Negro Labor as Determined by the Plantation Regime* (New York: D. Appleton, 1918). Robert E. Park, *Race and Culture*, ed. Everett C. Hughes (Glencoe, IL: Free Press, 1950). Frazier, *The Negro Family in the United States*. An early and programmatic case for the importance of works

like the tar baby to the battle against the Elkins thesis is given by Sterling Stuckey. Stuckey argues that "folk songs and tales" offered an alternative to the values that slavery "sought to impose," allowing slaves to "maintain their essential humanity" even as they were reduced to chattel. According to Stuckey, works like the tar baby were vital not only to the survival of slaves but also to any effort to understand history from the slave's point of view, as they supplied a point of access to an autonomous slave consciousness that did not register in the actuarial tables and statute books used as sources by historians like Phillips and Elkins. Sterling Stuckey, "Through the Prism of Folklore: The Black Ethos in Slavery," *Massachusetts Review* (1968): 417–37.

27. Jacobs, *Indian Fairy Tales*, 194–98. Gerber, "Uncle Remus Traced to the Old World,": 246. Espinosa, "Notes on the Origin," 173. Cline, "The Tar-Baby Story," 72–78. See also Dähnhardt, *Natursagen*, 4:27–30. For an account of the tar baby's diffusion in Mexico based on the assumed predominance of the stickfast motif, see George M. Foster, "Some Characteristics of Mexican Indian Folklore," *Journal of American Folklore* 58 (1945): 225–35. For an account of the diffusion of the stickfast motif to Malaysia, see R. O. Winstedt, "A History of Malay Literature," *Journal of the Malayan Branch of the Royal Asiatic Society* 17 (1940): 5–7. On its diffusion to Japan, see William E. Griffis, "The Original of Uncle Remus' Tar Baby in Japan," *The Folk-Lorist* 1 (1892): 146–49. See also William Elliot Griffis, *The Romance of American Colonization: How the Foundation Stones of Our History Were Laid* (Boston: W. A. Wilde & Company, 1898), 173–76.

28. Dähnhardt, *Natursagen*, 4:27–30. Espinosa, "Notes on the Origin," 173. Cline, "The Tar-Baby Story," 72–78. Espinosa, "More Notes," 170–77. Ananda K. Coomaraswamy, "A Note on the Stickfast Motif," *Journal of American Folklore* 57 (1944), 128–31.

CHAPTER 4. SAY MY NAME

1. Harris, *Uncle Remus: His Songs and His Sayings*, 23–25, 29–31.

2. The argument in this chapter relies on the substantial literature in economics and political science on commons institutions, most notably Elinor Ostrom, *Governing the Commons: The Evolution of Institutions for Collective Action* (Cambridge: Cambridge University Press, 1990). The literature on commons institutions is vast; see the following works for some foundational examples: Shepard Forman, *The Raft Fishermen: Tradition and Change in the Brazilian Peasant Economy* (Bloomington: Indiana University Press, 1970); Peter Kropotkin, *Mutual Aid*; Carl Johan Dahlman, *The Open Field System and Beyond: A Property Rights Analysis of an Economic Institution* (Cambridge: Cambridge University Press, 1980); William Cronon, *Changes in the Land: Indians, Colonists, and the Ecology of New England* (New York: Hill and Wang, 1983); Howard Barclay, *People without Government* (London: Kath and Averill, 1990); Richard White, *The Middle Ground: Indians, Empires, and Republics in the Great Lakes Region, 1650–1815* (Cambridge: Cambridge University Press, 1991); Robert C. Ellickson, *Order without Law: How Neighbors Settle Disputes* (Cambridge, MA: Harvard University Press, 1991).

3. Millington and Maxfield, "Visayan Folk-Tales," 311–14. Onofre D. Corpuz, "Land and Agriculture in the Philippines," *Philippine Review of Economics* 29 (1992): 137–60. Nirmal Sengupta, *Managing Common Property: Irrigation in India and the Philippines* (Thousand Oaks, CA: Sage Publications, 1991). Elinor Ostrom, *Crafting Institutions for Self-Governing Irrigation Systems* (San Francisco: ICS Press, 1992).

4. Hardin, "Tragedy of the Commons," 1243–48. Ostrom, *Governing the Commons*, 38–40.

5. Sylvia Federici, *Caliban and the Witch: Women, the Body, and Primitive Accumulation* (New York: Autonomedia, 2004), 71. A precedent for this thinking about the commons is the work of Peter Kropotkin, who argues that cooperation and not possessive individualism is the key to evolutionary adaptation. See Peter Kropotkin, *Mutual Aid: A Factor in Evolution* (London: William Heinemann, 1902).

6. Ostrom, *Governing the Commons*, 38–40. Ostrom develops the concept of substantive economy, which refers to the ways that people provide for themselves and others outside the market economy, while avoiding the polarization between premodern and modern society, substantive and formal economy, gift and commodity, which has constrained earlier influential accounts. On the problem of polarization in this discourse, see Arjun Appadurai, "Commodities and the Politics of Value," in Arjun Appadurai, ed., *The Social Life of Things: Commodities in Cultural Perspective* (Cambridge: Cambridge University Press, 1986), 3–63.

7. Jones, *Negro Myths from the Georgia Coast*, 7.

8. E. P. Thompson, "Custom, Law, and Common Right," in *Customs in Common* (New York: Penguin Books, 1993), 184. See also Marc Bloch, *French Rural History: An Essay on Its Basic Characteristics* (Berkeley: University of California Press, 1966), 197–213. On the criminalization of custom as conceived in the new social history, see the following: E. P. Thompson, *Whigs and Hunters: The Origin of the Black Act* (London: Allen Lane, 1975); Douglas Hay, Peter Linebaugh, John G. Rule, E. P. Thompson, and Cal Winslow, eds., *Albion's Fatal Tree: Crime and Society in Eighteenth-Century England* (London: Allen Lane, 1975); Peter Linebaugh, "Karl Marx, the Theft of Wood, and Working-Class Composition: A Contribution to the Current Debate," *Crime and Social Justice* (1976): 5–16; Peter Linebaugh, *The London Hanged: Crime and Civil Society in the Eighteenth Century*

(London: Verso Books, 1991); J. M. Neeson, *Commoners: Common Right, Encsure and Social Change in England, 1700–1820* (Cambridge: Cambridge University Press, 1993). For an important precedent to this scholarship, see J. L. Hammond and Barbara Bradby Hammond, *The Village Laborer, 1760–1832: A Study in the Government of England before the Reform Bill* (London: Longman and Green, 1911). For a contrasting perspective on the alienation that results from the transition to capitalism, see Michel Foucault, *Discipline and Punish: The Birth of the Prison*, trans. Alan Sheridan (New York: Vintage Books, 1977). "Landed property became absolute property," Foucault summarizes, and "all the tolerated 'rights' that the peasantry had acquired or preserved . . . were now rejected by the new owners who regarded them quite simply as theft" (85). The alienation from the body resulting from the commodification of labor is also a general theme in Marx's analysis. "The worker," Marx writes, "only feels himself outside his work, and in his work feels outside himself. He is at home when he is not working, and when he is working he is not at home." Marx, *Economic and Philosophical Manuscripts*, 74.

9. E. M. Gordon, *Indian Folk-Tales: Being Side-Lights on Village Life in Bilaspore Central Provinces* (London: Elliot Stock, 1909), 65–69. J. Alden Mason, "Cuatro Cuentos Colombianos," *Journal of American Folklore* 43 (1930): 216. J. Alden Mason, and Aurelio Espinosa, "Porto-Rican Folk-Lore. Folk-Tales," *Journal of American Folklore* 34 (1921): 164. Owens, "Folk-Lore of the Southern Negroes," 750–51. Charles L. Edwards, *Bahama Songs and Stories* (Boston: Houghton, Mifflin and Company, 1895), 73–75. Joyner, *Remember Me*, 52. Gender identification is sometimes less stable in the tar baby, including cases in which the trickster is female. See, for example, Honeÿ, *South-African Folk-Tales*, 73–83. There are also stories where the tar baby is feminized, but the rabbit's

approach does not have an explicitly sexual motivation. See, for example, Ortoli, *Contes de la Veillée*, 17–24.

10. Ortoli, *Evening Tales*, 7. Herskovits notes that this emphasis on good manners is a "significant Africanism." Herskovits, *Myth of the Negro Past*, 272.

11. See, for example, Christensen, *Afro-American Folk Lore*, 62–68.

12. Werner, "The Tar Baby Story," 285. Sapir, "Yana Texts," 227–28. Hose, "Bushy and Jack," 662. Melville J. Herskovits and Frances S. Herskovits, "Tales in Pidgin English from Nigeria," 462.

13. Here I am extending the empirical research on commons institutions by drawing on Axel Honneth's reading of Hegel's early Jena writing, in particular the essay "The Scientific Way of Treating Natural Law" (1802). In contrast to *The Phenomenology of Spirit* (1807), and especially in contrast to the agonistic interpretation of this later work popularized by Alexandre Kojève, Honneth aims to recover a moment in Hegel's thought in which recognition precedes struggle. "Hegel," Honneth writes, "merely wants to say that every philosophical theory of society must proceed not from the acts of isolated subjects but rather from the framework of ethical bonds, within which subjects always already move. Thus, contrary to atomistic theories of society, one is to assume, as a kind of natural basis for human socialization, a situation in which elementary forms of intersubjective coexistence are always present." In my understanding of the tar baby encounter, it is precisely the precedence of this "intersubjective coexistence" that is represented—albeit in a distorted or displaced form—through the expectations that the rabbit brings to his encounter with the tar baby. Axel Honneth, *The Struggle for Recognition: The Moral Grammar of Social Conflicts* (Cambridge: Polity Press, 1995), 14–15. Alexandre Kojève, *Introduction to the Reading of Hegel: Lectures on the Phenom-*

enology of Spirit, trans. James H. Nichols, Jr. (Ithaca, NY: Cornell University Press, 1980).

14. Ortoli, *Evening Tales*, 1–12. Millington and Maxfield, "Visayan Folk-Tales," 311–14. Christensen, "A Negro Legend." Fauset, "Negro Folk Tales from the South," 228–30. Katharine Berry Judson, *Myths and Legends of the Mississippi Valley and the Great Lakes* (Chicago: A.C. McClurg & Co., 1914), 111–15. Dennett, *Folklore of the Fjort*, 90–93. Elsie Clews Parsons, *Folk-Tales of Andros Island, Bahamas* (New York: G.E. Stechert & Co., 1918), 12–16. William Hubbs Mechling, "Stories from Tuxtepec, Oaxaca," *Journal of American Folklore* 25 (1912): 199–203.

15. In some cases, the property owner's moral condescension is imputed directly to the tar baby. "You are too proud," the trickster says, "to answer me!" Fansler, *Filipino Popular Tales*, 327. On the struggle for recognition as the recomposition of the struggle for self-preservation in the state of nature, see Honneth, *Struggle for Recognition*, 31–63.

16. Harris, *Uncle Remus: His Songs and His Sayings*, 23–25, 29–31. Millington and Maxfield, "Visayan Folk-Tales," 311–14.

17. Harris, *Uncle Remus: His Songs and His Sayings*, 23–25, 29–31.

18. Fauset, *Folklore from Nova Scotia*, 45.

19. On the potential positive resolutions to the struggle for recognition, see Charles Taylor, "The Politics of Recognition," in *Philosophical Arguments* (Cambridge: Harvard University Press, 1995), 225–56. The conditions that Taylor describes are objectively absent in the tar baby.

CHAPTER 5. THE BRIAR PATCH

1. For an example of the substitution ruse that closes many versions of the story, see Bain, "The Story of a Dam," 69–73.

For the rabbit's promise to work, see Porter, "Negro Stories," 28. For a story where the trickster is killed, see M. W. Waters, *Cameos from the Kraal* (Alice, South Africa: Lovedale Press, 1926), 28–30. For the trickster's enslavement, see Millington and Maxfield, "Visayan Folk-Tales," 311–14. See the following examples for versions of the story featuring a return to an unenclosed landscape: Hose, "Bushy and Jack," 662–63; "Negro Fables," 505–7. Owens, "Folk-Lore of the Southern Negroes," 750–51; Porter, "Negro Stories," 27–28; Harris, *Uncle Remus: His Songs and His Sayings,* 23–25, 29–31; Jones, *Negro Myths from the Georgia Coast,* 7–11; Edwards, "Some Tales from Bahama Folk-Lore," 50–51; Christensen, *Afro-American Folk Lore,* 62–68; Ortoli, *Evening Tales,* 1–12; J. Owen Dorsey, "Two Biloxi Tales," *Journal of American Folklore* 6 (1893): 48–49; Honeÿ, *South-African Folk-Tales,* 73–83; Talbot, *Shadow of the Bush,* 397–400; Swanton, "Animal Stories," 214–15; Lomax, "Yoruba Tales," 5; Parsons, "Aiken, S.C.," 4–5, 15; Bacon and Parsons, "Elizabeth City," 259–60; Fauset, *Folklore from Nova Scotia,* 45–46; Claudel and Carrière, "French Folklore of Louisiana," 39–41; Armistead, "Two Brer Rabbit Stories from the Eastern Shore of Maryland," 443–44.

2. "We know who we are," Neal chides, "and we are not invisible, at least not to each other." Larry Neal, "And Shine Swam On," in *Black Fire: An Anthology of Afro-American Writing,* ed. LeRoi Jones and Larry Neal (New York: William Morrow, 1968), 652. Albert Murray, *From the Briarpatch File* (New York: Pantheon Books, 2001), 11. Daniel Patrick Moynihan, *The Negro Family: The Case for National Action* (Washington, DC: United States Department of Labor Office of Policy Planning and Research, 1965). See also Larry Neal, "Beware of the Tar Baby," *New York Times,* 3 August 1969, in which Neal interprets being stuck to the tar baby as being locked into "a prison of distorted symbols and images." For a segregationist perspective on the briar patch as a sym-

bol for black community, originally published in 1930, see Robert Penn Warren, "The Briar Patch," in *I'll Take My Stand* (Baton Rouge: Louisiana State University Press, 1977), 246–64.

3. Elkins, *Slavery*. "The social organization of the quarters was the slave's primary environment which gave him his ethical rules and fostered cooperation, mutual assistance, and black solidarity," Blassingame insists, while "the work experiences which most often brought the slave in contact with whites represented his secondary environment and was far less important." Blassingame, *The Slave Community* (1979 ed.), 105. "While from sunup to sundown the American slave worked for another and was harshly exploited," Rawick argues, "from sundown to sunup he lived for himself and created the behavioral and institutional basis which prevented him from becoming the absolute victim." Rawick, *From Sundown to Sunup*, xix. Callahan, *In the African-American Grain*, 34.

4. Toni Morrison, *Tar Baby* (New York: Plume, 1987),48, 89, 193, 305. This allegorical strain is pinpointed by Angelita Reyes. The "central theme" in *Tar Baby*, Reyes writes, is that "Black people of the New World diaspora must not lose sight of their African consciousness." Angelita Reyes, "Ancient Properties in the New World: The Paradox of the 'Other' in Toni Morrison's *Tar Baby*," *Black Scholar* 17 (1986): 19.

5. Morrison, *Tar Baby*, 120, 184, 270–71, 306.

6. Rawick, *From Sundown to Sunup*, xix.

7. Hose, "Bushy and Jack," 662–63. Owens, "Folk-Lore of the Southern Negroes," 750–51. Swanton, "Animal Stories," 214–15. Christensen, *Afro-American Folk Lore*, 62–68. Edwards, *Bahama Songs and Stories*, 73–75. Fauset, "Negro Folk Tales from the South," 228–30. Lomax, "Yoruba Tales," 5. Fauset, *Folklore from Nova Scotia*, 45–46. Dorsey, "Biloxi Tales," 48–49. Honeÿ, *South-African Folk-Tales*, 73–83. For a story from Argentina where the trickster is a toad who

tricks his captor into throwing him into a pond, see Julio Aramburu, *El Folklore de los Niños: Juegos, Corros, Rondas, Canciones, Romances, Cuentos, y Leyendas* (Buenos Aires: El Ateneo, 1944), 177.

8. Espinosa, "Notes on the Origin," 162–83. Harris, *Uncle Remus: His Songs and His Sayings*, 23–25, 29–31. Owens, "Folk-Lore of the Southern Negroes," 750–51. Christensen, *Afro-American Folk Lore*, 62–68.

9. Christensen, *Afro-American Folk Lore*, 62–68. Ortoli, *Evening Tales*, 1–12. Lomax, "Yoruba Tales," 5. "Negro Fables," 505–7. Jones, *Negro Myths from the Georgia Coast*, 7–11. Carrière, *Tales from the French Folk-lore of Missouri*, 29–36.

10. Lester, "Brer Rabbit and the Tar Baby," 10–14.

11. Fernand Braudel, *The Perspective of the World*, vol. 3 of *Civilization and Capitalism: 15th–18th Century*, trans. Siân Reynolds (London: William Collins Sons and Company, 1984), 42. Pierre Clastres, *Society against the State: Essays in Political Anthropology* (New York: Zone Books, 1987). Gonzalo Aguirre Beltrán and Deward E. Walker, *Regions of Refuge* (Washington, DC: Society for Applied Anthropology, 1979). See especially James C. Scott, *The Art of Not Being Governed: An Anarchist History of Upland Southeast Asia* (New Haven, CT: Yale University Press, 2009). Scott describes the subsistence routines and norms of self-organization in these societies as adaptations designed to prevent capture by the state. More controversially, he claims that illiteracy is another one of these strategic adaptations. On maroons, see also the following: Richard Price, *Maroon Societies: Rebel Slave Communities in the Americas* (Baltimore: John Hopkins University Press, 1979); Gad Heuman, ed., *Out of the House of Bondage: Runaways, Resistance, and Marronage in Africa and the New World* (Totowa, NJ: Frank Cass, 1986); John Hope Franklin and Loren Schweninger, *Runaway Slaves: Rebels on the Plantation* (New York: Oxford University Press, 1999); Sylviane A. Diouf, *Slavery's Exiles: The Story of the American*

Maroons (New York: New York University Press, 2014). On marronage and philosophy, see Neil Roberts, *Freedom as Marronage* (Chicago: University of Chicago Press, 2015).

12. Christensen lets it slip at the beginning that the rabbit "lib in de brier-bush," a revelation that anticipates, if it does not exactly spoil, the ending. See Christensen, *Afro-American Folk Lore*, 62–68. One other version in which the rabbit's habitation in the briar patch is mentioned at the start is Mary Ross Banks, *Bright Days in the Old Plantation Time* (Boston: Lee and Shepard, 1882), 204–16. The tar baby story is a perfect example for Aristotle's account of deus ex machina. "It is obvious," Aristotle writes, "that the solutions of plots too should come about as a result of the plot itself, and not from a contrivance. . . . A contrivance must be used for matters outside the drama—either previous events which are beyond human knowledge, or later ones that need to be foretold or announced." Aristotle, *Poetics*, ed. Malcolm Heath (London: Penguin, 1996), 45.

13. Jones, *Negro Myths from the Georgia Coast*, 7–11. Joyner, *Remember Me*, 46. The approach to the story as a cultural retention is especially strong in this context, as the Georgia coast is one of the most important settings for studying African cultural retentions in the United States. The origin of stories like the tar baby, Ruby Andrews Moore would argue in 1894, was easy to determine in these locations. "A cargo from Congo," Andrews explains, "was brought to Liberty County . . . only a few years before the abolition of slavery." Their songs and stories were shared with the creole slave population, and so it was no surprise to Andrews that they would still be in circulation only a few decades later when she was writing. Ruby Andrews Moore, "Superstitions from Georgia, II," *Journal of American Folklore* 7 (1894): 305–6. On cultural retention among slaves and their descendents in coastal Georgia, see the following: Herskovits, "The Negro in the New World," 149–50; Georgia Writers' Project,

Drums and Shadows: Survival Studies among the Georgia Coastal Negroes (Athens: University of Georgia Press, 1940); Philip Morgan, "Lowcountry Georgia and the Early Modern Atlantic World," inPhilip Morgan, ed., *African American Life in the Georgia Lowcountry: The Atlantic World and the Gullah Geechee* (Athens: University of Georgia Press, 2010), 13–47.

14. Jones, *Negro Myths from the Georgia Coast*, 7–11. For a related version of the story from the same region, see Albert H. Stoddard, "The Tar Baby," in *Animal Tales Told in the Gullah Dialect* (Washington, DC: Library of Congress Division of Music Recording Laboratory, Folklore of the United States, 1955).

15. Erskine Clark, *Dwelling Place: A Plantation Epic* (New Haven: Yale University Press, 2005), 27–29, 48–50, 230–32, 313–14, 370–73. Timothy J. Lockley, *Lines in the Sand: Race and Class in Lowcountry Georgia, 1750–1860* (Athens: University of Georgia Press, 2001), 57–97. Mart A. Stewart, *"What Nature Suffers to Groe": Life, Labor, and Landscape on the Georgia Coast, 1680–1920* (Athens: University of Georgia Press, 1996), 135–36, 194–96, 238–39.

16. In the southern states, Sam Hillard reports, "nonfarm land and unimproved farmland added up to an almost incredible 87 percent of the land area in 1850 and nearly 82 percent even in 1860." Sam Bowers Hilliard, *Hog Meat and Hoecake: Food Supply in the Old South, 1840–1860* (Carbondale, IL: Southern Illinois University Press, 1972), 74; see also 98–100. For statistics on improved and unimproved acreage, see Donald B. Dodd and Wynelle S. Dodd, *Historical Statistics of the South, 1790–1970* (Tuscaloosa: University of Alabama Press, 1973), 2, 18, 26, 34, 38, 50, 54, 58. On unfenced land and the antebellum commons, see Stephanie McCurry, *Masters of Small Worlds Yeoman Households, Gender Relations, and the Political Culture of the Antebellum South Carolina Low Country* (New York: Oxford University Press, 1995),

5–36. On the commons in Liberty County, see the following: Ras M. Brown, "'Walk in the Feenda': West-Central Africans and the Forest in the South Carolina–Georgia Lowcountry," in Linda M. Heywood, ed., *Central Africans and Cultural Transformations in the American Diaspora* (Cambridge: Cambridge University Press, 2002), 289–318; Stewart, *What Nature Suffers to Groe*, 135–36, 194–96, 238–39; William Hampton, William R. Adams, Carolyn Rock, and Janis Kearney-Williams, "Foodways on the Plantations at Kings Bay: Hunting, Fishing, and Raising Food," in *Historical Archaeology of Plantations at Kings Bay, Camden County, Georgia*, ed. William Hampton (Gainesville: University of Florida Department of Anthropology), 225–27, 231–33, 241–42, 244–76.

17. "Historians have shown that the slaves' diet was objectively deficient in providing slaves with enough sustenance to reproduce their labor," Philip Morgan reports. Philip D. Morgan, *Slave Counterpoint: Black Culture in the Eighteenth-Century Chesapeake and Lowcountry* (Chapel Hill: University of North Carolina Press, 1998), 134–43. See the following on antebellum subsistence and food supply in Liberty County: Stewart, *What Nature Suffers to Groe*, 135–36, 176–78, 240–41; Elizabeth J. Reitz, Tyson Gibbs, and Ted A Rathbun, "Archaeological Evidence for Subsistence on Coastal Plantations," *The Archaeology of Slavery and Plantation Life* (Orlando, FL: Academic Press, 1985), 163–94; Tyson Gibbs, Kathleen Cargill, Leslie Sue Lieberman, and Elizabeth Reitz, "Nutrition in a Slave Population: An Anthropological Examination," *Medical Anthropology* 4 (1980): 175–262. On subsistence in central Georgia, see Joseph P. Reidy, *From Slavery to Agrarian Capitalism in the Cotton Plantation South: Central Georgia, 1800–1880* (Chapel Hill: University of North Carolina Press, 1992), 58–81, especially 69–73. On slave gardens, see Richard Westmacott, *African-American Gardens and Yards in the Rural South* (Knoxville:

University of Tennessee Press, 1992), 20–34, 88–107. On slave subsistence generally, see Hilliard, *Hog Meat and Hoecake*, 21–36, 70–91, 92–140, 172–85, 213–30. For first-person observation of the importance of hunting and fishing to slave subsistence, see Frances Anne Kemble, *Journal of a Residence on a Georgia Plantation*, ed. John A. Scott (Athens: University of Georgia Press, 1984), 89, 152–54, 172–73, 307. For a retrospective account of these practices after slavery, see Robert Q. Mallard, *Plantation Life before Emancipation* (Richmond, VA: Whillet and Shepperson, 1892), 65, 67–72.

18. See the following on the task system, especially as it was organized in the Georgia Low Country: Philip D. Morgan, "Work and Culture: The Task System and the World of Lowcountry Blacks, 1700 to 1880," *William and Mary Quarterly* (1982): 564–99; Morgan, *Slave Counterpoint*, 179–87; Peter A. Coclanis, "How the Low Country Was Taken to Task: Slave-Labor Organization in Coastal South Carolina and Georgia," in *Slavery, Secession, and Southern History*, ed. Robert Louis Paquette and Louis Ferleger (Charlottesville: University Press of Virginia, 2000), 59–78. On slaves and common property, independent production by slaves, and the informal economy in the Low Country and elsewhere, see the following: Thomas Armstrong, "From Task Labor to Free Labor: The Transition along Georgia's Rice Coast, 1820–1880," *Georgia Historical Quarterly* 64 (1980): 432–47; Philip D. Morgan, "The Ownership of Property by Slaves in the Mid-Nineteenth-Century Low Country," *Journal of Southern History* 49 (1983): 399–420; Ira Berlin and Philip D. Morgan, eds., *The Slaves' Economy: Independent Production by Slaves in the Americas* (London: Frank Cass, 1991); Betty Wood, *Women's Work, Men's Work: The Informal Slave Economies of Lowcountry Georgia* (Athens: University of Georgia Press, 1995); Morgan, *Slave Counterpoint*, 134–43; Dylan C. Penningroth, *The Claims of Kinfolk: African American Prop-*

erty and Community in the Nineteenth-Century South (Chapel Hill: University of North Carolina Press, 2003), 46–79. For discussions of the "peculium" as a phenomenon of world slavery, see Patterson, *Slavery and Social Death*, 182–84.

19. Penningroth, *Claims of Kinfolk*, 46–79.

20. Penningroth, *Claims of Kinfolk*, 41, 86, 89, 97, 100. Dylan Penningroth, "Slavery, Freedom, and Social Claims to Property among African Americans in Liberty County, Georgia, 1850–1880," *Journal of American History* 84 (1997): 411–12. The term "informal economy" was coined by anthropologist Keith Hart. See Hart, "Informal Income Opportunities and Urban Employment in Ghana," *Journal of Modern African Studies* 11 (1973): 61–89. This concept has sometimes seemed problematic because it presumes its opposite— a transparent state-sanctioned economy—under circumstances where it does not exist. For critique and elaboration, see Alejandro Portes, Manuel Castells, and Lauren A. Benton, *The Informal Economy: Studies in Advanced and Less Developed Countries* (Baltimore: Johns Hopkins University Press, 1989).

21. Leon F. Litwack, *Been in the Storm So Long: The Aftermath of Slavery* (New York: Vintage Books), 292–449. Amy Dru Stanley, "Beggars Can't Be Choosers: Compulsion and Contract in Postbellum America," *Journal of American History* 78 (1992):1265–93. Reidy, *From Slavery to Agrarian Capitalism*, 215–41. On white recreational hunters and fishermen objecting to ex-slaves hunting, fishing, and foraging for subsistence, see Scott E. Giltner, *Hunting and Fishing in the New South: Black Labor and White Leisure after the Civil War* (Baltimore: Johns Hopkins University Press, 2008), 45–77.

22. On the shift from the encouragement of open-field grazing and other subsistence activities during the antebellum decades to their criminalization after emancipation, see also Alex Lichtenstein, " 'That Disposition to Theft, with Which They Have Been Branded': Moral Economy, Slave Manage-

ment, and the Law," *Journal of Social History* 21 (1988): 413–40. On this shift specifically in the wiregrass counties in northern Georgia, see Reidy, *From Slavery to Agrarian Capitalism*, 69–71.

23. Steven Hahn, "Hunting, Fishing, and Foraging: Common Rights and Class Relations in the Postbellum South," *Radical History Review* 26 (1982): 37–64. Lichtenstein, " 'That Disposition to Theft' ": 413–40. Pippa Holloway, " 'A Chicken-Stealer Shall Lose His Vote': Disfranchisement for Larceny in the South, 1874–1890," *Journal of Southern History* 75 (2009): 931–62. Stewart, *What Nature Suffers to Groe*, 135–36. Giltner, *Hunting and Fishing in the New South*, 10–44. Reidy, *From Slavery to Agrarian Capitalism*, 69–70, 151–52, 224–27, 240–41.

24. Thomas R. R. Cobb, *A Digest of the Statute Laws of the State of Georgia: In Force Prior to the Session of the General Assembly of 1851* (Athens, GA: Christy, Kelsea & Burke, 1851), 18–19, 260, 261. Richard H. Clark, Thomas R. R. Cobb, and David Irwin, *The Code of the State of Georgia* (Atlanta, GA: John H. Seals, Crusader Book and Job Office, 1861), 269–70. *Harrel v. Hannum*, 56 Georgia 508 (1876). Washburn and Moen Manufacturing Company, *The Fence Question in the Southern States as Related to General Husbandry and Sheep Raising* (Worcester, MA: Snow, Woodman, and Company, 1881). Forrest McDonald and Grady McWhiney, "The Antebellum Southern Herdsman: A Reinterpretation," *Journal of Southern History* (1975): 147–66. Charles L. Flynn Jr., *White Land, Black Labor: Caste and Class in Late Nineteenth-Century Georgia* (Baton Rouge: Louisiana State University Press, 1983), 84–149. Steven Hahn, *The Roots of Southern Populism: Yeoman Farmers and the Transformation of the Georgia Upcountry, 1850–1890* (New York: Oxford University Press, 1983), 50–86, 239–68. Reidy, *From Slavery to Agrarian Capitalism*, 8, 40, 69–70, 151–60, 215–41. Shawn Kantor, *Politics and Property Rights: The Closing of the Open Range*

in the *Postbellum South* (Chicago: University of Chicago Press, 1998). Penningroth, *Claims of Kinfolk*, 47–50, 64–67. R. Ben Brown, "Free Men and Free Pigs: Closing the Southern Range and the American Property Tradition," *Radical History Review* 108 (2010): 117–37.

25. *Rust v. Low*, 6 Massachusetts 90 (1809). "Memorial from the State Grange of Patrons of Husbandry," 7 February 1874, in Petitions and Memorials, Record of the House and Senate, Georgia Department of Archives and History, Atlanta, Georgia.

26. Charles C. Jones, *The Religious Instruction of the Negroes in the United States* (Savannah: Thomas Purse, 1842), 146. "*You can not afford to be idle,*" Clinton Fisk insists. "The world is full of profitable work," he continues, "and nothing is impossible to the industrious." Idleness, on the other hand, "destroys a man's health," makes him "feel mean," and "sends him on a short road to ruin," if not to "prison" or "the gallows." Clinton B. Fisk, *Plain Counsels for Freedmen: In Sixteen Brief Lectures* (Boston: American Tract Society, 1866), 17, 67. Helen E. Brown, *John Freeman and His Family* (New York: A.M.S. Press, 1864). Jacqueline Jones, *Soldiers of Light and Love: Northern Teachers and Georgia Blacks, 1865–1873* (Chapel Hill: University of North Carolina Press, 1980), 109–66. Hartman, *Scenes of Subjection*, 125–40. James C. Bonner, "Charles Colcock Jones: The Macauley of the South," *Georgia Historical Quarterly* 27 (1943): 324–38.

27. Gordon Noel Hurtel, "Brer Rabbit and the Collard Patch," *Atlanta Constitution*, 10 January 1902. Bailey's alibi is also crucial to consider. "I axed Brudder Jones before Chrismus ef I mite hab some ob his collard greens an' he lowed dat atter de fall ob de nex' fros' I mout hab er mess," Bailey explains. Walking past the collard patch, Bailey recalled the promise, hopped the gate, and helped himself, only to find a police officer waiting. "Hello, Brer Rabbit," the officer said before hailing him to jail. This sketch draws on the tar baby

and similar trickster stories to make a joke of Bailey's criminal tendencies. We know the greens do not belong to Bailey, because it was Jones, not Bailey, who devoted labor to their cultivation. We know too that no credence should be given to Bailey's excuses, either his claim to Jones's promise or his claim to contingent labor, as his testimony is self-defeating, like the rabbit's claim to subsist on the dew.

28. Howard W. Odum and Guy B. Johnson, *Negro Workaday Songs* (Chapel Hill: University of North Carolina Press, 1926), 71–72. John Blassingame interprets this song as an example of political consciousness under slavery. Blassingame, *Slave Community* (1979 ed.), 122.

29. On convict leasing in Georgia and elsewhere, see the following. Alexander C. Lichtenstein, *Twice the Work of Free Labor: The Political Economy of Convict Labor in the New South* (London: Verso Books, 1996). David Oshinsky, *Worse than Slavery: Parchman Farm and the Ordeal of Jim Crow Justice* (New York: Free Press, 1996). Edward Ayers, *Vengeance and Justice: Crime and Punishment in the Nineteenth-Century American South* (New York: Oxford University Press, 1983) 185–222. On criminal justice and the transformation of racial categories after slavery, see Khalil G. Muhammad, *The Condemnation of Blackness: Race, Crime, and the Making of Modern Urban America* (Cambridge, MA: Harvard University Press, 2010).

30. On turpentine labor in the pine forests in south Georgia and northeast Florida, see the following: Thomas F. Armstrong, "The Transformation of Work: Turpentine Workers in Coastal Georgia, 1865–1901," *Labor History* 25 (1984): 518–32; Jerrell H. Shofner, "Forced Labor in the Florida Forests, 1880–1950," *Journal of Forest History* (1981): 14–25; Robert N. Lauriault, "From Can't to Can't: The North Florida Turpentine Camp, 1900–1950," *Florida Historical Quarterly* 67 (1989): 310–28.

31. Frederick Douglass, *Narrative of the Life of Frederick Douglass, an American Slave* (Boston: Published at the Anti-slavery Office, 1845), 16. On contextualization cues, see Richard Bauman and Charles Briggs, "Poetics and Performance as Critical Perspectives on Language and Social Life," *Annual Review of Anthropology* 19 (1990): 59–88.

32. This conviction that expropriation is an ongoing process, and not a one-time event, has led scholars like David Harvey and Patrick Wolfe to coin new terms in order to reframe Marx's discussion of the preconditions for capitalism. On "accumulation by dispossession," see David Harvey, *The New Imperialism* (New York: Oxford University Press, 2003). On "preaccumulation," a term referencing both the "historical endowment that colonisers bring with them" and "the native's countervailing historical plenitudes," see Wolfe, *Traces of History*, 19–24.

EPILOGUE

1. On the permeable boundary between bound and free labor in these contexts, see Tomlins, *Freedom Bound*, 193–331. See also Sven Beckert, *Empire of Cotton: A Global History* (New York: Alfred A. Knopf, 2014).

2. Hannah Arendt, *The Human Condition* (Chicago: University of Chicago Press, 1958), 3. The "right to have rights," Arendt proposes, is the "right to belong to humanity." Hannah Arendt, *The Origins of Totalitarianism* . 2nd ed. (New York: Harcourt Brace, 1968), 296–97.

3. Aristotle, *The Politics and the Constitution of Athens*, ed. Stephen Everson (Cambridge: Cambridge University Press, 1996), 13–14. The idea about the impossibility of animals speaking remained influential at the time when thinkers, including John Locke, were deducing the natural right to prop-

erty. See, for instance, John Locke, *An Essay Concerning Human Understanding*, ed. P. H. Nidditch (New York: Oxford University Press, 1975), 159–60, 402, 408, 614. This was far from a unanimous position in European philosophy of mind. See, for instance, Michel de Montaigne, "The Apology for Raymond Sebond," in *Complete Essays*, ed. M. A. Screech (London: Penguin Books, 1993), 489–683. See also R. W. Serjeantson, "The Passions and Animal Language, 1540–1700," *Journal of the History of Ideas* 62 (2001): 425–44.

4. *Primitive Culture*, 1:409–10. See also M. de Fontenelle, *Oeuvres de Monsieur de Fontenelle*, 8 vols. (Paris: Chez Brunet, 1753), 3:270–96. On the "method of folklore," see Andrew Lang, *Custom and Myth* (London: Longmans, Green, and Co., 1884), 11. "Folklore," Lang writes, is a "form of study" that "collects and compares the similar but immaterial relics of old races, the surviving superstitions and stories, the ideas which are in our time but not of it." On anthropomorphism as category mistake, see Thomas Nagel, "What Is It Like to Be a Bat?" *Philosophical Review* 83 (1974): 435–50. For the claim that anthropomorphism is unavoidable and is productive for thought, see Daniel C. Dennett, *The Intentional Stance* (Cambridge: MIT Press, 1987). See also Jacques Derrida, "The Animal That Therefore I Am," *Critical Inquiry* 28 (2002): 367–418.

5. *Aesop's Fables*, trans. Laura Gibbs (New York: Oxford University Press, 2008). On these fables as political parables of everyday life, see the following. Annabel Patterson, *Fables of Power: Aesopian Writing and Political History* (Durham, NC: Duke University Press, 1991). Michel de Certeau, *The Mystic Fable* (Chicago: University of Chicago Press, 1992). Sara Forsdyke, *Slaves Tell Tales and Other Episodes in the Politics of Popular Culture in Ancient Greece* (Princeton, NJ: Princeton University Press, 2012).

6. [Christensen], "A Negro Legend." Alice Werner understands this anthropomorphism not as intentional design but as a sign of confusion. "This sort of thing constantly occurs," she says, "the narrator apparently forgetting that his characters are not in human shape." Alice Werner, "The Bantu Element in Swahili Folklore," *Folklore* 20 (1909): 443–44. See also Nassau, *Where Animals Talk*.

7. Jane Bennett, *Vibrant Matter: A Political Ecology of Things* (Durham, NC: Duke University Press, 2010). Donna Haraway, *When Species Meet* (Minneapolis: University of Minnesota Press, 2008). Cary Wolfe, *Animal Rites* (Chicago: University of Chicago Press, 2003).

8. Johnson, "Three Mexican Tar Baby Stories," 215–17. [Christensen], "A Negro Legend." Swanton, "Animal Stories," 214–15.

9. On unstable irony, see Wayne Booth, *A Rhetoric of Irony* (Chicago: University of Chicago Press, 1974), 240–52.

10. Locke, *Two Treatises*, 179, 183, 273, 279. On Alberico Gentili, see Tomlins, *Freedom Bound*, 129–30, 134–35. Hobbes holds that "to make covenant with bruit Beasts is impossible; because not understanding our speech, they understand not, nor accept any translation of Right, nor can translate any Right to another: and without mutuall acceptation, there is no Covenant." Hobbes, *Leviathan*, 97. Vitoria agrees that "barbarians . . . are little or no more capable of governing themselves . . . than wild beasts." Vitoria, *Political Writings*, 290–91. On the controversy over recursive thought in humans and nonhuman animals, see Michael C. Corballis, *The Recursive Mind: The Origins of Human Language, Thought, and Civilization* (Princeton, NJ: Princeton University Press, 2011). Also relevant here is the argument made by David Brion Davis over a series of books that slavery sought to reduce humans to a condition in which they had "no more autonomy of will and consciousness" than an "animal."

David Brion Davis, *The Problem of Slavery in Western Culture* (Ithaca, NY: Cornell University Press, 1966), 62.

11. Donna Haraway, *The Companion Species Manifesto: Dogs, People, and Significant Otherness* (Chicago: Prickly Paradigm Press, 2003), 5. Maurice Leenhardt, *Do Kamo: La Personne et Le Mythe dans le Monde Mélanésien* (Paris: Gallimard, 1947). If the tar baby is not *about* animals, it is also not *about* humans, at least in any sense that would isolate humans from the natural world. The story's anthropomorphism destabilizes these points of reference. To borrow Brian Massumi's terms, we might say that the story's anthropomorphism breaks down "our image of ourselves as standing apart from other animals . . . based on the specious grounds of our sole proprietorship of language, thought, and creativity." Brian Massumi, *What Animals Teach Us about Politics* (Durham, NC: Duke University Press, 2014), 3.

12. On the separation of politics (the domain of subjects) and science (the domain of objects) in modernity, see Bruno Latour, *We Have Never Been Modern* (Cambridge, MA: Harvard University Press, 1993). As I have shown, the tar baby story does not bolster the regime of knowledge that Latour associates with modernity. Instead, the story questions how its own characters (such as the rabbit) and props (such as the tar baby) came to count as subjects and objects in the first place.

SELECT BIBLIOGRAPHY OF PRIMARY SOURCES, 1865-1945

Abernethy, Francis Edward. "V. The Centennial Years 1934 to 1938," in *Texas Folklore Society: 1909–1945* (Denton, TX: University of North Texas Press, 1992), 118–19.

Andrade, Manuel José. *Folk-Lore from the Dominican Republic* (New York: G.E. Stechert and Co., 1930), 210–13.

"[Annie Reed Interview]," in George P. Rawick, ed., *The American Slave: A Composite Autobiography: Supplement, Series 2* (Westport, CT: Greenwood Press, 1979), 2209.

Aramburu, Julio, *El Folklore de los Niños: Juegos, Corros, Rondas, Canciones, Romances, Cuentos y Leyendas* (Buenos Aires: Librería y Editorial, 1944), 177.

Armistead, Samuel G., "Two Brer Rabbit Stories from the Eastern Shore of Maryland," *Journal of American Folklore* 84 (1971): 443–44.

Bacon, A. M., and Elsie Clews Parsons, "Folk-Lore from Elizabeth City County, Virginia," *Journal of American Folklore* 35 (1922): 259–60.

Bain, Robert Nisbet, ed., *Cossack Fairy Tales and Folk-Tales* (London: A.H. Bullen, 1902), 139–43.

Bain, Thomas, "The Story of a Dam," *Folk-Lore Journal* 1 (1879): 69–73.

Baissac, Charles, "Le Folk-lore de L'Ile-Maurice," in *Litteratures Populaires de Toutes Les Nations: Traditions, Legendes, Contes,*

Chansons, Proverbes, Devinettes, Superstitions (Paris: Maisonneuve et Ch. Leclerc, 1888), 27: 2–14.

Banks, Mary Ross, *Bright Days in the Old Plantation Time* (Boston: Lee and Shepard, 1882), 204–16.

Barker, William Henry, and Cecilia Sinclair, *West African Folk-
Tales* (London: George G. Harrap & Company, 1917),
69–72.

Beckwith, Martha Warren, *Jamaica Folk-Lore* (New York:
American Folk-Lore Society, 1928), 64.

Beckwith, Martha Warren, and Helen Heffron Roberts, *Jamaica Anansi Stories* (New York: G.E. Stechert & Co.,
1924), 23–26, 64–66.

Bladé, M. Jean-François, *Contes Populaires de la Gascogne* (Paris:
Maisonneuve Frères, 1886), 104–19.

Boas, Franz, "Notes on Mexican Folk-Lore," *Journal of American Folklore* 25 (1912): 235–39.

P. O. Bodding, ed., *Santal Folk Tales*, 2 vols. (Oslo: H. Asche-
houg & Co., 1925), 1:179–85, 213–17.

Boas, Franz, and C. Kamba Simango, "Tales and Proverbs of
the Vandau of Portuguese South Africa," *Journal of American
Folklore* 35 (1922): 162–64.

Boehm, Max, and Franz Specht, *Lettisch-litauisch Volksmärchen*
(Jena: E. Diederichs, 1924), 147–48.

Bompas, Cecil Henry, "The Jackal and the Chickens," in *Folklore of the Santal Parganas* (London: David Nutt, 1909),
322–25.

Braga, Teófilo, *Contos Tradicionais do Povo Português*, 2 vols.
(Lisbon: J. Rodrigues, 1919), 1:83, 2:165–68.

Brown, Charles Edward, *Wigwam Tales: Indian Short Stories for
the Fireside and Camp Fire* (Madison, WI: C.E. Brown,
1930), 20.

Brown, Wenzell, "Anansi and Brer Rabbit," *American Mercury*
69 (1949): 440.

Burlin, Natalie Curtis, C. Kamba Simango, and Madikane

Čele, *Songs and Tales from the Dark Continent* (New York: G. Schirmer, 1920), 45–47.

Cabrera, Lydia, *Cuentos Negros de Cuba*, trans. J. Alberto Hernandez-Chiroldes and Lauren Yoder (Lincoln, NE: University of Nebraska Press, 2004), 124–26.

Carrière, Joseph-Médard, *Tales from the French Folk-Lore of Missouri* (Evanston, IL: Northwestern University, 1937), 29–36.

Cascudo, Luis da Camara, *Contos Tradicionais do Brasil* (Rio de Janeiro: Americ-Edit, 1946), 56, 183–89, 295.

Chatelain, Héli, *Folk-Tales of Angola* (Boston: G.E. Stechert & Co., 1894), 183–89, 295.

[Christensen, Abigail M. H.], "A Negro Legend: De Wolf, De Rabbit and De Tar Baby," *Springfield Daily Republican*, 2 June 1874.

Christensen, Abigail M. H., *Afro-American Folk Lore: Told Round Cabin Fires on the Sea Islands of South Carolina* (Boston: J.G. Cupples, 1892), 62–68.

Claudel, Calvin, and J.-M. Carrière, "Three Tales from the French Folklore of Louisiana," *Journal of American Folklore* 56 (1943): 39–41.

Coelho, Francisco Adolpho, *Contos Populares Portuguezes* (Lisboa: Plantier, 1879), 317–18.

Cox, John Harrington, "Negro Tales from West Virginia," *Journal of American Folklore* 47 (1934): 342–47.

Cronise, Florence M., and Henry W. Ward, *Cunnie Rabbit, Mr. Spider and the Other Beef* (New York: E. P. Dutton and Company, 1903), 101–9.

Dähnhardt, Oskar, *Natursagen: Eine Sammlung naturdeutender Sagen Märchen Fabeln und Legenden*, 4 vols. (Leipzig und Berlin, 1907–1912), 4: 27–30

De Huff, E. W., *Taytay's Tales: Folklore of the Pueblo Indians* (New York: Harcourt, Brace, and Company, 1922), 61–64.

Dennett, R. E., *Notes on the Folklore of the Fjort* (London: David Nutt, 1898), 90–93.

Dewar, Emmeline H. *Chinamwanga Stories* (Livingstonia, Malawi: Mission Press, 1900), 57.

Dixon, Roland B., "Shasta Myths," *Journal of American Folklore* 23 (1910): 34–35.

Dobie, J. Frank. *Puro Mexicano* (Austin, TX: Texas Folk-Lore Society, 1935), 13–19.

Dorsey, George Amos, *Traditions of the Osage* (Chicago: Field Columbian Museum, 1904), 24–25.

Dorsey, J. Owen, "Two Biloxi Tales," *Journal of American Folklore* 6 (1893): 48–49.

Edwards, Charles L., *Bahama Songs and Stories* (Boston: Houghton, Mifflin and Company, 1895), 73–75.

Edwards, Charles L., "Some Tales from Bahama Folk-Lore," *Journal of American Folklore* 4 (1891): 50–51.

Ellis, Alfred Burdon, *The Ewe-Speaking Peoples of the Slave Coast of West Africa* (London: Chapman and Hall, 1890), 275–77.

Ernst, Adolfo, *Tio Tigre und Tio Conejo: Venezuelanische Thierfabeln dem Volke nacherzählt* (Berlin: Verhandlungen der Berliner anthropologischen Gesellschaft, 1888), 275, 277.

Espinosa, Aurelio M., *Cuentos Populares Espanoles* (Stanford, CA: Stanford University Press, 1923), 80–82.

Espinosa, Aurelio M., "Pueblo Indian Folk-Tales," Journal of American Folklore 49 (1936): 85–86.

Espinosa, Aurelio M., "Three More Peninsular Spanish Folktales That Contain the Tar-Baby Story," *Folklore* 50 (1939): 366–77.

Espinosa, Aurelio M., "A Third European Version of the Tar-Baby Story," *Journal of American Folklore* 43 (1930): 329–31.

Fansler, Dean S., *Filipino Popular Tales: Collected and Edited with Comparative Notes* (New York: G.E. Stechert & Co., 1921), 326–37.

Farrand, Livingston, "Shasta and Athapascan Myths from Oregon," ed. Leo J. Frachtenberg, *Journal of American Folklore* 28 (1915): 218.

Fauset, Arthur Huff, *Folklore from Nova Scotia* (New York: G. E. Stechert & Co., 1931), 45–46.

Fauset, Arthur Huff, "Negro Folk Tales from the South (Alabama, Mississippi, Louisiana)," *Journal of American Folklore* 40 (1927): 228–30.

Fauset, Arthur Huff, "Tales and Riddles Collected in Philadelphia." *Journal of American Folklore* 41 (1928): 532.

Federal Writers' Project, "Tar-Baby," in *South Carolina Folk Tales: Stories of Animals and Supernatural Beings* (Columbia, SC: Federal Works Agency, 1941), 29–31.

Fortier, Alcée, "Bits of Louisiana Folk-Lore," *Transactions and Proceedings of the Modern Language Association of America* 3 (1887): 101–15.

Frachtenberg, Leo Joachim, *Alsea Texts and Myths* (Washington, DC: Government Printing Office, 1920), 12.

Gamaleya, Boris, "Contes Populaires de la Réunion," *Bardzour Maskarin* 4 (1977): 18–27.

Goddard, Pliny Earle, "Myths and Tales from the San Carlos Apache," in *Anthropological Papers of the American Museum of Natural History* (New York: Order of the Trustees, 1920), 24:74.

Gomes, Lindolfo, *Contos Populares Brasileiros* (São Paulo: Melhoramentos, 1948), 82–84.

Gonzales, Ambrose E., *The Black Border: Gullah Stories of the Carolina Coast* (Columbia, SC, 1922), 15.

Gordon, E. M., *Indian Folk-Tales: Being Side-Lights on Village Life in Bilaspore, Central Provinces* (London: Elliot Stock, 1909), 65–69.

Harris, Joel Chandler, *The Tar-Baby: and Other Rhymes of Uncle Remus* (New York: D. Appleton and Company, 1904), 3–18.

Harris, Joel Chandler, "Uncle Remus's Folk Lore: Brer Rabbit, Brer Fox, and the Tar-Baby, II," *Atlanta Constitution*, November 16, 1879.

Harris, Joel Chandler, "Uncle Remus's Folk Lore: Showing

How Brer Rabbit Was Too Sharp for Brer Fox, IV," *Atlanta Constitution*, November 30, 1879.

Harris, Joel Chandler, "The Wonderful Tar-Baby Story" and "How Mr. Rabbit Was Too Sharp for Mr. Fox," in *Uncle Remus: His Songs and His Sayings, the Folk-lore of the Old Plantation* (New York: D. Appleton and Company, 1881), 23–25, 29–31.

Held, Toni von, *Märchen und Sagen der afrikanischen Neger* (Jena: H. W. Schmidt, 1904), 72.

Helser, Albert D., *African Stories* (Chicago: Fleming H. Revell Company, 1920), 67.

Herskovits, Melville J., and Frances S. Herskovits, *Rebel Destiny: Among the Bush Negroes of Dutch Guiana* (New York: Whittlesey House, 1934), 13–15.

Herskovits, Melville J., and Frances S. Herskovits, *Suriname Folk-Lore* (New York: Columbia University Press, 1936), 163–8.

Herskovits, Melville J., and Frances S. Herskovits, "Tales in Pidgin English from Ashanti," *Journal of American Folklore* 50 (1937): 55–56.

Herskovits, Melville J., and Frances S. Herskovits, "Tales in Pidgin English from Nigeria," *Journal of American Folklore* 44 (1931): 460–63.

Hill, W. W., "Navaho Coyote Tales and Their Position in the Southern Athabaskan Stock," *Journal of American Folklore* 58 (1945): 333.

Holland, Madeleine, "Folklore of the Banyanja," *Folklore* 27 (1916): 116.

Honeÿ, James A., *South-African Folk-Tales* (New York: The Baker & Taylor Company, 1910), 73–83.

Hose, Mary, "Bushy and Jack," *Harper's New Monthly Magazine* 34 (1867): 662–63.

Huffman, Ray, *Nuer Customs and Folklore* (London: Oxford University Press, 1931), 100–102.

Hughes, Langston, and Arna Bontemps, eds., *The Book of Negro Folklore* (New York: Dodd, Mead & Company, 1958), 1–2.

Jacobs, Joseph, "The Demon with the Matted Hair," in *Indian Fairy Tales* (London: David Nutt, 1892), 194–98.

Johnson, Frederick, "Kiniramba Folk Tales," *Bantu Studies* 5 (1931): 328–30.

Johnson, Jean Bassett, "Three Mexican Tar Baby Stories," *Journal of American Folklore* 53 (1940): 215–17.

Johnson, John H., "Folk-Lore from Antigua, British West Indies," *Journal of American Folklore* 34 (1921): 53.

Johnston, Sir Harry H., *Liberia*, 2 vols. (London: Hutchinson and Company, 1906), 2: 1087–89.

Jones, Charles Colcock, Jr., *Negro Myths from the Georgia Coast Told in the Vernacular* (Boston: Houghton, Mifflin and Company, 1888), 7–11.

Judson, Katharine Berry, *Myths and Legends of the Mississippi Valley and the Great Lakes* (Chicago: A.C. McClurg & Co., 1914), 111–13, 114–15.

Junod, Henri A., *Les Chants et les Contes de Ba-Ronga de la Baie de Delagoa* (Lausanne: Georges Bridel & Cie., 1897), 96–98.

Kalibala, E. Baintuma, and Mary Gould Davis, *Wakaima and the Clay Man and Other African Folktales* (New York: Longmans, 1946), 245.

Kidd, Dudley, *Savage Childhood: A Study of Kafir Children* (London: Adam and Charles Black, 1906), 240–43.

Koch-Grünberg, Theodor, *Vom Roroima zum Orinoco*, 2 vols. (Stuttgart: Strecker und Schröder, 1916–22), 1:47–48.

Kootz-Kretschmer, Elsie, *Die Safwa*, 3 vols. (Berlin: Dietrich Reimer, 1929), 2:159–61.

Kunst, J., "Some Animal Fables of the Chuh Indians," *Journal of American Folklore* 28 (1915): 356.

Lederbogen, Wilhelm, "Duala Fables," trans. M. Huber, *Journal of the Royal African Society* 4 (1904): 58–60.

Lomax, John A., "Stories of an African Prince: Yoruba Tales," *Journal of American Folklore* 26 (1913): 5.

Lyra, Carmen, *Los Cuentos de Mi Tia Panchita* (San Jose, Costa Rica: Soley & Valverde, 1936), 132–34.

Mänchen-Helfen, Otto, "Zu den Zwerghirschgeschichten," *Anthropos* 30 (1935): 554–57.

Mason, J. Alden, "Cuatro Cuentos Colombianos." *Journal of American Folklore* 43 (1930): 216.

Mason, J. Alden, and Aurelio Espinosa, "Porto-Rican Folk-Lore. Folk-Tales," *Journal of American Folklore* 34 (1921): 164.

McNair, J.F.A., and Thomas Lambert Barlow, "The Farmer, the Crocodile, and the Jackal," in *Oral Traditions from the Indus* (Brighton: Cranbourne Printing Works, 1908), 54–60.

Mechling, William Hubbs, "Stories and Songs from the Southern Atlantic Coastal Region of Mexico," *Journal of American Folklore* 29 (1916): 549–51.

Mechling, William Hubbs, "Stories from Tuxtepec, Oaxaca," *Journal of American Folklore* 25 (1912): 199–203.

Meinhof, Carl von, *Afrikanische Märchen* (Jena: Eugen Diederichs, 1917), 18.

Metelerkamp, Sanni, *Outa Karel's Stories: South African Folk-Lore Tales* (London: Macmillan and Co., Limited, 1914), 88–100, 101–7.

Millington, W. H., and Berton L. Maxfield, "Visayan Folk-Tales III," *Journal of American Folklore* 20 (1907): 311–14.

Mitterrutzner, Johannes C., *Die Sprache der Beri in Central Afrika: Grammatik, Text, und Wörterbuch* (Brixen: A. Weger, 1867), 13–15.

Mockler-Ferryman, Augustus F., *British Nigeria* (London: Cassell and Company, Limited, 1902), 288–89.

Mockler-Ferryman, A[ugustus] F., *Imperial Africa: The Rise, Progress and Future of the British Possessions in Africa* (London: The Imperial Press, Limited, 1898), 1:464–65.

Mooney, James, *Myths of the Cherokee* (Washington, DC: Government Printing Office, 1902), 271–73, 450.

Mudge-Paris, David Benji, "Tales and Riddles from Freetown, Sierra Leone," *Journal of American Folklore* 43 (1930): 320.

Nassau, Robert H., *Where Animals Talk: West African Folk Lore Tales* (London: Duckworth & Co., 1914), 18–26.

"Negro Fables." *Riverside Magazine for Young People* 2 (November 1868): 505–7.

Norris, Thaddeus, "Negro Superstitions," *Lippincott's Magazine* 6 (1870), 94–95.

Opler, Morris Edward, *Myths and Tales of the Jicarilla Apache Indians* (New York: American Folk-Lore Society, 1938), 310–12.

Ortoli, Jean-Baptiste Frédéric, *Evening Tales*, trans. Joel Chandler Harris (New York: Charles Scribner's Sons, 1893), 1–12.

Ortoli, Jean-Baptiste Frédéric, *Les Contes de la Veillée* (Paris: Librairie d'Éducation Nationale, 1886), 17–24.

Owen, Mary Alicia, *Old Rabbit, the Voodoo, and Other Sorcerers* (London: T. Fisher Unwin, 1893), 169–85.

Owens, William, "Folk-Lore of the Southern Negroes," *Lippincott's Magazine* 20 (1877): 750–51.

Parsons, Elsie Clews, "Folk-Lore from Aiken, S. C.," *Journal of American Folklore* 34 (1921): 4–5, 15.

Parsons, Elsie Clews, *Folk-Lore from the Cape Verde Islands*, 2 vols.(New York: G.E. Stechert & Co., 1923), 1:30–33, 90–96.

Parsons, Elsie Clews, *Folk-Lore of the Antilles, French and English Part II* (New York: American Folk-Lore Society/G.E. Stechert and Co., 1936), 291, 325–26, 399, 401–4, 416, 418–19, 434, 454–55.

Parsons, Elsie Clews, *Folk-Lore of the Antilles, French and English Part III* (New York: American Folk-Lore Society/G.E. Stechert and Co., 1943), 51–52, 94–97.

Parsons, Elsie Clews, *Folk-Lore of the Sea Islands, South Carolina* (New York: G.E. Stechert & Co., 1923), 25–29, 60.

Parsons, Elsie Clews, "Folk-Tales Collected at Miami, FLA.," *Journal of American Folklore* 30 (1917): 222.

Parsons, Elsie Clews, *Folk-Tales of Andros Island, Bahamas* (New York: G.E. Stechert & Co., 1918), 12–16, 83.

Parsons, Elsie Clews, "The Provenience of Certain Negro Folk-Tales," *Folklore* 28 (1917): 408–14.

Parsons, Elsie Clews, "The Provenience of Certain Negro Folk Tales: The Tar Baby," *Folklore* 30 (1919): 227–34.

Parsons, Elsie Clews, "Spirituals and Other Folklore from the Bahamas," *Journal of American Folklore* 41 (1928): 500, 515–16.

Parsons, Elsie Clews, "Tales from Guilford County, North Carolina," *Journal of American Folklore* 30 (1917): 171–72.

Parsons, Elsie Clews, *Taos Tales* (New York: American Folklore Society, 1940), 136–38.

Parsons, Elsie Clews, *Tewa Tales* (New York: American Folk-Lore Society, 1926), 1:69.

Parsons, E[lsie] C[lews], "Zapotec and Spanish Tales of Mitla, Oaxaca," *Journal of American Folklore* 45 (1932): 296–99.

Pendleton, Louis, "Notes on Negro Folk-Lore and Witchcraft in the South," *Journal of American Folklore* 3 (1890): 201–2.

Pimentel, Figueiredo, *Histórias da Avózinha* (Rio de Janeiro: Weiszflog Irmãos, 1917), 217–18.

Porter, Anna, "Negro Stories," *The Independent* 30 (1878): 27–28.

Posselt, F., *Fables of the Veld* (London: Oxford University Press, 1929), 127–28.

Preuss, Konrad Theodor, *Die Nayarit-Expedition* (Leipzig: Teubner, 1912), 1:289–90.

Radin, Paul, *El Folklore de Oaxaca* (Havana: Imprenta de Aurelio Miranda, 1917), 153–54, 186, 195–98.

Rattray, Robert Sutherland, "The Rabbit and the Elephant," in

Some Folk-Lore Stories and Songs in Chinyanja (London: Richard Cray & Sons, Limited, 1907), 139–42.

Recinos, Adrian, "Cuentos Populares de Guatemala," *Journal of American Folklore* 31 (1918): 472–73.

Reid, John Turner, "Seven Folktales from Mexico," *Journal of American Folklore* 48 (1935): 121–24.

Renel, Charles, *Contes de Madagascar*, 3 vols. (Paris: E. Leroux, 1910), 1:111–13.

Rodrigues, João Barbosa, *Poranduba Amazonense* (Rio de Janeiro: G. Leuzinger & Filhos, 1890), 245.

Sylvio, Romero, *Contos Populares do Brasil* (Rio de Janeiro: Livraria Classica de Alves & Comp., 1897), 317–18.

Santa-Anna Nery, F. J. de, *Folk-Lore Brésilien* (Paris: Perrin et Cie., 1889), 213.

Sapir, Edward, "Takelma Texts," in *University of Pennsylvania Anthropological Publications of the University Museum*, 2 vols. (Philadelphia: The University Museum, 1909), 2:86–89.

Sapir, Edward, "Yana Texts," *University of California Publications in American Archaeology and Ethnology* 9 (1919): 227–28.

Sellers, Charles, "King Robin," in *Tales from the Lands of Nuts and Grapes: Spanish and Portuguese Folklore* (London: Field and Tuer; Simpkin, Marshall and Company, 1888), 112–16.

Seidel, August, *Geschichten und Lieder der Afrikaner* (Berlin: Schall and Grund, 1896), 336.

Simmons, D. C., "Specimens of Efik Folklore," *Folklore* 66 (1955): 418–19.

Simpson, George Eaton, "Traditional Tales from Northern Haiti." *Journal of American Folklore* 56 (1943): 256–57.

Smith, Rev. Edwin W., and Captain Andrew Murray Dale, *The Ila-Speaking Peoples of Northern Rhodesia*, 2 vols. (London: MacMillan and Co., Limited, 1920), 2:394–98.

Speck, Frank G., "The Creek Indians of the Taskigi Town," in *Memoirs of the American Anthropological Association* (New York: Kraus Reprint Co., 1974), 2:149–50.

Speck, Frank G., "Ethnology of the Yuchi Indians," in *University of Pennsylvania Anthropological Publications of the University Museum*, 2 vols. (Philadelphia: The University Museum, 1909), 1:152–53.

Swanton, John R., "Animal Stories from the Indians of the Muskhogean Stock," *Journal of American Folklore* 26 (1913): 214–15.

Swanton, John R., *Myths and Tales of the Southeastern Indians* (Washington, DC: Government Printing Office, 1929), 68, 110, 161, 208–9, 258.

Talbot, Percy Amaury, *In the Shadow of the Bush* (New York: George H. Doran Company; London: Heinemann, 1912), 397–400.

Theal, George McCall, *The Yellow and Dark-Skinned Peoples of Africa South of the Zambesi* (London: Swan Sonnenschein and Company, 1910), 88–91.

Tremearne, Arthur John Newman, *Hausa Superstitions and Customs: An Introduction to the Folk-Lore and the Folk* (London: John Bale, Sons & Danielsson, 1913), 212–14.

Tremearne, Mary, and Arthur John Newman Tremearne, *Fables and Fairy Tales for Little Folk, or Uncle Remus in Hausaland* (Cambridge: W. Heffer and Sons Ltd., 1910), 87–89.

Twente, Theophil H., and Dorothy R. Fyson, *Folk Tales of Chhattisgarh, India* (North Tonawanda, NY: Bodoni Press, 1938), 46–47.

Waters, M. W., *Cameos from the Kraal* (Alice, South Africa: Lovedale Press, 1926), 28–30.

Weeks, John H., *Congo Life and Folklore* (London: Religious Tract Society, 1911), 388–90.

Weeks, John H., "The Leopard in the Maize-Farm: a Lower Congo Folk-Tale," *Folklore* 20 (1909): 209–11.

Winstedt, Richard Olof, *Literature of Malay Folk-lore: Beginnings, Fable, Farcical Tales, Romance* (Kuala Lumpur: Federated Malay States Government Press, 1907), 44–48.

INDEX

stickfast motif, xiv, 9, 53–54, 56–73, 151–152

subaltern, 12–16, 20–23, 49–50, 51–53, 65, 74–75, 80–82, 83–84, 97–99, 119–120

Swanton, John, 37, 38–39

Talbot, P. Aumary, 152–155

Tanzania, 165–168

tar, 54–56, 110–112

tar baby: African origin, 2–6, 11; American Indian origin, 6–7, 24–25; epithet, ix, 63–65, 69–70, 130–139; European origin, 6–7; figure of speech, ix, 69; human sciences, xi, 2, 8, 12–13; unknown trajectory, xii, 2, 6, 11–12, 19, 173, 188–189; variation, 1, 10, 31, 174–175

Taylor, Archer, 9

Thompson, E. P., 80, 209–210

Thompson, Stith, 9, 171–172

trickster, xi–xii, 4–5, 6–7, 13–14, 20–22, 81

Tylor, E. B., 61, 117–118

United States: California, 151–152; Louisiana, 4, 7, 36–37; Missouri, 95; New Mexico, 25, 37, 199–200; North Carolina, 39, 55–56, 97, 217–218; Oklahoma, 24, 37; Pennsylvania, 30; South Carolina, 31–34, 39, 83–84, 94, 98, 115, 120; Texas, 6, 30–32, 48, 93; Utah, 6; Washington, 25. *See also* Liberty County, Georgia

Vattel, Emer de, 46

Venezuela, 63

Vila, Herminio Portell, 31

Vitoria, Francisco de, 45–50, 48, 115

Waldron, Jeremy, 34

war, 45–50

Warren, F. M., 7

waste, 34–35

water, 24–31, 34–39, 77–78, 126–130

Weeks, John, 6, 60–61

Wells, David, 4

Werner, Alice, 4

Wofford, James, 57

Wolfe, Bernard, 29

zanjeras, 77–78